PATHS
LESS
TRAVELLED

PATHS
LESS
TRAVELLED

Dispatches from the Front Lines of Exploration

edited by

RICHARD BANGS AND
CHRISTIAN KALLEN

project director

MARTHA FREEMAN

ATHENEUM   NEW YORK   1988

Copyright © 1988 by Sobek Productions, Ltd.
"Arabia Felix" copyright © 1988 by Edward Hoagland

Atheneum
Macmillan Publishing Company
866 Third Avenue, New York, N.Y. 10022
Collier Macmillan Canada, Inc.

Library of Congress Cataloging-in-Publication Data
Paths less travelled : dispatches from the front lines of exploration
/ edited by Richard Bangs and Christian Kallen : project director,
Martha Freeman.
    p.   cm.
ISBN 0-689-11819-8
    1. Safaris.   2. Authors, American—20th century—Journeys.
I. Bangs, Richard, 1950-   II. Kallen, Christian.   III.   Freeman,
Martha, 1956-
G516.P37   1988
910.4—dc 19   88-14521
                                                           CIP
Macmillan books are available at special discounts for bulk purchases
for sales promotions, premiums, fund-raising, or educational use.
For details, contact:
    Special Sales Director
    Macmillan Publishing Company
    866 Third Avenue
    New York, N.Y. 10022

Title page photo by Stan Boor
10 9 8 7 6 5 4 3 2 1

Printed in the United States of America

CONTENTS

ABOUT THE AUTHORS

Max Apple teaches at Rice University in Houston. His books include two novels, *The Propheteers* and *Zip*, and two collections of short stories, *Free Agents* and *The Oranging of America*.

Roy Blount Jr. is a Georgian but not a cracker. He lives in Mill River, Massachusetts. His books include *It Grows on You: The Hair-Raising Story of Human Plumage*, *Crackers*, *Not Exactly What I Had in Mind*, and, most recently, *Soupsongs–Webster's Art*. He is a contributing editor of *The Atlantic*.

William Broyles is the former managing editor of *Newsweek* and the author of *Brothers in Arms*.

Tim Cahill's books include *Buried Dreams: Inside the Mind of a Serial Killer*, *Jaguars Ripped My Flesh*, and *A Wolverine is Eating My Leg*. He is a contributing editor for both *Rolling Stone* and *Outside* magazine.

Edward Hoagland is the author of *African Calliope: A Journey to the Sudan* and *Notes From the Century Before: A Journal From British Columbia*.

Barry Lopez is the author of *Arctic Dreams*, *Of Wolves and Men*, a recent collection of essays called *Crossing Open Ground*, and several works of fiction. He contributes regularly to several publications, including *Harper's* and *North American Review*, and is a recipient of the National Book Award.

Jay McInerney's novels are *Bright Lights, Big City*, *Ransom*, and *The Sportswriter*.

Bobbie Ann Mason is the author of *In Country*, *Shiloh and Other Stories*, and *Spence and Lila*. She is a native of Kentucky.

David Roberts is a contributing editor of *Outside* magazine and the author of several books on travel and climbing, among them *Moments of Doubt and Other Mountaineering Writings*.

Tom Robbins is a former newspaperman who made it big as a novelist. His books are *Another Roadside Attraction*, *Even Cowgirls Get the Blues*, *Jitterbug Perfume*, and *Still Life with Woodpecker*.

James Salter's novels include *A Sport and a Pastime* and *Light Years*. His most recent collection is entitled *Dusk and Other Stories*. He is also a screenwriter and editor, and he lives on Long Island.

Alex Shoumatoff is a staff writer at *The New Yorker*. His most recent books are *In Southern Light: Treks through Brazil and Africa*, and *The Capital of Hope: Brasilia and Its People*.

ACKNOWLEDGMENTS

One summer afternoon on the patio of a delicatessen in Angels Camp, California, Richard Bangs bought me a cheese sandwich and told me about his new idea for a book: a series of first person adventure travel essays by world renowned authors who would glean their material by actually taking Sobek expeditions around the world.

If I could convince him I was literate, he'd give me a fancy title like Project Director and put me to work recruiting and coordinating these authors. My responsibilities would be a snap. All I had to do was write alluring letters offering great authors great adventures. I'd receive a few dollars, a collection of Smithsonian quality autographs, and enough droppable names to bore new acquaintances for a lifetime.

Richard was favorably impressed with my spelling, and the next thing I knew I was on the phone with James Dickey. Asked the courtly author who claims his book *Deliverance* kicked off the adventure travel industry, "What about wampum? You know us Hollywood types don't do anything unless there is a lot of wampum involved."

Looking through my files now, I see half a dozen letters to James Dickey. Each was enticing as all get-out, but if you scan the table of contents herein, you'll see there's no essay by him. To his credit, wampum wasn't the problem. Books, movies, students, and finally surgery interfered. Still, I'd like to begin by thanking Mr. Dickey. He took my entreaties seriously when I myself wasn't so sure.

The authors who did contribute, of course, deserve the greatest credit for bringing this book into existence, and I thank them for believing in the big adventures I described in my little voice over the phone, and for actually going, experiencing, returning, and writing about it all.

But also to be credited are the many, many people who wheedled, cajoled, and sweat to send these writers to the ends of the earth. In particular I want to thank Sobek's entire staff and especially its team of crack travel agents, including Gail Cameron, Leslie Agee, Leslie Jarvie, Laura Taylor, Shaun Manuel, Sharon Walker, Debra Godfrey, Nigel Dabby, and Randy Reimers. Also thanks to John Yost, Sobek's vice-president, and Erin Brogilo, the organizing personality behind all the chaos.

And thanks to the following:

Ruthann Russell Roberts of Yemen Airways, Abu Taleb of the Yemen Tourist Association, Nick Reynolds and Jon Bjornsson.

Maggie Valera Henry and Explorandes, Dan Chin at Air Jamaica, and Aeroperu.

Jack Morison at White Magic Expeditions, Bob Moore of Premiere Marketing, and Robert Elsaesser at Pan American World Airways.

Patricia Ackerman Blount and Ney Olortegui.

Mike Pometta and Bill Blair at KLM.

Frank DeClara at Air New Zealand, Glenys Shearer and Roxanne Emory at Rainbow Travel.

Jodi Coleman at Malaysian Air Systems, and Ahmad Yosuf at the Malaysia Tourist Office.

Roger Rakotomalala at Lemur Tours, and Air Madagascar.

Rick Laylin of United Airlines, San Francisco.

Yvonne Nichie and Gail Knopfler of Mallory Factor, Inc.

Genet Expeditions.

Marie Brown of Bhutan Travel.

Trish Lande, who helped conceive this book.

Judy Kern, our editor.

Finally, I want to acknowledge the two people whose roots in reality have ever balanced Richard's giddy optimism: Sobek's tirelessly diligent accountant, Paul Henry; and the dour editor with the heart of marshmallow, Christian Kallen.

Paths Less Travelled turned out to be a little more complicated than Richard "This'll Work, Trust Me" Bangs told me it would that summer afternoon. I can measure the eighteen months I spent on it in long distance bills, stationery, floppy disks, friends (and enemies) made. Still and all, I ended up with the money promised, the autographs, and all those droppable names. Looking for a project director who can spell? I'm available.

Martha Freeman
Project Director

INTRODUCTION

> Of the gladdest moments in human life, methinks, is the departure upon a distant journey into unknown lands. Shaking off with one mighty effort the fetters of Habit, the leaden weight of Routine, the cloak of many Cares and the slavery of Home, man feels once more happy. The blood flows with the fast circulation of childhood... Afresh dawns the morn of life...
>
> —RICHARD BURTON
> Journal entry
> December 2, 1856

Adventure is a step down the overgrown path, a step that can make all the difference in the world, as Robert Frost proffered in his 1916 poem, *The Road Not Taken*. He who never walks save where he sees men's tracks, makes no discoveries. To push aside the tangle, to venture beyond the mainstream, to taste heart in mouth is to vitalize the impulse of life, to reassert the play of passion, and to shed luster on the little gleam of time between two eternities. It is a grand difference.

This is a book that explores that difference, but with a difference. Twelve of America's most eloquent, accomplished authors took to the zetetic trails, turned the unturned stones, and got up before the day to try the fair adventure of tomorrow. And they were asked to put pen to paper and share their experiences, insights, discoveries, disappointments, joys. Fifty of today's most eminent writers were invited to participate in this experiment. Each was sent a Sobek catalogue describing some 300 different adventure tours to the ends of the earth and beyond, all organized by Sobek Expeditions, a company that has been leading such outings since 1973. The world then became a fantasy dart board for the invitees. Any author interested in the project could select the destination and adventure of his or her choice, and Sobek would arrange it, gratis, with hopes of sparking inspiration, and of the author contributing an essay for this book.

About a third of those invited didn't write back; they were probably too busy writing, or adventure just wasn't in their dictionary. Another dozen sent regrets. Tom Wolfe, in florid calligraphy worthy of framing, said he couldn't get away. William F. Buckley Jr. said he didn't have the time, but not to give up on him. Garrison Keillor wrote that he kept the Sobek catalogue on his bedside table and dreamed of it many nights, but he was involved in the adventure of a new marriage. Ed Abbey was still working on his fat novel, and begged a raincheck. Tom McGuane was in the midst of building a new Montana house. Ann Beattie said she had three book contracts, was writing two articles, and was trying to remember to drop off the dry cleaning and pick it up. Norman Mailer had his priorities mixed and was chairing the PEN conference, and preparing to direct his novel. Judy Blume was moving to Connecticut. Annie Dillard had a new baby; as did Sara Davidson and Jayne Anne Phillips. Jan Morris was travelling. John Irving didn't reply to the first two invitations, so a third was sent, emphasizing the colorful characters he would encounter on an adventure travel trip. He responded: "I am thrilled by the interest taken in me by Sobek Expeditions, but I must inform you that although I am a writer, I am not a seeker of colorful characters; my characters do not emerge from such seeking... Perhaps what is exciting in your expeditions and what is exciting in my fiction is not at all the same thing?... Regardless, I remain transfixed with interest just to hear about your expeditions, and I would become depressed should you cease to invite me to attend; I am thrilled to be asked—if you are not now tired of being rejected, because I am in the middle of a new book, which holds (for me) all the adventure I can bear (or understand). When I'm between books, one day—I promise you!—I would be deeply interested in one of your voyages."

John D. MacDonald wrote "Your current book does indeed spark the imagination, juices up the wanderlust, but at the same time brings the welling of a few tears of regret. I feel as if I should resign from the Explorer's Club as an act of penance," and then goes on to say he has booked a three month world cruise. E. L. Doctorow wished he could venture to Africa, but, like most of us, couldn't find the time. Nora Ephron called to say her idea of high adventure was catching a cab in the rain, and she had little interest in expanding those horizons. William Kennedy wrote that he was "too busy riding my own horse—a new novel." And John Sayles said he was "immersed in the adventure of making an independent, large-scale, low-budget film." Many others wrote they were simply too occupied to take an adventure vacation.

Then there were those who committed, but for one reason or another couldn't make the trip. D. M. Thomas signed on for Peru, but days before departure found himself in the hospital with a kidney stone. Germaine Greer volunteered to join a tour called Fabrics and Festivals of the Andes, but cancelled when word leaked of her participation and too many of her fans sent in deposits. James Dickey wanted to raft Alaska's Tatshenshini, but had to undergo brain surgery (he is fully recovered). Frances FitzGerald said yes to New Guinea, but fell behind on a deadline. And Rita Mae Brown threw her hat in for a hike through Scotland, but also bumped into conflicting commitments.

That left fourteen authors who were ready to venture across the river and into the trees, and they followed up on the impulse, packing duffles, visiting obscure consulates to secure the correct visas, and winging off to unknown sights, sounds and smells. All fourteen returned from their various adventures just slightly worse for wear, though just twelve essays could be included herein.

The distillation of these efforts is a fine wine of modern literary adventure, served with a warmed plate of unimaginable exotica. The courses include entrees from four continents; the conversation weaves from the Amazon to the Zambezi, from Botswana to Borneo, from the Andes to the Himalayas, and points between. And the common path is one of discovery, of understanding, of the reconsideration of habits, routines, cares and home that can only come from viewing them at such a distance. A theme is freedom, a liberation from the perpetual hurry of civilization. To be free is to be footloose in a trackless wilderness, unbounded by geography or history, utterly unconstrained by social bounds. The Mrs. Malaprops object, saying that allegories should stay on the banks of the Nile, that each being has his assigned place, and to wander afield is not a civilized pursuit. But it is, it is, and the writings herein prove as much.

On the other end of the spectrum, there are those who travel too much, too fast, pockets full of frequent flier coupons, but empty of a compass. They reach a lot of places, but have no grasp of the world.

In 1948 S. J. Perelman wrote in *Westward Ha!*, "I suggested that she take a trip round the world. 'Oh, I know,' returned the lady, yawning with ennui, 'but there's so many other places I want to see first.'"

More than a pearl of travelling truth swirls through Perelman's anecdote—the more one journeys beneath the overview, the more there is to behold and to ken. The universe gets bigger as we look closer; smaller as we pull back. The tourist who signs up for the round-the-world-in-eight-days jetlag special is left with bleary eyes and blurred memories. Yet the journeyer who immerses himself in a rain forest, clutches the side of a mountain, or punches the spray of a wild river discovers wells with unfathomed depths; windows overlooking infinity.

"This dim spot," some men call our earth. But they are those who drive to the rim of the wilderness and see with clouded eyes. To others, those who breathe the crisp morning air of adventure, who buckle their boots and are ready for the walk down oblique and less travelled paths, the view is clear . . . and sometimes stunning. Notions resonate, spirits soar, and the frontiers of the mind rival topographical boundaries. T. E. Lawrence wrote in *Seven Pillars of Wisdom*, "All men dream, but not equally. Those who dream by night in the dusty recesses of their minds wake in the day to find that it was vanity; but the dreamers of the day are dangerous men, for they may act their dreams with open eyes to make them possible." These writers are dangerous people, dreamers of the day who dared to act, who wouldn't allow their lives to be just accidents, who sought new perspectives in their adventures. For them it was worth the long, strange trip, in spite of storms, cataracts, crocodiles, piranhas, mosquitoes, and blisters.

This is a collection of what Perelman called "other places," and other ways to see them. This is an exploration of "this *bright* spot." The authors here haven't come close to taking that trip round the world. But they've seen many places, and for those who would as lief take the less-travelled path, this book is an exhilarating journey.

—RICHARD BANGS
Kunming, China
November, 1987

THE SOUTH ISLAND COAST (BART HENDERSON)

Bobbie Ann Mason

▼

THE ODD TOURIST

New Zealand is far, far away. I went there on what is called an adventure tour. Just thinking about distant, exotic New Zealand felt adventurous. And flying the virtual length of the Pacific, from Los Angeles to Auckland, in an Air New Zealand Boeing 747 packed with over six hundred people and eleven tons of cargo was almost as amazing to me as the fact that men have walked on the moon. But that little excursion was just the warm-up. I had traveled Down Under to go hiking on the famous Milford Track, a rugged mountain trail known as "the finest walk in the world." It's a Class III adventure in a I-V range of difficulty. But before getting really reckless, I spent a week getting acquainted with New Zealand, a country of overwhelming beauty.

The scenic variety in such a small country—about a thousand

miles long and not very wide at all—is remarkable. New Zealand has alps, fiords, volcanos, tropical beaches, and convoluted hills dotted with grazing sheep. The climate is temperate, though it varies from North to South and is colder in the South, which points toward Antarctica. It's a sort of paradise, I guess. It doesn't have any snakes or poisonous insects or scary predators. Without predators, birds like the kiwi, the weka and the kakapo didn't develop their wings. There are no dangers in this landscape—except maybe from wild boars. I saw a wild boar in captivity. She looked intelligent, shy, and sad. She had recently had piglets. Actually, the wild boar in New Zealand is the domestic pig gone off to the bush to live the Class V life. It's not a jungle native. In fact, New Zealand has only two native mammals, and both are species of bats (the short-tailed and the long-tailed). The Polynesians, who migrated there beginning in 1350, brought the rat. Captain Cook (the first European to land in New Zealand, in 1769) brought the first sheep, in 1773. The Europeans introduced deer and goats and hares and other small mammals, including hedgehogs, which were brought to control the snails and slugs. All the mice are of one species, *Mus muscuclus*, descended from the European house mouse. Possums came from Australia, along with the wallaby. You see dead possums and wallabies on the road.

The vegetation is lush and unusual, strewn with lots of flax plants and ferns. The rangiora shrub, with its broad shiny leaf, is known as the bushman's toilet paper. The native pepper plant is an insect repellent. The Maoris, descendants of those Polynesian immigrants, now numbering ten percent of New Zealand's population, once used the purple berry of the poroporo plant for birth control. The toetoe grass is a native flowering grass, but the similar, bushier South American pampas grass has invaded the hills west of Auckland. Its leaves are double-edged razors, and kids call it "cutty grass." "It looks pretty, but it's a swine of a plant," said my guide to Piha Beach, a black-sand surfing beach not far from Auckland, the capital. Ferns flourish in New Zealand. The silver fern is the national fern. The underside of its leaf is phosphorescent, and the Maoris used it to light their paths at night. Tree ferns are common, and sometimes you see the moss-covered trunk of a tree fern standing alone— beheaded by possums. Moss grows on all sides of the tree in New Zealand. Shelter belts of poplars are planted between pastures. They stand tall and stately like rows of guards. The pohutukawa, a myrtle with large bright red brush-like flowers, is the New Zealand Christmas tree. If left alone, it grows into a huge ornamental tree with great climbing branches. The largest tree in New Zealand, the kauri, unique to this country, used to cover North Island, but when the European settlers came they started sawing down those gigantic old trees (some as old as two to four thousand years), milling them and selling the wood, until they decimated the forests. Most of the large old trees are gone now.

Kiwis. The kiwi fruit, brought from China, was originally marketed to the English as the Chinese gooseberry. The fruit was named after the kiwi bird because it was small and round and fuzzy. New Zealanders call themselves Kiwis. And they call goats "Kiwi lawnmowers." In a nocturnal kiwi house at a park, I saw two kiwis sleeping together like cats, their beaks hidden in their furry-looking feathers. Another kiwi was running around energetically, scratching and poking its beak into the leaves on the ground, more frantic than a chicken. It probably had a lot to do in its short time awake, since kiwis sleep eighteen hours a day.

Not many places in the world have glowworm caves. I explored the Waitomo Caves, not far from the Bay of Plenty, where there had recently been a devastating earthquake. A million years ago, these caves were created by earthquakes lifting residue out of the sea. I read somewhere that the glowworms, which send down threads of silk to trap their prey, are

really a species of arachnid. Spiders—my number one phobia. Earthquakes are number two. As far as I was concerned, this was a Class V adventure. But the caves seemed still and solid and eternal. The cathedral area is forty-seven feet high. The acoustics are just about perfect. The Vienna Boys Choir and Kris Kristofferson and Rita Coolidge have all sung here. Weddings have been performed. There are broad wooden floors like a beach boardwalk. Some of the sculptured stones resemble an elephant—or maybe it's possible to see George Washington at Mt. Rushmore, or Howard Hughes, or even Disney's Goofy in the formations, depending on the kind of mind you have. In a darkened area, you begin to see the glowworms appear as pinpoints of light high above. Later, when you get on a boat and the guide propels it through a dark canal by grasping guide wires overhead, you see the ceiling of glowing worms like a magnificent sky full of stars. I looked for the Southern Cross. Later, in the real night sky, I located the Southern Cross, which we can't see in the Northern Hemisphere.

Facts about New Zealand: 3.3 million people, seventy million sheep. Cat and dog food are called Jellimeat. Speed bumps are called control humps. Woolworth's Superstore is a chain of supermarkets. McDonald's is down there, but not Wendy's. Road signs are wooden pointers clustered on a pole, like the sign in M*A*S*H. Some grocery stores are painted red all over with Coca-Cola signs. Butcher shops sell "banged steak" and "crumbed chops." Granny Smith apples were developed in New Zealand. Everyone says "Ah, yeah!"

I traveled around the beaches and caves and geothermal hot-spots of North Island, then went to South Island and spent a couple of days in the Victorian-style city of Christchurch, with its own Avon River, before flying over New Zealand's highest mountain range down to Te Anau to begin preparations for the official adventure—the Milford Track, a thirty-three-and-a-half-mile inland route to Milford Sound on the Tasman Sea. This is one of the few accessible hikes through the four hundred thousand acres of Fiordland National Park. Quinton Mackinnon, a Scotsman, discovered the Mackinnon Pass in 1888, and right away the trail he blazed became a tourist trek. The first woman made the trip in 1890. Now the track is run by the New Zealand government, which restricts the flow of traffic and keeps the track impeccably maintained. Along the way, three lodges with dorm-style accommodations and hot meals handle about forty hikers a day during the warm seasons. About

forty Freedom Hikers are also allowed through each day. They carry their own gear and food, stopping at several primitive huts for shelter. No camping is allowed in the bush.

I was ready for adventure, but I knew I could never be a Freedom Hiker. I knew exactly what I could carry in my little blue day-pack—about eight pounds. But I had brought all the wrong stuff. The track officer who met our group at the Te Anau Resort Hotel scoffed at my Gore-tex parka and insisted that I take a heavy yellow slicker from his stack in the office. Gore-tex won't work when it really comes to rain, he insisted. We were going into the rain forest, where it rains 282 inches—more than twenty feet—a year. There had just been severe flooding, stranding hikers on some other trails in the park. And my rubber overpants, although recommended gear in the trek brochure, wouldn't do to wade rivers. He told me to throw away those and my long canvas pants and thermal underwear. The proper costume, he informed the trekkers, is polypropylene long johns worn under shorts. The polypropylene keeps the legs warm even when fording streams and battling sudden storms. He said not to worry about what you look like wearing long johns under shorts.

I had to abandon my day-pack and use their day-pack, which was large enough to hold the slicker. In addition, I carried some sandals and sweatpants (evening wear), an extra

T-shirt, an extra pair of wool socks, and a few miniaturized toiletries in a sort of dollhouse travel kit. They also gave us an envelope-style bedsheet to tote from hut to hut. Luckily, we didn't need canteens, since the water in the streams is so pure. The track officer said the yellow slicker weighed only half a pound, but in fact it weighed about thirteen and a half pounds, according to my shoulders on the morning of the first day of the hike. After lunch, the pack was a lot lighter. (We carried our lunches too.) "We need pack sheep," my companion said. She and I shared feet fleece—a package of wool to stuff between our toes. We also shared a "torch" (flashlight) and toothpaste. The generators at the lodges shut down at ten and we needed torches.

On the first day, our cheerful group of forty hikers rode two hours in a launch up Lake Te Anau, the same boat that has carried trekkers since 1899, then walked a mile in the rain to Glade House, our first stop. Glade House is a lodge in a glade encircled by austere mountains. We waited for a long time to see the moon come over the mountain that night. Earlier, during dinner, we were alerted by the sharp cry of birds outside the window of the dining hall. It was a pair of weka birds. Phil Turnbull, the manager of Glade House, told us about these flightless wood hens, which look something like kiwis. A female had showed up one day, he said. She had lost her foot in a possum trap. She hung around Glade House and became tame, but the stoats got her eggs. One day she was screaming on the edge of the river that runs through the glade. Across the river a male was screaming back, so Phil kindly caught her and took her across the suspension bridge to the male. Some time later, the pair showed up at the lodge. "She brought him here," Phil said. "But how? She couldn't climb the steep riverbank with one foot. Yet they must have swum across. I couldn't imagine they had gone upriver and crossed the bridge. They're nesting now and the male has started eating out of people's hands."

To describe the scenery on the Milford Track, one risks falling into a syrup of superlatives. This is beautiful scenery gone crazy. You can't take in the profusion of picturesque tree ferns, mossy trees, light-flecked beech forests, breathtaking waterfalls, rushing streams, stark mountain walls hiding the sun. After a while, paradise is numbing; you grow satiated, drunk on prettiness. In 1908 the London Spectator described the Milford Track as "the finest walk in the world" and the name stuck. According to Maori legend, the goddess of the underworld was so alarmed at the beauty of the land—created by the god Tu-te-Rakiwhanoa—that she was afraid men who saw it would want to live there forever. To thwart this desire, she released a large namu (sandfly). Sandflies are the chief scourge of the Milford Track trekkers, but I have a feeling that their peskiness is exaggerated because there is little else to complain about. The real danger is the weather. It could snow any day of the year, and it's always likely to rain.

From Glade House, the first major leg of the journey was an easy ten and a half miles through red beech forest, beside the fast-flowing aqua-tinted Clinton River. The weather was pleasant, the birdsong as alive as a Hollywood musical. The trail was broad, sometimes rocky or muddy. I wasn't used to organized group adventure, so I tended to fall behind and talk to the guide bringing up the rear. Charging off early and getting there first seemed to be the goal of many. I don't see how they noticed much at that swift pace. I was confused and overwhelmed by all I was seeing. I wanted to look at the birds—the large wood pigeons whooshing their wings low across the paths, the friendly bush robin stopping to tell us what was on its mind, and the flirtatious fantail, which kept fanning its tail open in bushes along the trail. I wanted to identify the trees. I was lost in mosses. I photographed scenes for later study. I tried to hurry. If you go *too* slowly the guides may decide you can't make it and turn you back.

I kept photographing moss, a shag carpet on a four-inch foam cushion. The tussocks of moss reminded me of those hooked rugs with raised, knobby designs, and the old-man's-beard moss hanging on everything made one think of sluts' wool (dust fluffs). The tall mossy stumps (tree ferns beheaded by possums) were like cat scratching-posts. There were doll-house gardens. And in the river a whirlpool acted like a washing machine rinse cycle; the river suddenly curves and water hits the bank and whirls off giddily. The pebbly bottom shines like a laminated mosaic ash tray. In places, moss enveloped everything like plush-covered plumbing fixtures, and sometimes on rock walls moss dripped water like sopping-wet sponges. It's wall-to-wall beauty. All these domestic images must have come to mind because this rain forest is so thoroughly benevolent, compared to the tropical forest in Australia I had heard about—where snakes abound, along with plants that embed hairlike stickers into your skin that have to be surgically removed, and vines that hook you with a nasty thorn and then wrap themselves around you like packing string.

New Zealand has kea birds, however. At Pompolona Lodge that night, we were warned about the mischievous kea birds. They like to destroy hiking boots, picking out the eyes and stitches, and they'll vandalize a room if they can sneak in the door. At dawn, they screech and slide down the tin roofs with bone-chilling sounds. They steal your food right out from under your nose. They're big birds, with wicked-looking talons. Later in the trip, after finishing the Milford Track, we saw a little sports car convertible that had been stripped by keas—everything plucked bare, from upholstery to wiring to hubcaps. They're pretty birds, though, green parrots with red-orange under their wings. The kea is similar to the kakapo, a flightless nocturnal parrot that is almost extinct. (The kakapo displays like a bower bird and browses like a sheep. There's one valley where it lives that's so carefully protected planes aren't even allowed to fly through it.)

Meals on the trail were enormous and practical. Breakfast included porridge and bacon and eggs and toast and canned fruit and milk and Nestle's Milo (a powdered chocolate drink) and Nestle's Classic coffee and tea. (Down Under, Nestle's rhymes with trestles.) Orange juice is like something astronauts would drink. And in New Zealand, they eat a concentrated yeast paste called Vegemite. (Recall "Vegemite sandwiches" in a line from the song "Down Under" by Men at Work.) They spread it on toast—just a minute amount—with butter. It's said to repel sandflies, because of the Vitamin B. The jars of Vegemite seemed to grow larger as we traveled further into the bush.

The second day was the hard day. From Pompolona Lodge (named for pompolonas, scones Quinton Mackinnon fried in melted-down mutton-fat candles), we hiked over Mackinnon Pass (3,570 feet in elevation) down to Quinton Hut. The pass separates the Clinton River Valley from the Arthur River Valley. Most of the morning walk is flat and fern-filled, along the Clinton River; then it's a steep climb on a zig-zag trail. It's five zigs, six zags up to Mackinnon Pass. A guide named Murray led us up, and Louis brought up the rear. Then Donald followed us down the other side. The guides were young, healthy, athletic guys, equipped with first aid packs and track lore. On the way we saw fuchsia trees with peeling tan bark, and Louis encouraged me to eat some of the purple berries. They were sweet. "What we don't have in wildlife we make up for in moss," he said. We saw an exotic shiny purple mushroom and liverwort and rayolia, which is known as vegetable sheep. "We feed our vegetarians vegetable sheep so everyone can eat sheep," joked Murray. As we climbed, the vegetation changed from moss and forest to scrub and tussock. Paradise ducks flew over. When we reached the pass, someone said, "There's the can!" and I thought she meant the toilet, the Pass Hut Longdrop, built of concrete to keep it from blowing off the mountain, but it was just her New Zealand accent. She meant the cairn—the round rock memorial constructed in honor

of Quinton Mackinnon. It has a cross on top. The pass is wide, about three hundred yards, and spotted with tarns (little lakes, what I'd personally call ponds). It was cooler up there than down below, but the weather remained clear. Sometimes it can be dangerously windy, and more often than not it's rainy and chilly. We could see forever in all directions. A woman in our party drove a golf ball off the edge of the pass with her walking stick, sort of on the same principle that Alan Shepherd did on the moon that time when he sneaked a collapsible golf club aboard the Apollo. We were near the Twelve-Second Drop, a big rock that juts out over the edge of the pass. Anything falling from there takes twelve seconds to hit ground. That day we met a young woman from the Quinton Hut staff; she had a day off and had trotted up to the pass that morning for something to do. As we started down the trail, she tripped lightly past us, dancing down those rocks like a mountain goat.

From Mackinnon Pass, it was rocks all the way down. I looked at my feet the rest of the way. A nasty fall was a real risk. "Banged toes," I moaned, unpacking the feet fleece from between my aching toes at the end of the day.

Surprises awaited us at Quinton Hut: beer and wine and ice cream flown in on a Mount Cook Line Cessna 185 by a pilot named Gary. But first, Gary took hikers up for sightseeing rides through Clinton Canyon and over Sutherland Falls. The tiny aircraft, with three passengers, rumbled down a short, bumpy dirt strip straight toward a mountain and lifted up, wafting among the mountains but not above them. We flew over the mountain pass we had just hiked over. We buzzed the Pass Hut, where we had eaten our lunch. We drifted down the canyon and circled here and there, getting various angles on our route of the previous two days and our coming day's route. Several times Gary seemed to be heading straight toward a mountain and that's when he'd turn around and talk to the passengers in the back through his microphone. For fifteen minutes, we were birds, which must be better than being famous for fifteen minutes. It's hard to overstate how thrilling this ride was, soaring on wings through the canyons, gliding over Quill Lake—which spills down over the mountain and creates Sutherland Falls, a three-leap waterfall that's the third highest in the world. The Maori name for it is Te Tautea, the White Thread. It was a calm, clear day. Our wings caught the updraft, and we hung there in the air, eventually floating back down to earth.

At Quinton Hut, there was a souvenir shop—T-shirts and post-cards. Waylon Jennings and Willie Nelson were singing "Ladies Love Outlaws" on a cassette player in the kitchen. Todd Vesey, the manager, dispensed the wine and beer, and told us we could have our packs flown out the next morning to our hotel at Milford Sound. That evening we saw slides of where we had been and where we were going, including one of an inversion layer in Clinton Valley, where we had just been flying. It was warm down low and sunny above, causing a cloud to fill the valley. From above, it was like a pot of milk boiling over, white froth spilling over Mackinnon Pass.

The next morning, Todd announced that the weather was so clear—an anti-cyclone (a high)—that we could send our despised yellow rain slickers out on the plane with our day-packs! I decided to keep my pack for carrying my lunch and sweater and a few essentials, and I crammed the rest of my stuff into a garbage bag and sent it on the plane out to the hotel in Milford. With a light step, then, and no fear of chilling rain, we hiked a mere 13½ miles (more rocks) to Sandfly Point to catch the launch to the Milford Sound Hotel. Our guide Donald followed us, over numerous suspension bridges, past more waterfalls and mossy grottoes. Wood pigeons swept over the path and landed on low branches. Whooshers, someone called them. Some of the bush was so mossy and misshapen and eerie, it was like something out of a fairy tale. All the guides made that observation. They said it was an unusual rain forest because it had so many plants growing on the ground and so few animals living in it. It was creepy and thick, with bottomless moss—so soft you felt you might sink, not a place you'd want to crawl into to relieve yourself.

A word about that: we were many miles from civilization but it was hard to find a private place. Forest, forest everywhere and not a place to pee. There were toilets at intervals, but in between it was hard to get far off the trail because the bush was so thick. I ran into a man behind a tree.

At Sandfly Point, where we photographed ourselves with the 33.5-mile marker to document our achievement, someone asked Donald, our guide, "Now that it's over, has anyone ever died on the trail?"

"Ah, yeah. In fact, only last December a bloke died on the track. He was on the second zigzag. He had heart disease and shouldn't have been along. Murray and I had to carry him back down to Mintaro Hut. It had a bad effect on the group." He shuddered. "For a long time I hated to pass that spot." That's the only time he knows of that it has happened, because the operators of the track insist on a reasonable level of fitness. The track is not for the person who rarely gets out of the house, but anyone in good shape should have no trouble.

The boat rounded a bend and suddenly we saw the glorious sight of Mitre Peak, surely New Zealand's most popular tourist photograph, the star of Fiordland National Park. It's a tall peak rising 5,560 feet straight out of Milford Sound—one of the highest mountains in the world to shoot straight up from the sea. Mitre Peak is supposed to resemble a mitre, a bishop's headdress, but it also looks like the mountain at the beginning of Paramount movies.

At Milford Sound, we had real hotel rooms waiting with the baggage we had sent ahead, as well as our garbage bags of trek gear. That night, spruced up, we had a banquet, which included Pompolona Stopover (Southern crayfish sautéed with spring vegetables) and Fiordland fruit cocktail and blue cod fillets. And we received our certificates of achievement (decorated with a drawing of a kea bird). A satellite dish brought us live news programs from the United States. Nothing much had happened that seemed important.

The Milford Track adventure ended the next day with a cruise on Milford Sound—Fiord World itself, where the mountains rise straight out of the water, waterfalls stream at random down the granite sides, and fat, playful seals loll on the rocks at the base of the peaks. Cruise ships haunt the sound, but there is no place to anchor because it is so deep. One mountain is shaped like an elephant, another like a crouching lion—some of those same guys that were down in Waitomo Caves. The captain of the boat said, "We have an average of one earthquake a day here in Milford Sound. The walls can burst open at any time, so they are constantly changing faces." We were gazing straight up Mitre Peak at close range— a gray wall decorated with clumps of greenery. It was calm. There was no rain. The seals were rolling luxuriously on the rocks. We cruised straight out into the Tasman Sea through a three-hundred-yard-wide opening, then on the return journey, we dipped briefly into a waterfall, the closest we got to a drenching on the whole trip. The captain said of the seals, "Now and then the odd one gets attacked by fiord sharks." He pointed out "the odd starfish and the odd octopus." The man standing next to me said, "I'm wondering about the odd tourist who now and then falls off the boat."

It was soon time for the odd tourist to say goodbye to New Zealand—the land of benched paths, banged steak, crumbed chops, Vegemite sandwiches, Nestle's Classic, cricket, a variety of kiwis, and seventy million nuclear-free sheep. As well as more scenic beauty than can be remembered or reported or believed. Ah, yeah!

"Some of the bush was so mossy and misshapen and eerie, it was like something out of a fairy tale."

YEMEN IS A COUNTRY OF CONTRASTS WHOSE GAUDY HISTORY PERVADES ITS MODERN GUISE. (RICHARD BANGS)

Edward Hoagland

▼

ARABIA FELIX

Ma'rib was the Queen of Sheba's capital nearly three thousand years ago—a burgeoning garden spot and trading center on the spice, myrrh and frankincense caravan route that wound north from the Gulf of Aden through Mecca and eventually to Gaza on the Mediterranean. It was the largest city in Old South Arabia, or Arabia Felix, "Happy Arabia," as the region later came to be called (versus Arabia Petrea, "Stony Arabia," the Romans' idea of Saudi Arabia). The magnificently engineered dam a couple of hundred yards long that had captured "seventy rivulets" flowing out of the mountains and had irrigated the four thousand acres of orchards and fields of this breadbasket city didn't break once and for all until around A.D. 570. Now the broken ruins atop Ma'rib's citadel are all that remain to be seen of a city otherwise under sand dunes at the edge of the vast Saudi Arabian Empty Quarter. And this whole major archeological site is virtually unexcavated—the first and last team to make a real start managed to flee by a ruse from threatening Murad tribesmen thirty-five years ago—and is a rarity for that, though oil was discovered nearby in 1984 by the Hunt Oil Company of Texas.

Ma'rib is a pleasant four-hour drive on a road built by Swedes through the mountains east of Sana'a, the capital of the present-day Yemen Arab Republic, better known as North Yemen. Sana'a itself is a most ancient town, founded according to legend by Noah's son Shem, who must have hiked down from Mount Ararat in Turkey, where the Ark landed, to accomplish the feat. The name means, appropriately, "Fortified City," but since the revolution in 1962, which overthrew the absolute rule of the last of the Zaydi imams, it has been expanding way past its walls in low gray cement-block constructions, with the din of Toyotas, Suzukis, Mitsubishis, Datsuns, Nissans, Daihatsus, Hyundais and Mazdas tooting along raw new roads. In the old quarters the best-kept houses are chocolate-brown with whitewashed trim, built of rows of mud brick above striped layered limestone or igneous foundations, on a narrow yet feudally lofty impulse, and painted like six-story palaces, with high-up, monastic, filigreed windows of stained glass and alabaster, and sometimes a garden hidden behind. Gardens with vegetables thickly growing in them and apricot, almond or walnut trees still seem to abound in Sana'a, which was built to withstand a siege. The latest, in the winter of 1967–68, lasted for seventy days before the republicans inside succeeded in breaking the renascent royalist lines; but in 1905, when the Imam Yahya besieged a Turkish occupying force, half the populace died. (He then besieged it again in 1911, and after he was assassinated in 1948, his son, the new Imam Ahmad, sacked the city arbitrarily on general principle.)

Sana'a, with its dagger markets and raisin markets, its cramped, medieval mud skyscrapers that look like cliff dwellings, its steam baths heated by human dung, and blindfolded camels underground turning oilseed grindstones, its hundred mosques with muezzins crying out over every neighborhood at dawn, noon and bedtime, blending their voices with a passion appropriate for a land converted to Islam within the Prophet's own life span (indeed, Sana'a's inaccessible Great Mosque is rumored to be the only one outside Mecca that has a kaaba), lies at seventy-five hundred feet, surrounded by mountains more than four thousand feet higher, and thus catches both the tail end of the Mediterranean's spring rains and the late-summer rainfall from India's monsoon. Highland Yemen traditionally could feed itself with rain-grown sorghum raised on the plateaus, as well as a gamut of vegetables and fruits planted on the intricacy of terraces that whorl down every slope not too sheer to hold soil, and used to export its world-famous mocha coffee and some cotton from the port of al-Mukha, also. But this is true no more. Yemen has a remittance economy based on payments sent home by the million Yemeni men who work in the Arab oilfield countries and the billion dollars a year of direct foreign aid funneled in by Saudi Arabia, which frets about every untoward event in this alarmingly martial Nebraska-sized nation on its southern border that has a population (seven million) about the size of its own in one-tenth as much space.

Sana'a, established perhaps by Sabaeans (Saba = Sheba), and then invaded by Himyaris, Abyssinians, Persians, Egyptian Mamelukes, and Ottoman Turks—sending its merchants as far afield as India, Indonesia and Moorish Spain, although not itself propelled into modernism until Gamal Abdel Nasser galvanized the imagination of the Middle East—now blares with construction and vehicular noise. But Ma'rib's citadel, caving and peeling, sand-blown and silent except for a few shepherd squatters and their flocks of sheep, comes further unstrung with each seasonal splatter of monsoon rain. Close by, several columns of Sheba's own supposed temple remain, along with another dedicated to the moon god Almaqah. Islam is a sister religion to Christianity and Judaism, and most Christians and Jews are familiar with

votaries of their own faiths who quite correspond to the range of Muslim practice and belief. But how does one go back in the mind's eye to an astral religion?

Well, there are ways, in fact, and the astral religion of Old South Arabia was similar to Babylon's, from which our astrology derives. However, in the midday heat Martha, Bjorn and I weren't really attempting to do this, except for appreciating why the moon rather than the pummeling sun was the Sabaeans' main deity. Martha, a slim, black-haired Californian with an innocent air and a freckled face whose physiognomy indicated her Boston ancestry, was celebrating her thirtieth birthday in Yemen. Bjorn, a tall shambly Norwegian, was several years older than that, with a fluffy mustache, kind inquisitive eyes, and hair that winged out above his ears. He'd trained as an architect and had worked at betterment projects here for eight years, so he was doing the translating for us. Ali, from the town of Wadi Dhar near the capital, was our driver, and because the car was actually his, a man of property as well, with seven children and a coolly hopeful mien, always trying to get us, and maybe principally his car, past the incessant dramas of travel in this Balkanized region.

We had just picked up the "Director of Antiquities" at Ma'rib, a bumptious, nattily white-robed, callow, clerkly young man named Mohammed who told us in Arabic that no, he had never attended a university, but nevertheless clearly did play a supervisory role among the half-dozen soldiers who were there to see that no stones were taken away—though the fabled seventeen original temples and other structures of the site have already been picked apart by local villagers through the ages to the point where you will notice old houses in neighboring hamlets with friezes of ibises flying upside down set into them as building blocks.

"I'll spray you if you grab anything," Mohammed joked to Bjorn, waving his assault rifle. Like practically every man in northern Yemen, he wore a curved foot-long dagger belted in front of his belly, as well as a Russian AK-47 slung on one shoulder, with ammunition clips at his waist, and a pistol peeping out from under his shirttails. Yet he didn't seem a warlike fellow—more like a grown-up mama's boy whose father was influential and had found him his job. He took us to the ruins of the dam, which is still an eloquent presence in its dry corkscrew ravine, and later, inside the moon-temple compound, where again it was a matter

"Tiger skins, ostrich eggs, peacock feathers, Chinese silks, Indian textiles, ebony, ivory, pearls and gold, dexterous monkeys and fanciful slaves."

of attempting to stretch one's mind back to imagine the mystery and power of this kingdom (circa 1000–115 B.C.) from which not only the known world's incense and spices were thought to originate, but also tiger skins, ostrich eggs, peacock feathers, Chinese silks, Indian textiles, ebony, ivory, pearls and gold, dexterous monkeys and fanciful slaves. The Red Sea was dangerous to navigate, and so goods from India, Punt (now Somalia) and Ethiopia travelled north by this same camel route, commingled with valuables from Arabia Felix itself, paralleling but safe from the sea.

The outlines of Ma'rib's plantations remain too, although as much veld as desert once surrounded them. Lions and giraffes roamed Arabia then, and giraffe horns still make the most favored dagger handles in Yemen, costing even more than rhino horn. Rhinos have been driven to the brink of extinction in Africa to fill this market, but the average man will buy cow horn (and a poor man, goat). When the Sabaeans built their twenty-story palace in Sana'a, with each side crafted of different-colored stone, they put bronze lions at the four corners of the roof, aimed outward in such a way that at least one would roar, whichever direction the wind blew.

The featureless, monochromatic heat made pondering these ecological and cultural complexities so difficult that we went to a little restaurant and enjoyed a sumptuous lunch of sorghum dough and sheeps' vertebrae dipped in a foamy green fenugreek broth. Also rice and stir-fried tomatoes and eggs and fava beans boiled in fat, with chilies on the side, and flat bread to dip the dishes up, plus lots of the good bottled *Shamlan* water from a well outside Sana'a that middle-class Yemenis drink. The restaurant was crowded and loud. Lunch is the main meal and with liquor forbidden, is imbued with the sort of festivity that elsewhere accompanies a six-pack of beer. Husky Mercedes trucks with eyes painted on their hoods were parked outside, powerful vehicles that have for many years proven ideal on the smugglers' run across the roadless Empty Quarter from Oman to here. The drivers were celebrating what has lately become the end of the working day, and like them, we went to the market square after eating to buy a lapful of qat.

Qat probably came to the Arabian peninsula from the Horn of Africa during the fifteenth century, and although it is either forbidden or not popular in other Arab countries, it is more pervasive than ever in Yemen. If Saudi Arabia sometimes seems God-struck—all else subsumed in religion—Yemen is qat-struck. Qat is a woody shrub five or ten feet high with birchy-looking leaves that contain an ephedrinelike addictive drug with effects like a mild amphetamine—excitement, insomnia, loss of appetite, constipation—though if you swallow them you'll get a bellyache. But you don't swallow them. You hold a freshly cut branch and slowly pluck off the tenderest leaves, as you chat with your friends and smoke a water pipe or hubble-bubble and sip from a glass of water, while gradually wadding the leaves into one cheek, which at the end of an hour will bulge as if you had a toothache or a chaw of tobacco there. Taking care not to shift the wad, lest bits of leaf fall into your throat, you squeeze, suck and swallow the juice. Nibbling these leaves makes even the solemnest citizen appear somewhat goatlike and the juice's astringence causes a continual thirst, so that even Bedouin who might otherwise get by even in the hottest weather on a few cups of water a day are drinking and spitting, drinking and spitting, incongruous-looking in their desert robes and head cloths, cradling more twigs on their knees.

The stalls in the souk were thronged with bargainers fingering the separate batches of qat, which were closely wrapped in banana leaves; a rifle hung muzzle-down from each man's shoulder like a third arm. Bjorn, who is a connoisseur and had been missing the drug during the past two years, which he had spent in Cairo, was unusual in that he was looking specifically for insect tracks on the plants to show that they hadn't been doused with insecticide. The rarest type of qat tastes like licorice, but we settled for something less expensive that had the flavor of spearmint and cost about six dollars per portion, or about half the nation's median daily wage. (The use of qat, therefore, has become a major cause of malnutrition among children in North Yemen.) Yemenis seldom haggle much over price. Nor do they practice the more general Arab custom of extending special courtesies to foreigners. North Yemen, which has never been occupied by a Western power, feels no awe or deference toward Western technological and cultural achievements and tends to consider Americans who operate within the country as agents of Saudi Arabian foreign policy, not vice versa. It would no more look to Europe and America for inspiration in solving its problems than Americans might look to it. (Indeed, even in South Yemen, which was heavily British-influenced for a century beforehand, the Sultan of Lahej, just outside the port of Aden, as recently as 1934 had publicly crucified three of his slaves in the marketplace on Christmas Day.)

A YEMINI CHILD (JIM SLADE)

But both the Sunni and Shiite branches of Islam are moderate in tenor in their Yemeni form, invoking neither "fanatical" excesses of hospitality to strangers nor religiously sanctioned assassination and martyrdom. Rather, in this Afghanlike cockpit of undiluted tribalism, daggers are drawn, shots are fired and hostages are taken in kinship quarrels. Hostage-holding was a tool of governance during North Yemen's lengthy imamate. In 1939 Yahya had around four thousand immured in various castles after a "unifying campaign"—the boys were said to be in "boarding school." And Ahmad, as late as the 1950s, had two thousand, some of whom he even carried off with him when he went to Rome for medical treatment. Yahya fathered more than forty children, who brought him much sadness. He had ruled for nearly two decades before he saw the sea, but confronted the Turks and Saudis and British fearlessly, warring with the Saudis along the coast; then when the British during World War II cut off his kerosene because he'd been negotiating with the Italians in Ethiopia, he cut off Aden's qat. Ahmad was more mercurial—sadistic at beheadings, and so suspicious that he liked to have the treasury's gold transferred among a series of hiding places by slaves who afterwards were killed. When Ahmad's palace doctor succeeded in evoking an erection in him with hormonal shots after eighteen months of impotency, he is said to have called his whole household together to witness the phenomenon.

In Ma'rib's souk there were veiled Arab women, among whom I glanced in vain to catch a glimpse of Sheba's countenance, masked but perhaps still extant after all these years. Also bold-faced, black-skinned women of the street-cleaner caste who had travelled inland from the Red Sea coast and gazed unveiled, with smoldering eyes, at any white man who might be persuaded to give them money. Such people have their own tribes or clans, and may be descendants of African slaves. Or, on the other hand, they may have had as antecedents the conquering army of Christian Ethiopians who invaded South Arabia in A.D. 525 at the instance of Emperor Justinian of Constantinople and overthrew the Jewish convert king, Dhu Nuwas (apart from an eighth-century A.D. king of the Khazars of Crimea, the only Jewish king ever to reign outside of Israel) after Dhu Nuwas' massacre of some of the area's Christians. Tubba (King) Dhu (Lord) Nuwas (of the Forelock)—called Joseph by the Jews—is said to have spurred his horse straight into the Red Sea after his defeat and was never seen again. Whereupon, after suffering Christian rule a while, the Jews who were left called in the Persians to defeat these Christian Ethiopians. Whereupon, after another fifty years, in A.D. 628, the last Persian satrap in Yemen embraced the newborn religion of Islam.

Yemen's history coils gaudily from dynasty to dynasty—Ya'furis, Ziyadīs, Rasuli sultans, Rassī Zaydis, an abortive Roman invasion, Tahirīs, Qu'aitis, Fatamid caliphs, Ayyubīs, Wahabis, and the Ottoman Empire. The Apostle Thomas probably passed through on his way to India (cathedral ruins underlie part of Sana'a's Great Mosque); and Mohammed did, as

well, during his early career as a trader. Before the Sabaeans' ascendancy, Yemen had been the home of the Minaeans, a people shadowed now by more than three thousand years of wind and sand, and after the fall of the Sabaeans, the Himyarī tribe was dominant until Dhu Nuwas was beaten.

Our Mohammed, director of Ma'rib's antiquities, offered to take us to another pre-Islamic ruin called Baraqish, which was presently off-limits to visitors but had been a district capital of the Himyarīs from perhaps the time of Christ. First, we needed to get through a roadblock, but this was not an unusual procedure. On any trip outside Sana'a we carried photocopies of our travel permit to leave with the security men at each station, but here the soldier decided he didn't want one because our trip was unauthorized except by the antiquities director; he simply moved the barricade. We had thought this sector of the province might be closed off because of military camps or maneuvers, not realizing it was still a zone of "insolence." For much of the period after the 1962 revolution, the entire stretch of the country north and northeast of Sana'a, extending to the Saudi border, had been known as the Zone of Insolence, and, in the fevered tribalism of Yemen, Bjorn had often had to cross the lines to visit his girlfriend, an Algerian aid worker who lived in former royalist territory—where cars then bore no license plates and bootleg gasoline was sold from tanker trucks beside the road—using no pass at all except for the insouciant bulge of qat leaves in his cheek and the clutter of qat twigs next to him on the front seat.

After fifty miles we picked up a hitchhiker at a tiny store, and turned down a dry stream bed, or *wadi*. Martha and I, cautious in our consumption of the drug, were still suffused with the soothing initial effects qat has, but Bjorn, Mohammed and the hitchhiker began gabbling happily at a pitch of intensity, as if they'd each just drunk six cups of coffee—swigging bottled water too, and lighting one cigarette from another, as qat-chewers do when they have no hubble-bubble. We remembered that our new friend had been skulking inside the store, not hustling for a ride out front where he might have been better able to flag down a car, when he told Bjorn in Arabic that although he worked on the coast at the port of Hudayda, he was rushing home to his village near this *wadi* "to help with the killing." His village and the next one were at war and his uncle had been shot. He apologized to all of us for having only a hand grenade with him. People living in Hudayda or travelling through Sana'a were not allowed to carry a rifle—but with Mohammed's two guns and his grenade we could put up a brief fight if his village's enemies should corner us.

Poor Ali's four-wheel-drive Toyota was taking a beating because we couldn't even follow the main *wadi* track; we'd now had to dodge off onto rougher paths more suitable for camels, where a truck patrol from the other village would be less likely to catch us. Our hitchhiker pointed up at two promontories on the rock ridges above us where enemy outposts faced each other, and, laughing, lifted the grenade from his coat pocket, saying he hoped it wouldn't go off accidentally from this jouncing. Though he was glad to be with foreigners whose presence might help to protect him, he was scared. Qat often kites people into a red-eyed daze like peyote after the first storm of conversation, but not under these circumstances.

Anyhow, we reached the gallant-looking, crumbling, red, wild ramparts of Baraqish, which was set between the rival villages, within sight of each, and scrambled up over a caved-in portion of the wall to climb inside. We discovered that a space possibly equivalent to two football fields had been enclosed, with several shells of old buildings still visible, including two temples, beautifully proportioned, that had been dedicated first to a stellar religion and later to Islam but were now deeply smothered in sand. The windy silence was exhilarating, like the height of the rude battlements and the sense of the abyss of history here. Near the center of this little fort was a wide-mouthed well, out of the depths of which a flock of blue

THE IMAN'S PALACE ON THE ROCK—"A JUMBLED TALL CASTLE BUILT OF SAND-STONE, BRICKS AND BASALT ATOP A HUNDRED-FOOT ROCK." (JIM SLADE)

desert doves came laboriously beating. We would have examined every building, three-fourths covered in sand (though the friezes on the porticoes of the temples showed), if the sun hadn't been low and Ali hadn't begun anxiously honking his horn for us to return to the car almost as soon as we'd left it. The local villagers themselves guarded this site as a matter of pride, and the only reason they hadn't already come out to interrogate us was that during the current hostilities it lay in no man's land; they were scared of being trapped by their enemies.

We dropped our friend safely within gun range of his relatives, and he invited us to spend the night, telling us that they would slaughter a sheep for us, and throwing pinches of dust on us, a traditional gesture by which a reluctant guest may be persuaded that he should come with you into your house to wash and stay over. Nevertheless, we took off, now able to follow the main *wadi* bed directly (though a pickup truck full of young men pulled close to scout us), and struck the paved road just at dark. Mohammed rode on into Sana'a with us, checking his rifle, as required, at the army roadblock on the city's outskirts, and argued with Bjorn so long and vociferously for an outlandish guiding fee at the door of his dark caravansary that the high pitch of good fellowship they had shared on the strength of the qat was totally dissolved.

"So you're here to promote tourism?" our Lebanese landlady in Sana'a asked me when she heard that Yemenia Airways had given me a ticket and was providing the services of Ali and his Landcruiser for free. "I hope the Yemenis don't kill the tourists if they come," she added with her sharp Beirut laugh. In a hostile town north of Sana'a, she and her American husband had been waved away at gunpoint when they'd stopped for coffee. At her villa, specializing in American scholars, we were guarded unobtrusively by two or three plainclothes government security agents, who watched over us from a van parked not far from the gate or while loitering in the butcher shop across the street, whose proprietor sat in the doorway in a cloud of flies most of the day, spraying bug dope on the meats that he had on display. This newer sector of the city was sparsely but convivially lit by thin neon signs after the sun set in the dusty sky, and there was a continual din of high-pitched horns. Streams of pedestrians swung quickly along, sure-footed as people who'd walked everywhere until a dozen years ago. We were near a big Health Department facility called the Blood Bank which I could ask for when lost. Sana'a has the complexity of a capital city, and I had astonishing difficulty in mastering its riddle of antique fiefdoms and hasty alleys. Half the denizens sported a foot-length *jambia* (dagger) like a rampant penis poking up from under their belts while the other half were swathed from head to foot in robes and capes and veils. (Somehow the *jambia* in its sheath is regarded as no more dangerous than a woman's face: unholster either and somebody's life will be altered forever.) No street in the old city ran straight enough to see ahead more than a couple of blocks. Each just curved in among its brothers and sisters till suddenly blocked, and there were no street signs and few billboards to catch one's eye as landmarks.

In Yemen one meets a good many expatriates who have been displaced by the Lebanese fighting, including surviving *bons vivants* of the Beirut "Dangerous Diners Club" who had managed to quit the city before they got blown up or kidnapped from a restaurant. The Palestine Liberation Organization, too, has used North Yemen as a kind of rest camp, designating the country its military headquarters after fourteen thousand of its fighters were evacuated from Beirut with American help at the time of the Israeli invasion—Tunis became its political headquarters. Their tents are located in a small valley on the road running south from Sana'a, where they have "made the desert bloom" not far from a campsite previously occupied by Yemeni refugees from the Vietnam War. Palestinian militias of more radical factions have bases in South Yemen, whose 1967 Marxist revolution from British rule was partly godfathered in its preliminary stages by the Palestinian leftist George Habash.

Yemen's highlands, because of the twenty or thirty inches of rainfall they catch in a year, were abundantly populated from early on, and spun off many wanderers and traders who had all of East Africa and the Indian subcontinent to sail to, or beyond, though they usually wished to return home toward the end of their lives. They still come back—also from the Arab neighborhoods near the Ford factory in Dearborn, Michigan—and often to the lush, scenic hills and mild climate around the city of Ibb, among the Sunni Shafiis who constitute most of the nation's bureaucrats, merchants, truck farmers and scholars, to a culture that does not look askance at a man in his sixties with a pension from overseas who marries a girl in her teens and starts over. Indeed, with an infant mortality rate of fifty percent (as we were told at hospitals in two different regions) and virtually no opportunity for a woman to do more than raise children, it's not such a bad idea for her to marry an avuncular man who can provide her family with plenty of food and clean bottled water and an education.

Eight hundred years ago Ibb was the seat of power of perhaps Yemen's pleasantest dynasty: Queen Arwa's. She was an Ismaeli, a member of a Shiite splinter group more recently followers of a holy man who lives in Surat, India, and a woman of legendary beauty, masterly at "stratagems," who devoted her peaceable reign mainly to road-building and other graceful good works. We stayed overnight in the lovely medieval hill town of Jibla, with a ninth-century mosque where Ismaeli dignitaries are buried, in a jagged, auger-twist valley where twenty years ago a farmer strangled the last local leopard with his bare hands. The streets were lightless, cobbled with boulders, and only the width of the ribs of a donkey. When I went walking alone, two black-garbed women with bell-like voices asked me if I had any chocolate through the mask of their veils.

We celebrated Martha's milestone thirtieth that evening with a dinner of beans, red tea and bread in the town's cafe, talking with Jibla's gloomy druggist, who had studied in Alexandria, in what had been for him a happier day, and gazed out at the modest yellow gleam of kerosene lamps in the huts across the wide gap of the *wadi. We* were cheerful, at any rate; Martha teasing me that after reading one of my books she had decided it would be better if she didn't sleep with me. I said she would keep her girlish freckles forever then; that she was our official "adventuress," being the in-house representative of Sobek Expeditions of California, which was feeding and housing me in exchange for mention of their services. Sobek is a company of trek guides and river runners who have named themselves after a Nile crocodile-god, and I said she herself, being the one unveiled woman in Jibla, was a river-god. She said I was the proverbial toad whom no princess had ever kissed and might remain so. She was cooking raisin-oatmeal for me in the mornings, however, and since she wasn't sleeping with the younger, handsomer Bjorn either, our jigsaw bedroom arrangements in these little *funduqs* (inns) were painless.

Beyond Ibb, the American-cut, German-paved highway that connects Sana'a with Ta'izz, North Yemen's principal southerly city, climbs a pass and descends by sumptuous switchbacks—each with a peddler sitting beside baskets of tomatoes, carrots, onions, potatoes or corn—to this *Aruzat al-Yemen*, "Bride of Yemen," as Ta'izz is sometimes called. Only seven hundred years old, it has an ease and tolerance, a vibrancy and buoyancy. People spice their qat with betel nuts occasionally, or sauce their tea with opium. The market is full of unveiled businesswomen from Jebel Sabor selling wheelbarrowloads of dates, oranges, papayas, and mangoes, barrels of millet, wheat, barley and lentils, sacks of saffron, turmeric, cardamom and caraway seeds, and especially qat. What with the old university and theo-logical centers like Dhamar, Zabid, and Bayt al-Faqih having slid into decay (Yemenis claim Zabid is where algebra and logarithms were invented), it was in Ta'izz that one could imagine poetry being argued over and politics of a less violent stripe being plotted. The Shafiis of this part of Yemen were tribal mostly in theory, long-sedentary taxpayers who were warlike only when they needed to protect themselves from the Zaydis of the north. They're the scribblers and traders, the modernists of Yemen.

Bjorn being full of an architect's zeal, we were soon climbing to the heights of the city to inspect a six-hundred-fifty-year-old mosque whose painted interior had been whitewashed or cemented over during the bad days of some benighted conquest when the mosque had been turned into a tannery. Now it was being restored wherever the cement hadn't damaged the decorations irretrievably. The confident, well-knit, old, short-bodied, white-haired master mason who was in charge told Bjorn he was working for free and said gaily in Arabic, "Ever since I was sixteen, I've walked so straight in life that I could walk on the ocean now if I wanted to." He led us up the circular staircase inside the fat minaret to gaze over the rolling, ocher-colored, mostly four-storied little city cupped in the curve of a mountain—at its broken outer walls, its domed baths, squat, square tenements, and tan and white towering religious edifices. Way overhead was the former Turkish citadel on a knife-edge spur above us.

We stayed at al-Ganad Hotel, a fine four-square downtown villa which, although inexpensive, boasted bougainvillaeas in the garden and servants "British-trained," who had fled the Communist takeover in Aden. (Newly constructed tourist hotels are on "Baboon Hill," where, until some of the firepower incidental to Yemen's civil war was brought to bear upon them, baboons used to live.) At dawn, a muezzin on a minaret coughed into his microphone briefly to clear his throat and then roused the whole city with a voice like a ram's horn:

> *God is greater.*
> *I bear witness, there is no god but God.*
> *I bear witness, Mohammed is the messenger of God.*
> *Come to prayer.*
> *Come to salvation.*

It sounded so stirring that all Ta'izz's dogs, roosters and donkeys chimed in. Even Haile Selassie's gift of a pride of lions, which are caged at the gate of Imam Ahmad's summer palace on a breezy elevated point of the city, sent forth a volley of roars.

The gates of the imam's winter palace, which was lower down, are bracketed not by lion cages but by the dungeons in which languished those of his prisoners whom he wanted closest to hand. Though he was a Zaydi Shi'i (like all the imams: caliph was the term for an equivalent figure among the Sunnis), maintained in power by the Zaydis' force of arms, he chose to locate his capital in this tractable Sunni city of Shafiis. Only once, in 1957, when he was sixty-eight and nearing the end of his turbulent, tyrannical reign, did he hold a press conference, which the British journalist David Holden, in "Farewell to Arabia," describes thus:

"His voice came in rapid, hoarse gasps, as if he was in pain ... his hands tugged at his black-dyed beard, and his eyes—starting from his head as if with goitre and the effort of speech—rolled like white marbles only tenuously anchored to his sallow flesh. At a glance one might have thought him literally staring mad. But if he was he remained uncannily alert. Nothing in the room escaped him: his eyes could be riveted in the instant upon the slightest movement, and he listened to every questioner with an intensity so fierce and so impatient that he seemed at times about to leap up, crying 'Off with his head!' "—meanwhile indulgently patting two of his small sons who were playing like puppies about his feet, but sharing a fearful, mocking smile with the newspapermen as he did.

"These flashes of grim, ingratiating humor, when the full lips were drawn back over broken teeth and the dark brows were lowered over popping eyes, gave an extraordinary humanity to what might otherwise have seemed a mere, broken monster. One grasped not only the power, cruelty and suspicion of a total despot, not only the weaknesses of pain, sickness and age with which his will seemed to be in open, tigerish conflict, but also the sense of a man fearfully alone."

Ta'izz is close to South Yemen's border and to its capital, Aden, which the British ruled as part of India for a hundred years, then as a separate crown colony for thirty more. Aden became known as "the Eye of Yemen," because it was the Yemenis' sole opening to the Western world, or as "the Coal Hole of the East," because ships sailing to India and the Orient were fueled and serviced in the harbor—six thousand a year by 1964. Only London, Liverpool and New York surpassed it as a bunkering port, and tens of thousands of tourists shopped there duty-free and explored the volcanic crater that holds the old city, while glancing northward perhaps toward the sealed-off, mysterious mountains of Yemen itself. Ta'izz received a trickle of goods from all this salt-water commerce, and injections of novel ideas, but South Yemen got such a flood of foreign entrepreneurs and ideologies that, with independence, it very soon wound up the only Arab nation in the Marxist camp, and it is still administered with tough severity against some of the ulema as well as the kin of former emirs, sultans and sheikhs.

Ta'izz, however, has the pep of a city just tasting new ideas, not swamped by them. We ate *kibda*—tidbits of liver sautéed with tomatoes and peppers—in cubbyholes off the street and drank *gishr*, the Yemeni version of coffee made from the husks after the precious coffee beans themselves have been sold for export. And we kept going back to the souk, bargaining for jewelry with an unveiled, fierce-faced sheikhly widow who casually but bafflingly juggled our money between us to shortchange us, then placated us when we complained with an ancient-looking copper coin apiece. Many Yemeni families, in response to the oil boom, have traded in their traditional silver pieces of jewelry for cookie-cut gold stuff that looks like a walking bank account, so she had handsome antique bracelets, rings, necklaces, snuff boxes and breastplates. Other booths offered brocaded belts and dagger sheaths, Persian pearls, Siamese fans, and long-barreled, scrimshawed guerrilla rifles from forgotten mountain fights in the Ottoman wars. Or simply pots and pans, Indian fabrics, gowns and scarves, vests and shirts, sandals, turbans, pillbox hats. In the morning it was a watchful place, the men sitting cross-legged and unsmiling in their pleated kilts (except that several gave me a thumbs-up sign when I walked back a ways to give a few rials to a beggar), as in the days when the motto of the markets here had been, "Chop one hand off: save a hundred." But in the afternoon, after the qat had taken effect, you could pass half a dozen stalls being watched over by the same men's young daughters or by boys under the age of ten; the stall owners were out of sight.

We were teasing Martha about how little she'd been eating of our millet porridges and sorghum pancakes, our spicy meats and fiery stews and yoghurt gruels. She had vegetarian tendencies, which I suggested might be the death of her in Yemen where the best food was meat, and she had also brought with her from California the notion that eggs contain harmful amounts of cholesterol, when of course it seemed to me we needed to burn all the cholesterol we could in order to keep going. But if Martha needed encouragement in eating, I was having trouble walking, having been weakened by a six-week bout with flu in the United States. She was protecting me from Bjorn's accesses of enthusiasm. His passion for Yemen was indefatigable and had even resulted in his designing buildings to be built of mud-brick, like the historic quarters of the cities, and losing some prospective architectural business from the impatient technocrats at the government ministry in Sana'a.

He was a touching man. Although flexible, reflective and gentle, he struck me as growing rather puzzled now in his late thirties by the ways of the world. Even Yemen had more citizens than Norway, and America more Norwegians, so he appeared to think that being Norwegian was in itself a precarious proposition. He had left there, returned, left, and returned again. Norwegians are travellers, and he had spent part of his childhood on the arctic island of Spitzbergen, where his mother had worked as a nurse and where the summer tourists had gawked at him and her, he said. Later, he had served as a steward on cruise ships carrying American tourists through the Pacific, which had probably reinforced the underdog spin that his perceptions already had; he spoke a bit bitterly of the rich "Love Boat" Americans, and of burning his hands holding hot teakettles for them. He wore his architecture school class ring, but after living in Sana'a and Cairo for a decade he hadn't had very much chance to practice his profession, and from living abroad he was losing his own language, he said. He thought as well as spoke in English more often than in Norwegian, but in English, as in Arabic, his vocabulary was limited, so that the free flow of his ideas was constricted; and meanwhile his Norwegian vocabulary had shrunk or rusted alarmingly. He was a man of ebullience and intuition but he was wondering what to do. Indeed, on most adventure treks (of which in a professional capacity I've made too many) one finds that the guides, though quite big-brotherly in their role and manner, are people who aren't practicing whatever kind of work they had trained for and are wondering what they ought to begin doing almost as soon as the trip ends. The customers, on the other hand, tend to have been maneuvering in a sleekly turned-out profession for decades, maybe too well.

South Yemen invaded the North as recently as 1979, almost cutting the road halfway between Sana'a and Ta'izz, with Russian military advisers facing each other on either side of the battle line until the signals were switched and a pullback arranged. So because in each town we had rambled into we'd enjoyed having a special errand to pursue, and because Ta'izz has been a Cold War "listening post" since the British lost Aden, we tried to figure out who the Americans' spymaster was, now that the American consulate, where one or two of the CIA's crack young Arabists had trained, has closed. We popped into the Danish consulate, close to our hotel, for want of an alternative, and asked who was "running agents into South Yemen for the West nowadays." The Consul (it's an honorary position) seemed to be an ordinary bustly Yemeni importer trying to keep track of a pile of inventory, and was nonplussed.

The most numerous, effective foreign agents in Yemen have been Egyptians, however. Nasserites helped plan and arm the overthrow of Ahmad's son, the more liberal sixty-sixth imam, Mohammed al-Badr, within a week of his accession in September, 1962. Then the Egyptian army, during a grinding, dreary, five-year war, which was regarded afterwards as "Nasser's folly" and "Egypt's Vietnam," repeatedly beat back tenacious Saudi-financed royalist tribesmen in their counterstrikes upon the republicans, amazing them sometimes with airpower. Tribal warriors equipped with Mausers, whose favorite tactic had been to loll on a crag and pick off an enemy toiling below, with the gunstock kissing one cheek and the muzzle cradled between two outstretched toes—and who'd been taught as boys that airplanes and even trucks were *djinns*—watched Migs do bombing runs over their walled villages in utter frustration.

THE MARKET AT TA'IZZ
(MARTHA FREEMAN)

Thus Egypt, more than any direct Western influence, effected radical changes upon North Yemen; and South Yemen's revolt against Britain, culminating in independence at about the same time that Egyptian troops were forced to withdraw from the North after the debacle of the Six Day War with Israel, drew confidence and inspiration from them. But Egypt's thinking altered after the Six Day War. Since Nasser's death in 1970, the cadre of thirty thousand Egyptian schoolteachers remaining in North Yemen have gradually become a far more conservative factor, together with their many Sudanese colleagues, who generally (like the Sudan with Egypt) follow their lead. They are the backbone of Yemen's Muslim Brotherhood. The Brotherhood is an international, fundamentalist, youthful but reactionary force in Arab societies whose governments are working for a secular future (whether socialist or Westernized) and a Puritan element in oil-boom nations with a new-minted devotion to worldly goods: in other words, a range of countries from Saudi Arabia to Syria and Egypt itself, where the Brotherhood was founded in 1928. Although they do engage in violent acts, the Brothers are typically of a more hortatory or intellectual bent, and find plenty to disapprove of anywhere, being determined that an unvarnished form of Islam stay paramount in the Middle East.

At the embassies in Sana'a people had talked to me "deep-background," for which they rather apologized but which, not being a newspaperman, I quite enjoy. Newspapermen need somebody to quote, whereas a free-lance larcenous soul like me may be content to appropriate any ideas he is told anonymously. Yet in fact the Western embassies were approving of what was going on politically in North Yemen. They did believe that the economics of allowing the fabulous thousand-year-old agricultural terraces to wash away down every mountainside, while the populace chewed up amounts of home-grown qat equal in cash value to the foreign food aid that has to be shipped in, was absurd and disastrous. (South Yemen permits qat-chewing only on weekends; Saudi Arabia will jail a chewer for five years.) But "Yemen (Sana'a)," as the country is known among diplomats, has a competent president, Ali Abdallah

Salih, who, though not a charismatic speaker, has succeeded in balancing Zaydi and Shafii, and Saudi and South Yemen, interests. He is a former sergeant and tribal fighter who sports a pistol low-slung on one hip and looks like a Mexican movie star in the still photographs that are posted up all over, or on the nightly news, when the camera pans endlessly across an auditorium full of delegates, candidates or graduates while a Sousa soundtrack is played and the announcer repeats the hopeful phrase, "the Homeland," in Arabic. His predecessor was killed when a briefcase chained to the wrist of an envoy from Aden blew up; and the president before *that* was poisoned, along with his brother and two French prostitutes with whom they had foolishly been dallying, all four bodies then being dragged into the same room and shot up together to make for a scandalous scene. Revolutionists from the National Democratic Front, who prefer South Yemen's model of governance, are a threat, but there is a religious sanction among the conservative Zaydis too that if a leader has committed substantial sins, others more appropriate for his position rise up and kill him.

The two most powerful and martial tribes in Yemen, the Hashid and Bakil—once known as "the wings of the imamate"—inhabit villages in a quilted pattern across the northern mountains. They dominated the Shafiis for centuries, but are so rivalrous that they have had to establish "confederations" to keep from flying at one another's throats. Salients of each tribe sold their talents to the highest bidder and then sometimes switched sides during the civil war, but both would generally have been thorough royalists if Imam Ahmad in one of his temper tantrums had not had the head of the Hashid's paramount chieftain chopped off (also his son's) during a supposed safe-conduct parley that the imam had arranged with them in order to settle a money dispute. Both maintain private armies and to oppose Marxism, with Saudi kibitzing, have set up an Islamic Front that would be a formidable countervailing element in case of a new insurrection from South Yemen by the National Democratic Front or a leftist putsch by officers of the army or security forces.

To hear anecdotes of political killings in the two Yemens—the machine-gunning of practically the whole Cabinet in Aden in January, 1986, as well as various smaller traps that have been set and sprung—is to imagine anarchy. But Ali Abdallah Salih has survived in office since 1978 by conciliation and negotiation, allowing two earlier presidents to return from exile and permitting a smattering of Yemeni Muslim Brothers to enter government service alongside the conventional Shafiis and Zaydis, some Islamic Front people and even, at the opposite pole, a few representatives of the NDF. The ten-thousand-man, black-beretted Security Force keeps a watch on the red-beretted, thirty-thousand-man Army, and the tiny Air Force wheels its several F-5 fighter planes over the middle of the country as yet another factor once a day.

From Ta'izz, we rolled down a spacious, loop-the-loop highway toward the Red Sea coast, past millet, tobacco and tomato fields, oxen plowing, banana plantations, hobbled camels browsing on the thorn trees, mangoes and oranges growing, and the rich-soiled bottomland to which the stick-plow sharecroppers and small landowners on the mountainsides used to descend after a rainstorm to carry back the soil that had washed down. We saw black goats, white sheep, brown dogs, and women herders striding serenely, garbed also in black. One girl walked toward a well with a pail on her head that she was rapping rhythmically.

Once we left the mountains, the desert created mirages that gave camels eight legs, and Ali used his headlights instead of his horn to warn approaching cars. Our immediate mission was to buy some bootleg whiskey for Bjorn's expatriate friends in Sana'a. The former coffee port of al-Mukha has silted in so much that sizeable ships seldom use it, but it's still suitable for smugglers' shallow-drawing craft that dart across the strait of Bab al-Mandab from the French protectorate of Djibouti in Africa. Founded by Himyarite traders, its fortunes peaked under the Ottomans during the seventeenth century, when it is said to have boasted three hundred mosques. It was the Turks' port in Yemen until the old Sabaeans' port of Aden, expanded by the British, eclipsed it.

Johnny Walker Red Label and Carlsbad beer cost less than they would have in New York City but had to be bought surreptitiously even by foreigners. We gave our order at a crossroads gas station to a slim, predatory-looking young man as swift and boneless in his movements as a snake, with a slave trader's deeply cruel and amused face—I was suddenly reminded that al-Mukha had been a slaving port too until rather recently. Our savvy party refused to receive the booze at the gas station but instead pulled down the road out of sight, where we lifted the hood of the car as if we had broken down. By and by along came the young man on his motorbike with a box strapped on the back, his face muddy-colored but aquilinely Arab, and that expression as though he were laughing at a slave girl's thirst on a march across the desert after he had decided that her thirst was not going to hurt her.

Al-Mukha is now a huddle of decrepit gray buildings covering a tenth of the historic city. But the Red Sea was a fresh jade-green, whipped silvery by the wind, with the eternal sand blowing hard in our faces, or spindrift when it shifted. We drove north on truck tracks that paralleled it closely, through date palm plantations, past salt evaporation pits and little settlements of round grass huts with conical thatched roofs, surrounded by wattle fences, just as in Africa. Among them walked a taller, chocolate-black, veilless people, and sometimes we saw small rowboats or rudimentary rafts on the beach, and the fishermen's throw-nets drying. Short bogs alternated with stretches of outright desert or dry scrubland or, again, a carefully irrigated patch of date palms growing fifty feet high, and a water pump thumping. We'd see some huts built of grass and palm leaves with a couple of children playing beside the rope beds set outside, three or four dogs asleep, and a goat wandering loose.

"These are just blacks," Ali said in Arabic with a laugh, driving hard to keep out of sand traps. Sometimes our path completely disappeared and he would need to swerve and speed up or grind down into first gear in order to keep going. Or else it ran straight into the surf, so that we had to backtrack. Deep sand gave way to miles of saltbush or lumpy, irrigated soil planted with sorghum. We found a derelict mosque whose oven-shaped domes were inhabited by swallows and bats, with animist amulets set into niches on the wall in the back; but later we saw another mosque in a further huddle of huts, neatly swept, beautifully cared for and gracefully structured, with a deep, cool, clean, blue-painted cistern where people could perform their ablutions before they prayed.

Ali did pray, with open fervor—the first time we had seen him do this—prostrating himself with his arms outstretched in the Sunni manner. (Shi'is keep their arms by their sides as they bend forward repeatedly from a kneeling position.) Praying five times a day with strenuous obeisances is good exercise, and it is said of the older Yemeni men that although chewing qat makes them impotent at a fairly early age, they keep fit otherwise by an austere regimen of prayer and mastering their mountainous terrain.

But we weren't in the mountains. We were by the wild sea, with spray hitting our noses, on a precarious track the high tide threatened as it thundered, or that could become completely obscured by a ten-minute sandstorm. We'd stop dead and sit as if night had fallen, and when that let up, would discover that the furrows we had been following had nearly filled in. Ali had to drive fast to keep from stalling, but to go fast was to risk flipping over or shooting off into a sinkhole or winding up in the sea.

Inshore, the sea was a lighter green than out beyond the reef. Whenever the sky cleared,

"Johnny Walker Red Label and Carlsbad beer cost less than they would have in New York City but had to be bought surreptitiously even by foreigners."

which it did abruptly, the sight was stunning—those splendid nuances of green, the curve of the waves and the froth on them, the conflicting angles that they ran from, and the white band of narrow beach they splashed against. Often the beachside grass grew head-high, so when we came upon a hut and *shamba* it was a surprise for the people who lived there. The women in their brightly-patterned cotton wraparounds, carrying thatch or firewood or household goods on their heads between compounds, seemed refreshingly personable because we could look at their faces as we passed. But whereas most Arab women would have made a show of ignoring us, not acknowledging the faintest possibility that they might ever be accosted by a stranger, these women acted agitated, if not actually frightened, as we approached. Especially if one of them was some little distance from her house, she was likely to break into a run in front of our van, glancing back over her shoulder, almost as though slavers still prowled the area and she might be scooped up and carted off. It was so startling to see a pretty woman scampering like a fearful deer in front of our van that predatory impulses were aroused in me; and I doubt I was the only person to want for just a second to grab her. Even in Sana'a, when Bjorn, Martha and I had sat chewing qat in a businessman's *mafraj* (chewing room), our host had jarred the otherwise placid proceedings by telling Martha in Arabic several times with a salacious grin that if Bjorn and I forgot about her and left her behind, "I'll lock you up in that closet under the stairs and sell you in the souk tomorrow."

Another sandstorm cut our visibility and threshed the surf vigorously. We ate dates, driving through the date groves, feeling that funny sensation of icing on our teeth, and finally camped close to al-Khawkhah, a fishing village with a fleet of old-fashioned longboats, each now equipped with a Yamaha outboard, beached on blocks for the night. Kids on bikes and men on motorbikes showed up to question us, while several camels stalked slowly by like elk. Overhead sailed a medley of black crows and brown hawks, blue doves, high vultures and fast kites.

"Why should I go to school? I can work on the sea," said a boy with a face like a pirate's, in Arabic, when Bjorn challenged him as he liked to do with the children who surrounded us in every village begging for ballpoint pens—"*Qolam, qolam*"—even when they had pens in their hands. He would ask them to show some pride, ask interesting questions, at least,

THE AUTHOR CONTEMPLATES TA'IZZ. (MARTHA FREEMAN)

and to think before they spoke, to be individuals instead of a mob, and to remember their geography when he told them he was from Norway, not assume Norway was part of America like Martha's California and my New York.

These were dark-skinned Arabs, the men with mussed hair and miscellaneous features like movie buccaneers, not kindly-looking, not people whose shores a castaway would want to wash up on. But the boy we'd talked to led over his Sudanese schoolteacher from the village, who walked with a stately posture in a spotless long white gown and asked for a book published in English that he could practice reading in the evening. He added, however, that he and two compatriots were working "night and day" with class preparations, teaching one hundred and sixty kids in all of the grammar-school grades, double-shifting them to fit everyone in.

"Only one or two are smart," he explained, with his big, even, benign-looking, Sudanese smile, though a discomfort fluttered just under the surface of it. "They're terrible to us, but also sometimes kind." He was a prepossessing, detribalized man from the Gezira cotton-growing region south of Khartoum, and he was working like an exile here in the punishing heat to save money to be married. We were sweating in February, but the summer's heat on Yemen's coastline has the reputation of hounding even British aid officials stark raving mad. When I asked, he said it was indeed worse than Khartoum's, and by his generous, philosophic manner made me homesick for that gentler city. But he left us with a hint of disapproval when Bjorn hauled out our dilettantish sack of qat.

All that moonlit night low foaming rollers dashed toward the beach. It was a cocoon of sound, but I woke up with an ache in the sinuses above my cheeks and my mouth still mildly stinging from qat. The fishermen were back to launch their boats, sitting in raucous yet ceremonious groups while each crew of six or eight established their plans and good cheer and rapport for the day. They gave a kind of yell in unison at the end like football players before running onto the field, because theirs could quickly become a life-and-death venture if a storm blew up, and was a hand-to-mouth existence at best.

We stopped in Zabid, the Koranic university town that was at its height in the thirteenth and fourteenth centuries. It has a ramshackle but imposing citadel and a big shell of a mosque where Yemen's Sunnis still bring their thorniest religious disputes, as well as a pleasant park full of birds, furnished with hammocks instead of benches, where I displayed to a crowd of children the parts of my Swiss Army knife.

Farther along, at Bayt al-Faqih, pickup truckloads of sweltering sheep waited to be sold, and twenty camels kneeled in a circle, each tethered to a stake by a thong through one nostril. Mainly, the vast market offered bags of coffee husks, boll cotton, leaf tobacco, walnuts, peaches, apricots, a motorcycle mart, and bales of Indian clothing and madras cloth. Old tribal costumes that looked like museum pieces were being proffered for a song, for want of foreign tourists to buy them. The market women wore straw hats wound around with bright scarves, and red, black and green dresses with a low décolletage. Disdaining a face-covering, they bargained with panache, while furloughed burros roamed the alleys, eating garbage with the dogs. Burros haven't the significance of camels in Yemenis' minds, and all over the country one sees them simply manumitted from labor by the arrival of Toyota cars and trucks.

From al-Hudeidah, the new port modernized by the Russians, we left the baking coast and drove into the mountains through a beautiful series of valleys planted with papaya trees, tamarisks and banana plants, with the remarkable sight of water sparkling in some of the *wadis*, and egrets flying up and down. Although the agricultural terraces spreading up the mountain slopes out of view were not being maintained any more, the kids we saw playing hopscotch still "terraced" the boundaries of their game instead of drawing lines on the ground. A shepherd was blowing his flute, firewood was stacked for sale next to the road, and corn was drying on the stone roofs nearby—though after all of the invasions of Yemen's highlands that have been launched along this route, most of the rock-built houses we passed were wedged precipitously onto cliffsides as far back, up and away from the road as the ancestors of the present occupants had been able to jimmy them. Some you would have needed a rope to climb to, and might have lost a dozen men in capturing the residents; an army of conquest hurrying toward Sana'a would just have gone by. All had gunslit windows, but several of the more cheerful ones were whitewashed and painted with jubilant-looking airplanes, like a child's drawings, in celebration of the safe return of somebody in the family from a *hajj*.

The reason that these valleys didn't appear entirely like a fairy tale is that they contained so many little castles, not just one in each. We slept in the chewing room atop a vertiginous *funduq* in the formerly much persecuted Ismaeli town of Manakhah, seven thousand feet up—the "Gibraltar of Yemen," its houses themselves pinnacles—which we reached by many switchbacks and which the Turks, early in this century, had held through many "risings." The view was giddy in the moonlight, and in the morning we breakfasted on puffy disks of pita bread laden with honey. Haggara, on an adjoining spur of Jebel Haraz, even higher, had fifteen hundred people living in seven-story houses painted with what resembled M's and X's and images of eagles, the latticed windows filigreed with gypsum. The children, as always, chased after us asking for *suras* and *qolams*, photos and pens, as if the very act of shaking hands with three large heathen was an adventure.

A woman carrying a pail on her head asked in Arabic what nationality we were; then joked, "I'm German." But after Bjorn started talking to her she soon spoke of "the time of the Old Ones," when people were wise. There is of course considerable poignancy to a country that has been propelled from feudalism into the late twentieth century in two and a half decades, and few of the older Yemenis we talked to were in love with progress, except for the money they could earn by leaving home to pump oil. The unreconstructed royalists, in particular, resent the thousands of little pickups penetrating every cranny of the country, hauling splintered trees out for a quick sale, hauling building cement in, or joy-riding all over as if God were no longer alive. Even republicans will often end up parked for a while at a turn in the road at a height of land, feasting their eyes like the mountain people they are. They'll bring a picnic to eat sitting on the rocks at the top of a pass, and may improve the time by changing their oil. Whole families turn out, with a man to handle the wheel but often more women and children because so many men are away earning foreign exchange. (Middle-class young men in Sana'a sometimes become part-time taxi drivers for the chance to talk to women unchaperoned; their girlfriends at the university will arrange to "call a cab.") The revolution brought pants to Yemen and a man's politics were sometimes judged by whether he adopted pants or stuck to the traditional skirt, but plenty of men who put on pants to go to work still wear a skirt on their days off, up here in the clean air, the paterfamilias draining the carburetor while enjoying the language of the rocks and birds.

All scenic highway edges are stained with motor oil and shoe-deep in plastic litter and tin cans. Plastic was never envisioned in the customs of tribal Yemen: that any kind of waste could be invented that goats and donkeys would not eat or that the day might come when goats and donkeys would seem to be in short supply. The blind leap of this small country toward hustly homogeneity with the rest of the world is poignant, and yet the reason that one's heart doesn't go out to the local people is that their previous existence was so far from a state of innocence. With slavery, serfdom, the bushwhacking of travellers and kidnapping of hostages, the infinitely variable autocracies that sultans, sheikhs and emirs (each with his prisoners and his harem) exercised over its patchwork of ranges and valleys, medieval Yemen was a knotty place. The dozens of walled towns that we caught sight of in the course of our tour, with their picturesque earth-colored battlements and tenementlike houses, bore the same message as scars—being the mark of sieges suffered and frequent or incessant war. To capture such a community, bashing down its log gates, sweeping over its mud fortifications, pulverizing its simple defenses, cracking it like an egg and biting it like an apple before bringing into play the proverbial slave headsman, must have increased the slaughter and rapine. After the revolution an army machine gunner replaced the imam's famous grinning executioner, whose sword was publicly broken. Instead, crowds witnessing the event would line an alleyway just wide enough for the volley of bullets to hit the doomed man without killing them.

Our road from Manakhah curved past Yemen's highest mountain and down again onto Sana'a's lofty plateau, where Egyptian and Chinese monuments commemorate the breaching of the final royalist siege only twenty years ago, when the Chinese road construction crew outside the city took up arms to help the Yemenis and Egyptians inside break through the Bakils' lines.

Spring rains arrived the night of our return to Sana'a, the city's first wetting in five months, and dawn erupted with birdsong. The people were equally happy, marveling at the deep mudholes over clogged drains at the crossroads. Taxicabs knew how to negotiate high water without stalling, but ordinary car-owning Yemenis driving to work were likely to steer right into the middle of a standing pool in a panicky fashion, lose their nerve and stop, while the pedestrians hollered. One thoroughfare is the riverbed, dry most of the year. Kids were splashing in it, throwing stones.

A butcher led a flock of sheep through the twisting streets with only the bait of a fresh green bough cradled in his arms. A good deal of a city is its food, and women walking to work were nibbling breakfast bread by slipping pieces of it underneath their veils, using the hand that wasn't carrying a briefcase. They are employed as bank tellers, secretaries and at other jobs requiring dexterous attentiveness, though as a matter of propriety they will still generally do their shopping after work with a young son along to speak to and convey their decisions to the storekeeper. And with their slim forms, straight postures and forthright, even peremptory air, their skirts drifting, their mantles blowing, their veils continually needing readjustment, the women's presence was very noticeable, at least for a foreigner unaccustomed to such scenes. Every woman looked extraordinarily "feminine," with her face left to the imagination while her hands manipulated the folds and billows of her unbelted clothing, as if somewhere under one of those gauzy veils and black, red and white tie-dyed *marmoukhs* that appeared to have been painted with huge ox eyes was the face and figure of Arwa or Sheba's Queen. They were probably closer to being chattel than queens, but several older women we encountered in back lanes were using their veils merely as scarves, so it was possible to see that they looked not unlike Greek or Italian women of sixty, and as they joked with us, that they had not been cowed by going around veiled from the age of nine.

Sana'a's Revolution Square holds the tank that first fired on the palace of the Imamate, and lots of concrete laid out in a lopsided triangle, with an ad for an orange drink on a rooftop at one end. It's ugly as such places go, but is an opening to fix on in the otherwise bewildering hive of passageways, cul-de-sacs and souks. Like Florence, Alexandria or Zanzibar, Sana'a is not a city where one can ever expect to see more happening than has occurred before. Yet like many great architectural sites of the distant past, it reaches not just the pre-

THE SMILING FACE OF
MODERN YEMEN (JIM SLADE)

Christian or pre-Muslim sources in us but goes back perhaps to neolithic experiences that can lend an intermittent, subterranean terror to perceiving oneself as an interloper here. And of course generations of Christian leeriness of Islam, with the bugaboos of current bigotry, leave a mark.

Sana'a has a population of four hundred thousand, and the two walled old quarters intersect like the halves of a figure eight at what used to be a natural choke-point for snuffing out a rebellion. The dirt or cobblestone streets loop like footpaths and the fanciful and teetery mini-castles and idiosyncratically tall mud tenements with gunslit windows that only begin four stories up are like cliff dwellings. But then you see a friendly and straightforward face, a market scene, or children playing and the illusion that this is a glimpse of pre-history is banished. People say one reason the houses are built of mud is that "mud swallows bullets" as stones do not; a bullet will ricochet off stonework and strike again somewhere else. On the other hand, a cannon shell that will knock down a stone house may pass right through a mud one. Yemenis most resemble the Omanis, another spiky, rigorously fractured mountain people, who live along the opposite side of the Empty Quarter, warring sporadically with central authority—in their case, a sultan assisted by British mercenaries. And in Sana'a, as in Muscat, one sees faces from the edge of India and East Africa, Zanzibaris, Mombasars, and so on.

Most Yemenis are cold-climate Arabs, with a faster idea of pacing and less patience for haggling than some hot-land peoples. A tick-tock rush of activity—white-turbaned laborers, black-turbaned craftsmen—prevails in Sana'a, as in other proud cities. Stalls selling bread or lettuce, stalls selling betrothal baubles. Blacksmiths, silversmiths, brass workers. By wandering we even found a hospice for donkeys with broken legs, fourteen animals hobbling about, nibbling clover, the remarkable charity of an old locksmith who looked like any average fellow in that central "Souk of the Cows," as the market area is called, but who was the object of hoots and catcalls from other stall owners when we located him; he got mad and wouldn't talk to us. Yemenis don't kill domestic creatures if they can help it, but often treat them inhumanely. A dog is considered good luck as a scapegoat—the family's bad luck

TOWERING MINARETS AND MUEZZINS' CRIES STILL PERVADE MODERN YEMEN. (RICHARD BANGS)

may fasten upon him, particularly if his ears have been cropped—but his saliva is ritually defiling; while a cat is respected as cleaner in the Prophet's eyes, and more generally for mousing. Yet both may be allowed to starve. Besides the six-story houses painted fantastically, with windows of stained glass and alabaster, there were plenty of hovels, but the massive, roan-red Bab al-Yemen, Gate of Yemen, with its fountain, the southern portal to the city, and the Gate of Constantinople, on the north, seemed mesmerizing, as though processions were still arriving from Mecca and Dar es Salaom.

Yemenis, and Yemeni Shi'is in particular, are not very public in their religious observance; one doesn't notice them touching their foreheads to the pavement the way a good many people do even in Cairo, for instance. This, and the vigor of commerce in the morning, might give rise to an impression that cultural relativism holds sway here; that jet-setters might soon be flying in to this zanily picturebook city to buy hideaways, as on the cozy island of Zamelek in the Nile, or Tuscany's quaint hill towns. But Yemenis are not like Cairenes or Italians. Drunkenness, bawdy noise, late-night visitors, unclad females glimpsed through an apartment window can provoke an anguish of concern, and in Sana'a the neighbors are not likely to let the matter drag. Nor is their means of bringing their grievance to a head easy to ignore. The European offender may first hear of it by the sound of bawling in the street and, looking out, discover that a leggy bull calf is being hauled unwillingly to his doorstep. There, the splash of blood as it is slaughtered signifies that an important parley must take place.

We drove north from Sana'a for five hours toward the walled district capital of Sadah, close to the Saudi border, through twisty, bouldery, banditty little valleys where every house was provisionally a fortress—though glyphed with gypsum and white-washed at the windows—and across a series of short plateaus planted to sorghum. Sometimes when the road curved we would see a small cairn memorializing the spot where a child or a goatherd had been run over and killed. The pavement would be interrupted where angry relatives had tried to manufacture bumps to slow the traffic down. Yet we met vehicles only every five minutes or so, most of them rag-tag cars making the once-a-year-or-two trek back from Saudi Arabia piled to double their natural height with brand-new tables, chairs, bureaus, refrigerators, mattresses, bedding, baled goods, and television sets and other appliances in packing boxes roped to the roof. Half a million Yemenis work in Saudi Arabia, earning thirty or forty dollars a day, which is three times the typical wage at home, so it's no wonder the road occasionally has bandits on it. Since the war, every man carries a Kalashnikov as a matter of custom, and needs only to slump one shoulder to let the magazine slide into his hand.

We paused to watch a crowd of vultures and carrion eagles feeding on a goat at the bottom of a cliff. The towns had boxy, earthen-colored dwellings with a staccato high row of window slits, the relative width of which, as well as their distance from the ground, provides a quick estimate of the relative friendliness of the residents to strangers and how much gunfire they and their ancestors have had to withstand. In some of the fields thousand-year-old stone watchtowers still mark the points at which grain was threshed, dried and stored. The houses are built upon the ruins of older houses at each defendable squeeze in the valley's walls, with cave-house remnants higher up, and maybe an Ottoman citadel or an older redoubt on the crags of a saw-edge ridgeline where Turkish soldiers holed up between tax-collecting expeditions until Arabia's revolt and their country's defeat in the First World War ended their empire.

In these self-sustaining villages one can see sights startling to a Westerner, such as a man wearing leg irons in lieu of serving a term in jail (with a string in his hand to lift the chain when he wants to walk somewhere), or a madwoman caged into a tiny store where she can sell candy, soap and sundries instead of being carted off to a harsher fate. Another woman might be walking around in a swarm of flies, with the odor of vaginal fistulas that cause her to leak urine continually. Tuberculosis is commonplace among the women of some villages, cooped up indoors, and bilharzia among the men. Cholera has been conquered, but typhoid can be renewed with the spring rains.

A bride's price averages $7,000 in Yemen (blood money paid to a victim's family after a wrongful death, Bjorn said, will be about $12,000), and she comes with no dowry, only her skills, but the money is refundable if either partner complains that the marriage cannot be consummated. There is the usual ceremony of the sheets being exhibited after the wedding night, but on the rare occasions when a match-up doesn't work out—the blood displayed need not be human blood if the two parties agree to pretend that it is—in this clannish culture the whole community is likely to feel collectively responsible. The ordeal is shared, not such a subject of derision as it might be in a more worldly setting.

Sons and mothers do get tied closely together in a society where women do not ordinarily have the chance to choose their husbands, and afterwards are cloistered from contact with the opposite sex—it makes for a certain predilection to nervous breakdowns among the young men. The one Bjorn remembered best had occurred when a boy's father insisted upon divorcing his mother in order to marry a fifth wife; Sharia law of course provided that he could have only four at once. Yet in this same region Sheikh Abdallah ibn Husayn al-Ahmar is said to be able to field an army of twenty thousand men in a matter of days if a woman of his Hashid tribe is insulted by a Bakil tribesman. Bjorn's girlfriend had been working here on various water projects for an international agency when she fell afoul of the national security service and was abruptly incarcerated in Sana'a's Women's Prison. But a hundred armed tribesmen journeyed to the capital, showed up at the prison gate, and forced her release. (The security men, nursing their grudge, spotted her at the airport a few months later, when she had slipped into town to see somebody off, and thrust her onto a plane bound for Cairo with just the clothes on her back.)

The dramatic small city of Sa'dah flourished at its peak about eight hundred years ago, and must still be entered through thick wooden gates at a double-looped entry point passing through immense mud-brick walls looming fifty feet high—the double-loop was first constructed to foil the use of a battering ram. Inside is a huge antique mosque, a good number of large residential tenements built of hand-slabbed, straw-strengthened mud, and the governor's lofty, imposing castle, as thick-walled as the city itself, with Yemen's red, black and white flag flying over it, and looking probably more grand and awesome than the Tower of London or Buckingham Palace because here it remains the seat of enormous power, including the possibility that one might be locked inside (which, I think, lends more pomp to a piece of architecture than anything else).

Sadah's pumphouse, thumpingly noisy, is fenced off and surrounded by a lush, diminutive garden of weeds and trees watered by the trickling runoff. As in all Yemen's earthen towns, however, we saw houses that rather recently had collapsed and returned to a state approximating nature, four or five stories now reduced to a mound of brown sand. Others still standing glistened with sinister seeps and streaks. One of the plagues of development in a desert country is that the local authorities become so elated by the extravagant availability of deep-well water such as they had never dreamed of before that they arrange to pipe it into the buildings but do not spend much extra money to drain it out again. The result is that sewage and other exit pipes are skimped on and running water leaks and leaches all through the structures, softens, soaks and undermines everybody's walls, and brings a bunch of them down.

We walked a circuit atop Sa'dah's city walls, which also are crumbling, not from piped-in water but from the seasonal rains, because they haven't been replastered since the oil boom began and lured away the laborers who used to attend to such chores. Yemenis learned anyhow during the civil war, with casualties of two hundred thousand, that walls couldn't protect them any more. But we were exuberant up there, shouting to children on both sides of the wall. A street-sweeping, garbage-picking outcast clan from Tihama lived in black tents on the outside, with a separate playground and tiny school. Inside, we watched a tumbledown house being rebuilt, a rapid, quite cheerful procedure of hand-shaped bricks thrown up from man to man to the mason straddling a scaffold who slapped them into rows that curved slightly upwards at each end for reinforcement. The householder meanwhile was pondering where he wanted his windows, not just the gothically narrow, arched, stained-glass jobs, but eccentric, oblong apertures out of which his wife and kids could poke their heads on a thousand mornings when the sun hit at a brief, happy angle, or perhaps a screened and outcanted window ledge with perforations through which his womenfolk without re-vealing their presence could peer straight down at the street below.

Sadah was the refuge of the first Zaydis after they had been defeated by other Shiites in a holy war in Iraq and retreated to Yemen in about the year 870. Shiites—the word means "partisan"—believe Mohammed's son-in-law Ali was Mohammed's proper successor, and had fought the Syrian precursors of the Sunnis over the question on the plain at Siffin near the Euphrates River in 657. (The Sunnis, whose name derives from the word for "tradition" and who now constitute ninety percent of Islam, believed in effect that the office of caliph or imam should be elective rather than hereditary.) The Zaydis' martyred leader, Zayd, was one of Ali's great-grandsons, and was the focus of only this one of several early Shiite schisms. But Sa'dah had already emerged as a mining and trading center on the caravan route from

Aden and Ma'rib toward Mecca and Gaza well before the arrival of this Bedouin band. Indeed, around the year 500 A.D., Sa'dah had been on the fringe of the short-lived Jewish kingdom in what is now extreme southwestern Saudi Arabia that was an outgrowth of what may be the oldest Jewish community in the Diaspora.

Jews first came to Yemen around 1000 B.C., some possibly sent by King Solomon in the Queen of Sheba's train when she returned from her visit to him, others after the sacking of Jerusalem in 922. More Jews had followed after the destruction of the Temple in the sixth century B.C., and after the fall of Jerusalem to Titus in 70 A.D. Yemen's Jews remained a mysterious, isolated sector of the community until the state of Israel was established in 1948 and, in the so-called Magic Carpet operation during the next two years, fifty thousand of them were airlifted out (with Alaska Airlines, curiously enough, doing a lot of the chartering). Only in the district surrounding Sa'dah is a remnant populace left, perhaps twelve hundred people who by the force of tradition in this most conservative region have been afforded a measure of security even in the present climate of opinion in the Middle East. Though they aren't treated in a friendly fashion, their right of residence is recognized and they aren't persecuted as much as might be the case where newer, more radical ideas hold sway. An example of the Zaydi attitude is Imam Ahmad's, who when Sana'a's Jews (who all departed in the exodus and had included the best handcraftsmen in his imamate) complained of being spit upon and struck in the streets, decreed that "one-third of an ox" was to be paid by the perpetrator to the victim of such an insult, the other two-thirds to go to the soldiery who enforced the edict. But no outsider can say whether the people still living near Sa'dah and working as carpenters, glass-makers, jacks-of-all-trades, chose to stay because some forty years ago most Jews there were anti-Zionist and believed their ancient community should be maintained, or simply because they were the farthest from the British airfield at Aden where the flights took off, a punishing walk of hundreds of miles through a succession of sheikhdoms and sultanates, each with its dangers and a head tax of Maria Theresa thalers to be paid, if the elderly among them survived.

In the town of Raydah we'd noticed a cobbler with sidelocks squatting by the sandal of an Arab who was chatting equably with him, though not so openly that we felt we could join them. Ali indicated he couldn't consider taking us off the main road to visit a Jewish settlement, but by dint of quietly pushing the issue, on our second day in Sa'dah we did manage to encounter two pairs of silent young men with sidelocks seated opposite each other in the souk with a modest but splendidly tooled display of silver set upon two blankets. Their faces, robes and headcloths were not very different from those of the Arabs around them, but in manner they were aloof and gingerly, volunteering nothing by way of salesmanship, as a crowd immediately gathered and a plainclothes policeman materialized and began to question Ali and Bjorn aggressively as to why we were there and whether any information or leaflets had been passed. In the hubbub the four young men grew still more unbending and disdainful of the attention they were receiving, allowing their nervousness to show only by the way their straight-postured bodies tipped and swayed a bit like ninepins under the volleys of words going over their heads. For their sake and our own, Martha and I hurried to purchase half a dozen filigreed rings and bicep-sized bracelets that had been worked in time-honored patterns by the older women of the families they came from, Bjorn said; and having purposely finished exploring Sa'dah beforehand, straightaway left town.

Bjorn and his North African womanfriend, while living adventurously in the Zone of Insolence, had not failed to pay a couple of visits to an off-road Jewish village, chewing qat and drinking the wine the residents are permitted to brew, although the neighborhood sheikh had showed up to check on them and had taken their supply of qat away with him (Muslims in Yemen do not drink wine). Bjorn added that once a strangely phlegmatic and yet a vigorous sort of man had turned up in Sana'a speaking a rudimentary but serviceable Arabic and telling people he was a German who had lived in Cairo for two years and now was going to buy fine silverwork for an art gallery in Bern. He had come from accomplishing the same feat in war-wracked Ethiopia, hiking with a backpack cross-country to remote settlements, but he said, when Bjorn mentioned Yemen's Jews, whose jewelry is renowned, that he hadn't known there were Jews in Yemen too. And so he started to go to the distant enclaves where Bjorn directed him and beyond them on the mountain paths, carrying out packloads of museum-quality silver artifacts among the multitudes of poor Arab tribesmen armed with Kalashnikovs, spending the night at any farmhouse he happened to land at.

"They like guts like that. They didn't hurt him," Bjorn explained.

"Did he seem brave?" I asked.

"It's two different things, being fearless and being brave. He was fearless."

"Do you think he was doing a census for Mossad?" I asked.

Bjorn was surprised at the idea but agreed that a German backpacker from Cairo speaking bad Arabic and buying silver adornments for a gallery in Bern might be a clever cover; he himself had fallen under suspicion occasionally when travelling in Yemen because he spoke Arabic so well. But an Israeli agent, as he pointed out, would not have told people that he had just been on the same kind of shopping expedition in Ethiopia; nor would he have been so touched by the isolation of Yemen's Jews after he'd met them that he not only smuggled in some Hebrew religious texts on his next buying trip but confided to Bjorn that he had done so.

Yemen's foreigners, Bjorn said, were often people "hiding out, running away," or embarked upon odd, crazy, self-imposed missions, or hurling themselves into fantastical love affairs of a kind most piquantly pursued in Sana'a's stern warrens—though generally also, I thought, waiting to hear news of jobs they had applied for elsewhere in the world, while whiling away the sunsets together over cups of mud-black coffee, leaning on the cushions of a *mafraj* with one leg bent and one stretched out in the approved fashion and listening to a dozen muezzins crying out in a holy bellow from the turrets of the capital, enhancing and harmonizing with one another as they exhorted the city to pray. In a sleepy provincial town, the muezzins will sometimes sound like frogs around a pond or hounds baying at the moon, but in Sana'a there's the fervor of Islam alive, God in the air, life as a matter of life and death. Nowadays the newspaper prints the exact minute at which each call to prayer ought to be made and the words are pre-ordained, but even so there must be a first man to start the call, and a last man to chime in, a high voice, a low voice, a monotone, and a musical voice that makes it into a song, a voice precise in diction, and a voice that attempts to sum it all up; and the politics or rivalry between individual mosques, the friendship or disaffection existing among six or a dozen muezzins who have been joining their voices five times a day above the city for many, many years, may well be imagined.

A discreetly glamorous Austrian woman with graying black hair, who was employed in the library of the Great Mosque conserving and restoring manuscripts, had rented a small house with a romantic battlement and a widespread view, where we would loll in the chewing room talking of byzantine politics and desert hardship, British theater, and tenure denied at somebody's university back in the United States. The British Embassy Club, located in a tatty blockhouse adjoining the embassy tennis court and swimming pool, was another resort for Western "expats"—that whole semipermanent contingent of airline help, contractors' assistants, U.N. personnel posted here for medical or development projects, and low-rung diplomats. A good many whom I met seemed a little misshapen, strangely beefy or unusually gaunt, with puzzled foreheads or bombastic chins. Despair or baffled intransigence seemed to lie in back of the eyes of some of them, with a muddled, interrupted, huffing and puffing air. While they were talking at the horseshoe bar their faces might go inattentive suddenly, as though yearning to be back at some previous stop-off or to leap fast-forward to their next date of departure and the bracing novelty of risk and difficulty they were anticipating at their next assignment. Many people live abroad partly to define themselves by where they are and where they've been, bolstering their sense of who they are by standing against the relief of a foreign backdrop, an ancient hierarchy or rigid religiosity that has molded their surroundings so profoundly as to prop them up also. And people postpone taking up the thread of their lives by travelling—the rush of airports, preoccupation with the new country, unpacking, settling in, learning the ropes, exploring, and *naturally* not being able to address any more lasting context in the meantime. Yet those of us who share their itchy feet, their rueful as well as gleeful addiction to being as far as possible from wherever they have lately been, making themselves special by the sights at hand, the rainbows, cliffs and islands seen, the destinations achieved, instead of internal factors, believe this is partly what life is about: that it's the world that's special more than us. On alternate Sundays in Sana'a, fifty or a hundred of the expats run with the "Hashhouse Harriers," a British-centered institution of the Near and Far East by which lonely Europeans will slowly jog through scenery especially chosen for its loveliness, watching for tokens and clues—scarves tied to bushes, and such things—left by the "hares" they are pursuing, and crying, "On, on! On, on!" whenever they find one.

Emerson said, "Travelling is a fool's paradise. They who made England, Italy or Greece venerable in the imagination did so by sticking fast where they were, like an axis of the earth." And again: "I am not much an advocate for travelling, and I observe that men run away to other countries because they are not good in their own, and run back to their own because they pass for nothing in the new places." It is still an appealing argument, although the notion of any nation now becoming a proper axis for the earth, or of its intellectuals and industrialists struggling to make it so is a funny one. Rather, the fondest wish of many

Western intellectuals and industrialists appears to be to travel. With the crush of worldwide tourism, the search for authentic pockets of "unspoiled" exoticism by the more expensive outfitters has reached every redoubt—places such as this, which hadn't been exploited because of chronic civil war. And Islam has not been domesticated for Americans by home-grown faddist versions that correspond to Zen Buddhism, or itinerant Hindu gurus expounding at weekend ashrams. On the contrary, decades of drumbeating bigotry on the subject of Islam have made that religion in itself a force for exoticism in the perceptions of the West; a Muslim country is always seen as alien, even dangerous.

Yemen is a miniature Afghanistan for connoisseurs of the tourist circuit, because of its mountain tribes (and you must have mountains now to have tribes). The very cisterns in which rainwater is collected are like gigantic bowls that have been artfully sculpted in the rock, and into which the villagers descend by ledges that coil down. Towns like Kawkaban are set incredibly on pinnacles scarcely to be scaled. In an Italian walled hill town, surrounded by passionate architecture from an epoch of schism, with bands of partisans and neighborhood armies and a God of sword, fist and martyrdom immanent everywhere, the traveller can try to imagine a life six hundred years ago that resembled Yemen's in the middle of our present century. But it's a decorous, sanitized experience, almost like visiting a large museum, whereas even close to his home, Ali felt obliged to drive us way around the next village instead of chancing a trip straight through. There are famous scenic towns such as Shahara, with its giddy, rock-pieced bridge, where the local people simply take over the guidance of visitors, at gunpoint if necessary. At the imam's Palace on the Rock, a jumbled tall castle built of sandstone, bricks and basalt atop a hundred-foot rock in Wadi Dhar, Martha and I spent our time closing windows and doors that were banging to bits in the wind—the walls were leaking, the fixtures falling off—so that its indoor curiosities might endure intact a little longer.

Wadi Dhar is known as *the* wadi in Yemen, and is used to illustrate to children what paradise perhaps is like, because of its green seethe of luscious trees—eucalyptus, sycamore, pines, palms, walnuts, apricots, cypresses, pepper trees, fig trees, mimosas, and huge oaklike *taluq* trees (*ficus vastus*)—its flocks of birds, and grape arbors growing black and yellow raisins in bountiful profusion, under the massif of Jebel an Nabi Shu'ayb, Yemen's highest mountain.

In Wadi Dhar we heard about the baboons, leopards and hyenas that had lived here until the civil war brought in armies and firepower, and about our first snake man, a tenant farmer who still caught snakes for part of his living when they appeared in other people's houses, or else would merely read the Koran to them for about ten dollars. Though Ali wouldn't take us to meet him, we enjoyed asking after such individuals when we stopped to chat in marketplaces or with women drying cakes of sheep dung for fuel or carrying green fodder on their heads, in villages built like hornets' nests with windows like knife punctures. In Yemen, musicians, barbers, butchers and blacksmiths are regarded as of a debased caste, and so, it seemed, were snake men. Most towns did have one, and a hoot would go up when we asked for him. He was generally said to be dark-skinned, of slave origin, *Abadi*, but able to draw a snake out of its hole by repeatedly dangling a string down inside and slowly pulling it out again, communing with the snake in the meantime, so that eventually when it emerged it might follow him about the room for a while, until he picked it up and pocketed it. These men were said never to kill the snakes they caught, but rather to carry them off and let them go again, though they might draw out the fangs of a viper before doing so. Even under everyday circumstances, they liked going around with a snake concealed somewhere in their robes. It sounded like a good magician's business for a man born into a feudal system of landholding where otherwise he would exist only to try to repay his father's debts.

In 1962, the yearly per capita income in Yemen was seventy dollars; there were a total of fifteen doctors, all foreign, and six hundred hospital beds. It's better now, but in the little fifty-six-bed facility near Sa'dah where we stopped, the administrator, Wilfrid Hufton, from Saginaw, Michigan, told us that twenty babies a day were being turned away from "the triage room" as too close to death to save. In the south, near Ta'izz, William Koehn, a Kansan who held a similar post at Jibla Baptist Hospital, with seventy-five beds to fill, said they were doing three thousand operations a year, charging twenty-eight dollars for the minor kind and a hundred thirty-five dollars for major surgery (a dollar-seventy to see a doctor, four dollars to see him quickly). Relatives must give blood before an operation, a serious issue because many people believe blood once given is never replaced—a superstition that makes any fight in which blood is drawn a terribly grave matter.

When we got tired or nervous after an adventure, Martha would empty and repack her luggage, and I would try to find new hiding places for my money. Arabic is a breathy language, full of exhalation and expostulation, but it seemed to me in my ignorance not to contain quite enough breadth to encompass all the faces we saw—the disgruntled, haughty Egyptian pedagogues in pajama costumes restlessly roaming backwater villages; stately, puzzled Sudanese; sleek, purposeful Saudis; Zaydis rich with wild-country hauteur; wary, mercantile Shafiis; and raffish-looking blacks engendering an élan of their own simply by being regarded as disreputable. Sana'a is a metropolis all eyes and as unapologetic as the cities described by Marco Polo, that glances at stray Westerners as if to say, *you burly, overanxious creature*, or *you skin-and-bones do-gooder, why are you so far from home?* But there are many more Russians working in Yemen than Americans—fifty or sixty times as many military advisers, the American embassy claimed—because in most Arab countries Russian military equipment is thought to be more durable and dependable than the Americans' faster, "smarter," elegant stuff. "The Egyptian Migs were as thick as mosquitoes over us. Our hair turned white defending our children," a retired officer in Sa'dah had said fervently of that worst time in his life.

The soldiers in red berets looked straightforward enough when we met them at roadblocks backed up by a light machine gun mounted on a jeep parked behind a piled-stone emplacement, but the security men, who maintained separate roadblocks, had older, subtler, more moody, sophisticated, amused, ominous faces. Schooled originally by Scotland Yard, they jockey with South Yemen's East German-trained security forces across "the" Yemen, as Arabists often call the whole region because the name translates in Arabic as "at the right hand" of Mecca (from the Red Sea). This passionate, endearing country of prickly-pear landscapes and hobbled camels, of tinkers, shawl sellers, snuff peddlers, spice merchants, of Indian sweetmeats, brooms of palm leaves, see-through harem clothing, and pamphlet biographies of Abraham Lincoln sold in Sana'a's Souk of Salt, where men friends stroll about holding hands, each chewing a cud, in the afternoon; this country of impromptu houses striped with red clay and blue paint, decorated with stick-man figures or windows depicted as eyes by means of whitewash, where foreigners are sometimes called Kaffirs and prisoners still must pay the salaries of the policemen who come to arrest them depending on how far they have had to walk—the circuit judges used to employ a man to follow behind them counting their steps as they travelled between villages, and set their fees arithmetically— winds up being irresistible.

The incantations, ululations, invocations, the whistle-blowing of Sana'a's watchmen signaling to each other all night; little girls in conical hats walking with fathers in skirts, jackets, and headcloths wrapped around pillbox hats; the bowls of *ful* (beans) eaten with "people's bread" and mango or guava juice drunk from a can, to the whack of dough being slapped against the round wall of a pot-shaped street oven with a white-gas flame hissing underneath: I would miss all of it. Bjorn had decided to stay longer than we'd planned, to check on a building project he had designed for the government, and he invited me to do the same. The bait he dangled before me was a rumor that had hit Sana'a's streets that the South Yemen army was going to invade "three days from tomorrow." Wouldn't a news hound like me want to witness that? Well, in truth if I'd been fresh to the country I would have, though I doubted the Russians, with their big naval base to protect in South Yemen—when they had been expelled from Somalia in 1977, they had simply fleated their drydock from Berbera to Aden—would actually allow the South Yemenis to invade anybody. They didn't, as it turned out. But I chose to fly back to London with Martha. Part of the purpose of travel is to slow down the incessantly accelerating velocity of one's life—not just to see new sights but to experience unexpected resistance, encounter obstacles that give one pause, to stand at the brink of a civilization that may seem spiky or unfathomable and makes the clock stop. It's sometimes chilling, sometimes tiring for a visitor to feel ignorant, awed or even fearful —America was undergoing one of its recurring convulsions of xenophobia at this point— when entering the heartland of a people like the Arabs who are distrusted or despised by many of one's countrymen, and where God is regarded as still for real and life as a matter of life and death, where the stones that a householder lifts to build his home may soon save his skin. I was tired.

The pilot for Yemenia Airways probably doubled as a fighter pilot, as many third-world pilots do. He lifted the Boeing very abruptly off the runway and into the sky, his voice on the intercom full of daring. And the stewardesses, who were refugees from the war in Eritrea and were willing to go unveiled, had about their pretty faces an air of glad desperation. Arabs have not forgotten that the Israeli air force deliberately shot down a civilian airliner that wandered off-course over the Sinai in early 1973, so we made calibrated adjustments that brought us from Saudi Arabian air space directly over Cairo's defenses before reaching the Mediterranean. (This is the line that flies Yasir Arafat to Sana'a so often, the CIA station chief had told me, that his agency had stopped bothering to log him in and out of the airport; but "Fiddler on the Roof" was playing on the sound system.) I was watching two husky, hardened-looking expatriates sitting on the nearly empty plane who looked like mercenary soldiers, although perhaps they were only mining engineers. I'd supposed that they were British, but when we landed in Paris after more than seven hours, they stood up with sighs and broad smiles of relief and murmured in soft-spoken French, just as if they weren't tough guys at all.

I had flown into Sana'a at daybreak with the pyrotechnics of the sunrise promising me adventure. But we landed in London at nightfall; and night is a good time to arrive in London, when people are going out to plays, clubs and restaurants dressed to the nines. The electricity was blazing, and this infinite city devised for commerce, industry and pleasure of every kind—designed, indeed, to rule the whole world, though it has become instead a favorite resort and refuge for all the world's exiles—laid out its evening charms. The lights were lovely, but the traffic gridlocked.

"TO STAND INSIDE DEER CAVE WAS TO TASTE THE SHARP THRILL OF THE UNKNOWN." (DAVID ROBERTS)

David Roberts

▼

MULU TO KINABALU

A JAUNT THROUGH
MALAYSIAN BORNEO

A two-pronged predicament often faces the traveller to remote and strange places. On the one hand, it may fall his task to make sense of some quite bizarre event which the natives yawn at as commonplace. On the other, he may have the luck to witness—or, God save him, perform—some seemingly ordinary act which suddenly elicits the wrath or ridicule of the whole populace.

On my first trip to Malaysia, I kept my usual lookout for such moments, which to my mind form one of the chief delights and bedevilments of travel. As I arrived in Kuala Lumpur, then, I was glad I was not in the shoes of the poor young German I read about in the newspapers, who had been wakened in his Malaysian hotel room and confronted by authorities with a sizeable stash of marijuana in a shoe-box in his closet. Bleary-eyed, he had claimed the dope had been planted on him by his roommates, who had escaped. This had happened three years ago; since then the German had languished in the clink. The penalty for conviction was death. Malaysia takes a tough line on drugs; not so long ago they hanged a Brit and an Aussie, international pleas be damned. And now, at last, the German was coming to trial.

I found the newspaper a rich source of oddities during my first Malaysian week, as I sauntered through an orangutan sanctuary, a Bidayuh longhouse, four museums, three city tours, a rubber forest, a batik cooperative, a Hindu cave, and a pewter factory. One day I read about a bust at a bar called the Fairy Lounge. "The owner of the lounge," sermonized a Kuala Lumpur tabloid, "learnt today that the recession was not an excuse for flouting the law when he was fined $2,000 for staging a striptease show." On another day, I was enlightened by *The People's Mirror* that the inhabitants of Seramban were facing a problem in the form of cattle that had developed a taste for underwear hanging on clotheslines. The cows ate only bras and panties.

Lest I forget the vigilance of Malaysian law, I read soon after in the *New Straits Times* that "Flogging will soon be introduced in the State as punishment for Muslims found guilty of illicit sex." A short delay in enacting this measure would be necessary, however, while prison officers "complete their training in the art of flogging."

On my tour of Kuala Lumpur. I was in the capable hands of Ivan, a guide of Indian extraction who spoke good English. Ivan bought me a durian ice cream cone as a benign introduction to the native fruit immortalized in the epithet, "the smell of hell and the taste of heaven." The yellow stuff reeked to my western nose like rotten onions. I am still waiting for the taste of heaven to kick in. Ivan also pointed out the many decorations hung about the city for the upcoming Chinese New Year—the Year of the Rabbit. My favorite showed Bugs Bunny speaking in characters.

I asked Ivan about Brunei, the tiny, oil-rich nation that had balked at incorporation in Malaysia twenty-four years ago, and which now boasts the second-highest per capita wealth in the world. "In Brunei," Ivan told me, unable to hide his disapproval, "when they run out of gas, they buy a new car." As we strolled through the excellent Kuala Lumpur museum, I asked my guide at what time Islam had spread to the Malaysian peninsula. He had proved himself a consummate historian, citing the exact dates of obscure events in the Communist Emergency or the discovery of tin. Now he smiled confidently and said, "It was in 300 A.D."

"But that can't be," I blurted. "Mohammed wasn't born till the sixth century."

Ivan looked sheepish. I wandered off, not wanting to embarrass the man further. No doubt as a Hindu he was rusty on Muslim dates.

Surrounded by giggling children, I was engrossed in a graphic diorama illustrating royal circumcision, when Ivan caught up with me. "I remember now," he said. "Islam come in 3000 A.D." I didn't argue.

At the pewter factory I gazed at life-size replicas of the boxing gloves of Muhammad Ali and Joe Bugner, who had fought in Kuala Lumpur in 1975. It was obvious why Bugner lost. In a police museum in Kuching, I admired photos of Malaysian G-men apprehending scrawny guerrillas in "a shabby hideout of the communist elements along the jungle fringe." I also perused a beheading platform, which fronted a shaded stand where VIPs used to take in the day's lesson in the march of justice.

In the longhouse at Benuk, I drank *arak*, the local rice wine, on the floor of a handsome living room, while I inspected my host's furnishings. These included priceless ancient Chinese vases and skulls, hanging in nets, which his grandfathers had gathered from unruly neighbors. But the man's pride and joy was his gallery of portraits clipped from slick English magazines and pinned to the walls. The honorees included British soccer stars, rock groups like Duran

Duran, starlets like Kim Wilde, motorcycle racers, Lady Di, models in brassiere ads, and a connoisseur's collection of Marlboro men. My favorite was a full-page photo of a rock climber leading a tough pitch. My host had mounted the picture sideways, so the fellow seemed to be crawling across a plateau of stone. Linguistic difficulties thwarted my attempts to find out if this was a Bidayuh joke on alpine machismo, or a simple misunderstanding that in no way diminished my host's appreciation of the weird sport of climbing.

I returned to the newspapers in quest of cultural insight. The German dope fiend, I was glad to hear, had been acquitted, mainly because the judge had stared into his eyes and believed he was telling the truth. In another item, I read that there were 119,713 registered dadah addicts in Malaysia, 97.9 percent of them male. Dadah is a catch-all term for drugs. Given the threat of the death penalty, I thought it quite magnanimous of all those potheads and poppy-sniffers to take the trouble to register; but no doubt I was missing some essential point.

The *Sabah Times* reassured me that rumors of an outbreak of headhunting in certain remote villages were to be discounted as the efforts of parents who had invented the stories to keep their children home at night. The Malaysian Sportsman of the Year had just been crowned. A bodybuilder had narrowly triumphed over a bowler, with a clutch of badminton stars also in the running.

I had come to Malaysia for what a newly booming industry had chosen to call "adventure travel," and I got my first whiff of it at the Semonggok orangutan sanctuary. Baby orangutans are cute as all get-out, but adults have a baleful glower and a tough-guy swagger that chill the anthropomorphist in his tracks. The keeper had warned me not to get near the cage of Bullet, a full-grown female saved from poachers who had shot her as an infant and killed her mother. Then he let the babies out to frolic in the grass. I forgot my warning as I backed up to get a good photo of the adorable primates. Suddenly the keeper yelled, "Watch out!," and at that moment I felt a Muhammad Ali-like blow that just grazed my buttocks. Bullet, who clearly lived for such moments, had almost nailed another tourist. A barking bear in a nearby cage sounded his approval.

Malaysia is an odd aggregation of territories. Peninsular Malaysia, which used to be called Malaya, is the relatively civilized land of hills and rice paddies and rubber plantations that dangles south from Thailand. At the time of federation in 1963, to the peninsula were added Singapore (which changed its mind two years later and became an independent state), and Sarawak and Sabah, the two states that form the northern part of

Borneo. Brunei, a small wedge between Sarawak and Sabah, had a hard think about its oil reserves and decided it wasn't about to share the riches with the bureaucrats in Kuala Lumpur.

In Malaysia as a whole, 55 percent of the residents are Malays (long-time Muslim residents most of whom originally emigrated from Indonesia); 34 percent are Chinese; 9 percent Indian; and a scant 2 percent "other," which includes Europeans and the many tribes of indigenous natives. But in the Bornean states of Sabah and Sarawak, the Indian population virtually disappears, the Malays dwindle to 20 percent, the Chinese are 30 percent, and the various tribes of more-or-less assimilated natives amount to a full 50 percent (topped by the Iban, at 30 percent). Sabah and Sarawak are much less technologized than peninsular Malaysia, and as you go upriver into the interior, you find yourself in real wilderness—relentless jungle that covers the whole island of Borneo, punctuated here and there by startling limestone cliffs and mountains reaching to thirteen thousand feet.

My eye, then, was on the Bornean states. I had two goals: to reach the Gunung Mulu caves, some of the largest and most beautiful in the world; and to climb Mount Kinabalu, the highest peak between the Himalayas and New Guinea.

From the Sarawak town of Miri, I was guided by an entrepreneur named Stanley Malang, who had grown up in the front yard of the Mulu caves. It is an exhausting nine hours by boat up the Baram River, one of the island's great waterways, to Stanley's base camp at Mulu Hot Springs. The first six hours are by express boat, a narrow, covered river ferry that bombs along at a surprising clip. To me, the banks of the Baram were mysterious and haunting, but to my fellow passengers, who lived on the river, the trip was as boring as a bus route. Thus the below-decks cabin is wholly given over to seats facing a VCR, on which tapes run throughout the ride, while speakers blast the sound track over the roar of the engines. I watched Chinese pop singers, Chinese game shows, and what looked like a Chinese western; but by far the most popular tapes were of American pro wrestling. The only escape is up on the roof, where you share a metal perch with old tires and sacks of rice and broil under the equatorial sun.

The last three hours are a blissful contrast, as a longboat takes you from the settlement of Long Panai up the Tutoh (a Baram tributary) toward the storied land of caves. You lounge in a kind of glorified dugout canoe, hand dangling in the spray, with background entertainment limited to the soothing purr of the outboard. Stanley's camp is a cozy outpost of bamboo huts, cold showers (which you crave in the tropics), decent food, and Tiger Beer for three Malaysian bucks a can (about $1.25).

The recently created Gunung Mulu National Park has been open to visitors for about two years. The more obvious caves have been known to natives for a long time, but the region is still largely unexplored. Three British science-and-caving teams had performed some extraordinary work starting in 1977, and had made mind-boggling discoveries underground. Yet in their own estimation, "Very little of the limestone surface has been trodden due to the extreme combination of jungle, steepness and corroded rock."

On our first day, Stanley guided our small group of clients (mostly Aussies) to Deer Cave. An hour's walk through the rain forest brought us suddenly face to face with a gigantic hole in the hillside. The first sight of that gaping immensity sent a very literal shiver down my spine. We turned on our flashlights and entered the largest known cave passage in the world.

Because Gunung Mulu is a national park, workers have begun laying a primitive handline through Deer Cave and placing stones for steps. This struck me as a minor tragedy, for here in the Bornean jungle lies a natural wonder as awesome as Mammoth Cave must have seemed to the Kentucky Indians. As our own commercial caves have proved, no wilderness is more easily trivialized than the subterranean. Light shows, rowboat rides, bleachers, homilies in stalactites—this sort of tourist hokum can denature the primordially disturbing underworld as no *téléphérique* will ever tame Mont Blanc.

Here in Deer Cave, however, we were still among the pioneers. For two hours, we clambered a mile and a half through the passage. The ceiling arches to the stupendous height of six hundred feet. It was easy going—mostly a walk, with a little scrambling over boulders, and a single short ladder. As we strode across centuries' accretion of slimy guano, whose acrid fumes filled our nostrils, we heard the plash of unseen streams and the ceaseless whir, high above us, of thousands of bats, mixed with the sonar clicks of thousands of swiftlets. Against the puny cones of light our flashlights threw, these raw quiddities of eternal night seemed overwhelming. I felt a first small bite of adrenaline, for to stand inside Deer Cave was to taste the sharp thrill of the unknown.

An oddity about the cave is that it is open on both ends; the passage, in fact, tunnels straight through a mountain. On the far side, we were in the deepest wilderness, and to circle around the mountain back to camp would have meant a day's desperate tramp through the jungle. Wilson, Stanley's assistant, built a fire; we lounged by the entrance stream, eating fried fish and sipping tea.

I had learned a lot about the caves of Borneo, and all of it astonished me. At one point we had crawled into a side passage full of bats, as Stanley had shone his powerful light on their panicked dance. It will be years before the image of that maelstrom of wings and eyes leaves my memory. The swiftlets, whose tiny nests we had fondled, feed, drink, and mate on the wing. Their clicks are far cruder than the bats' ultrasonic signals, yet a swiftlet can tell his own nest from all the others in blind darkness by click echoes alone. The birds' natural predator is the cave racer snake, which has the knack of catching a swiftlet in mid-flight.

The mounds of bat guano provide a gooey home for two kinds of cockroach, three kinds of moth, and many beetles. Swiftlet guano houses flies and the huntsman spider. (Wilson had found a five-inch-long specimen on one wall—by far the largest arachnid I had ever seen, and the most terrifying.) We had also seen fluorescent millipedes, which glow from irritation.

Scientists have found in these caves "living fossils"—species of crabs and scorpions that have gone extinct all through the forests of southeast Asia, but have hung on in these dim sanctuaries. One of the numbing puzzles of evolution inheres in the fact that the same species have also been found in caves in Australia, Europe, and South America.

My elation at entering the alien darkness had not been shared by all of Stanley's clients. Caves always unnerve a certain percentage of their visitors. In our group, a hypochondriacal math teacher from New South Wales had had enough. Through the rest of the trip, she not only refused to set foot underground, but insisted that her doting husband keep her company outside. On the other hand, Theo, a beefy, beer-loving plexiglass salesman from Perth, matched my zest. In Deer Cave he worked off a fierce hangover as he hopped from one boulder to another, cracking jokes as he went.

On the second day we toured Clearwater Cave. This cavern stands at the very head of a paradisiacal stream, up which Wilson had poled our longboat. We swung from vines, lunched on fish speared by Wilson, and bathed in a perfect swimming hole. Clearwater lacks the great height of Deer Cave, but it is far more elaborate. The British teams had pushed its passages to the dizzying combined length of thirty-four miles, making it the most extensive cave system yet found in southeast Asia. We could penetrate only the initial mile, but it was an even more marvelous adventure than that of the day before.

"The Penan listened to lizards and grasshoppers for omens that would tell them how to conduct their lives."

Clearwater is relatively clean, lacking the huge deposits of guano found in Deer Cave. A powerful stream rushes down its main channel, and to probe the cave at all, you must ford the stream in several places, going waist deep in the cool, crystalline water. Most of the route is along twenty-foot-high parabolic ledges grooved out of the side walls. These give onto exquisite niches and antechambers, some of which hint at deep mysteries beyond. Except for the darkness, the place had something of the feel of the canyons of the American southwest. We stopped where an old rope marked the beginning of the real technical difficulties. I am no caver, but it was a painful sacrifice to turn my back on those convolutions of limestone and return to the known world.

Stanley had been able to take us to only a handful of the Mulu caves. The tough British teams had discovered scores of them, yet concluded that there remained an even larger number lost in the jungle, waiting to be found and pushed. Most of the peaks in Gunung Mulu have yet to be climbed, and high on one ridge stands a forest of dagger-sharp limestone pinnacles, up to 150 feet high, that have never felt the touch of human hand.

On the way back to camp we made a brief visit to a Penan village. These people are often regarded as the most "primitive" in Malaysia. Traditionally they were skilled forest nomads, renowned for being able to track utterly silently through the jungle, and for their brilliance with blowpipe and poison dart. They were so leery of strangers that many an early European travelled for years through their territory without meeting a single Penan. Almost uniquely among the Bornean tribes, they avoided rivers, preferring the depths of the jungle.

It is as dangerous to read meaning into the looks of people whose language you cannot speak as it is to guess what an orangutan is thinking; but the small village seemed to me a sorry place. Several children had hideous infections on their legs, the oozing aftermaths of burns. Bare-breasted women carried their babies with a languid ennui. The people's large, dark eyes looked filmy with rheum, their cheeks hollow. Most of the men were away tilling the fields, having turned in one generation from forest gatherers of wild sago into riverbank rice farmers. One youth was banging away with a hammer, nailing a government-issue zinc roof in place—here, where his grandparents had never known houses. The handsome chief sat under a malaria eradication certificate in his hut, showed us his blowpipe with darts poisoned alternately for deer or small game, and chain-smoked. The young boys were missing their upper front teeth—knocked out to facilitate blowpipe technique. The beautiful young girls with their budding breasts stared blankly into our cameras.

As we were about to leave, Stanley said quietly to me, "These people, they are very poor. Also, they pray all the time." I felt stunned by the quandaries of acculturation I had witnessed. When the great botanist Charles Hose came among the Penan in the early years of the century, he had found robust nomads whom he described as "among the finest of the peoples of Borneo." They lived in small, democratic bands, rarely attacked other tribes, and were astonishingly skilled at finding their way in the jungle. They sang virtuosic songs around the campfire, played on the bamboo harp, and whittled pipes that imitated bird and deer calls. They believed in an afterlife devoid of moral judgment. They had never had the need to learn to count beyond the number three.

The Penan listened to lizards and grasshoppers for omens that would tell them how to conduct their lives. Their great god was Balu Penyalong, whose image was a crocodile carved in wood. Although they required few belongings, the Penan carried their crocodile icons from camp to camp as they moved through the forest.

I had seen in the Penan village no crocodile images, but an abundance of crucifixes. "Yes," said Wilson, "they pray all day long. They pray better than Christians." Later I came across a remarkable little book called *Drunk Before Dawn*. It is a true believer's account of the

exceptionally successful missionary effort—Anglican and Catholic—among the tribes of Sarawak and Sabah. The foreword begins, "This is the wonderful story of God at work in one of the most fascinating parts of the world. . . ." A passage recounts the travel of a missionary far up the Baram to preach among the Kayan tribe. One day an old, nearly deaf Penan woman had come into camp and asked, "What is all this praying?"

> As the missionary shouted the Gospel message into her ear, she opened her heart to the Lord. She was broken toothed, scraggy, itchy—she kept scratching her head with all ten of her fingers—and wore only the scantiest of "bikinis," but Christ came to dwell in her heart and she went away with a real assurance of salvation, to "tell the ones in the jungle about this."

With the missionaries' help, through the 1950s and 1960s the Penan stopped singing their campfire chants, gave up their bamboo harps, and mastered Christian hymns. They learned to read a Malay translation of the Gospel According to St. Mark. Although they were extremely reluctant to do so, they were finally persuaded to throw away their crocodile fetishes and set up crucifixes in their place.

A few days later I flew to Kota Kinabalu, the capital of Sabah. The climb up Mount Kinabalu is not very difficult—some fourteen thousand people try it every year and a large percentage reach the top. What makes the mountain virtually unique among tropical peaks is the beautiful granite plateau that crowns its jungle-hung sides, with bizarre prongs, knobs, and aiguilles strewn across acres of clean rock at thirteen thousand feet.

The hike is also interesting as a cultural experience, for the national park people have gone to great lengths to make sure visitors have a pleasant time on Kinabalu. I stayed the first night in a kind of concrete bunker motel room at the base. On the back of the door I read a warning against setting out for the top if you happen to be afflicted with arthritis, epileptic fits, jaundice, "severe aenemia," "muscular cramps," or "obesity."

By regulation, you must take a guide. Mine was a slight young fellow named Lanting, a Kadazan native in terrific shape, who spoke nary a word of English. We spent a taciturn two days together, nodding, grinning, and pointing. It took me four and a half hours to lug my body from the base, at 6,200 feet, to the splendid Gunting Lagadan hut at 10,800 feet. It was a dreary plod through incessant mist and rain, without a single view, but alleviated by a few piquant distractions. The trail is pedantically measured in "chains," eighty to the mile, and whether or not you want to know, you learn at the outset that you must pass exactly 431 of these markers to stand on the top.

Kinabalu's first conquerors, Hugh Low and Spenser St. John, took weeks to penetrate the jungle to reach the startling summit plateau during their two assaults in 1851 and 1858. It would still take weeks if you did not have use of the lovingly crafted trail that snakes up a ridge crest to the huts. Much of the path had been virtually corduroyed with sticks, and wherever the going gets steep, local wood has been hammered into a staircase, complete with handrail. At blessedly regular intervals, you can collapse in a cute gazebo, with running water spilling from a tank close at hand. Most surprisingly, a power cable runs along the path all the way to the huts.

Accustomed to the gloomy A-frames and quonsets that serve as huts on other tropical mountains such as Kilimanjaro in Tanzania or Wilhelm in Papua New Guinea, I was unprepared for the luxury of Gunting Lagadan. The place was like a small hotel, with a comfy lounge and plate glass windows giving onto the misty void. In the kitchen, a pair of bored teenage girls whipped up full-scale meals ranging from fresh-egg omelets to pork chops. There was a sign on the wall reading, "Do Not Spit," and a note on the posted menu, annotating the section devoted to steaks and chops: "Grill No Complain of Time Taken." There was electric light to read by, and, amazingly, a kind of portable radiator that I could plug in to warm my private room and dry off my clothes.

At 3:00 A.M. I got up to go for the summit, just as I had on Kilimanajaro and Wilhelm. The rationale for starting in the wee hours is that tropical mountains typically cloud over after sunrise. An unacknowledged second reason is that the guides like to get back home as soon as they can. At Gunting Lagadan, a chef heroically arose at 3:00 just to fix me (and the three other hikers on the route) French toast. With Lanting making sure I didn't stray off into no man's jungle, I set out by the light of a waning moon. It was so bright that I didn't use my flashlight at all.

The emergence at treeline onto the granite plateau is downright weird. It is as if you had suddenly stepped from Borneo into Tuolumne Meadows. I had felt tired and cranky in the rain the day before; now I raced ahead, charmed by the touch of open rock. The temperature was about forty degrees, by far the coldest I had yet experienced in Malaysia, but not in the least unpleasant. At places on the plateau where the rock angles up to all of twenty-five or thirty degrees, solicitous trail builders have installed fat blue, green, and white fixed

ropes. Even if you couldn't find the frequent cairns that mark the way to Low's Peak at 13,455 feet, you could guide yourself by the graffiti painted on the rock in a dozen languages (preponderantly Chinese).

I reached the top just before dawn, as the edge of a thick fog started lapping like a sea against the northeast flank of the mountain, obscuring the little-known gulf of Low's Gully. Gradually the sun gave shape and sparkle to the undulant granite. I felt a giddy sense of utter well-being, and I jabbered my pleasure at Lanting, who returned his best professional grin as he smoked a cigarette. The summit of Kinabalu struck me as a kind of inversion of the depths of Clearwater Cave. Instead of the joy of dark obscurity, of pushing into the hidden folds of the netherworld, I basked now in the joy of standing bare against the heavens, with the fathomless interior of Borneo far below me on the one hand and the gleaming South China Sea on the other.

By the time I was stumbling down the endless staircase of the trail at midday, back in the greenery and drizzle, my good mood had ebbed. I craved a beer down at park head-quarters, and maybe a cheeseburger to boot. My calves ached and I was soaked to the skin. Just as I was settling into a self-pitying stupor, however, I passed five tiny Kadazan women on their way up the mountain. They wore flip-flops on their feet, chewed betel nut, and bore gigantic wicker baskets on their backs, so weighty that they bent the women (one of whom looked sixty) close to the ground. In the baskets, I saw fresh meat, boxes of eggs, raw vegetables, cartons of milk, and—my God—cans of beer. These doughty Kadazans were making their semiweekly resupply trip to Gunting Lagadan, wearing themselves out on a 4,600-foot climb in the mud so that I (or, more accurately, my successors) could have French toast at three in the morning.

"No Complain of Time Taken," indeed! I wanted to thank these ladies personally and effusively, but my Kadazan was rusty. "Heavy," I said to Lanting, holding my arms apart. He grinned.

"MAJOR SURPRISE ATE US ALIVE." (STEVE CURTIS)

SHIVA WINKED

BEING A REVERENTIAL ACCOUNT OF WILDWATER RAFTING IN THE FOOTHILLS OF THE HIMALAYAS

"Ah," N. N. Badoni said, "your master will not seek you. You will seek your master. I believe you are seeking your master even while you deny this to me and to yourself."

A day before, rafting on a river that drops out of a snow field in the Himalayas, I had been thrown out of the boat in a rapid where I spent some time tumbling underwater in nature's frigid spin and rinse cycle. This was followed by a rush through a couple more downriver rapids that featured numerous unpleasant collisions with boulders of varying sizes and unvarying solidity. The successive impacts necessitated some predictably unsuccessful attempts to breathe underwater. My life had not passed before my eyes but somewhere in the middle of the third rapid, cartwheeling along ass over teakettle, caroming off rocks, the phrase "holy shit, this is serious," began ringing through my mind. It was high noon and, even deep underwater, I could see the bright mountain sun above. It shimmered on the surface of the water, nuclear bright, and I fought towards it, feeling the surface retreat from me even as I swam. It was like a bad dream, a real tooth-grinder, and I longed to rise to the light, to breathe, to break through to the other side of the sun. Now, thirty hours later, sitting in a hotel restaurant, there was a lingering congestion in my lungs and I felt as if someone had taken a baseball bat to my entire body. N. N. Badoni, a sweet-shop owner in this north Indian town of Dehra Dun, suggested that I might consider my swim a religious experience. N. N. was an avid trekker and a devout Hindu.

I am not much of a fan of the Hindu religion, associating it as I do with those pestiferous weenies known as Hare Krishnas whose panhandling presence in American airports results in such mind-boggling exchanges as "We're giving away copies of this book: it's five thousand years old."

"Five thousand years?" Stunned disbelief. "It looks brand new."

My experience with with holy types in India thus far, I told N. N., made the Krishnas seem like a class act.

N. N. agreed that some of the holy men who populate the subcontinent like rats in a granary were undoubtedly transparent frauds and despicable money-grubbers. Still, he felt there were teachers of spiritual distinction: teachers who did not come to you. They were men you searched for in your soul. And when you found them, you would know. He mentioned a pair of Swamis, now deceased, whose teachings had enriched his life.

I nodded politely and N. N. bought me another beer. He was of the priestly Brahmin caste and did not, himself, drink. N. N. had provided research for Gary Weare's book, *Trekking in the Indian Himalaya,* and had spent many years studying the Garhwal region, north of Dehra Dun, where I had just been. Located in the lush Himalayan foothills that rise above the blistered plains of northern India, the Garhwal is considered the Abode of the Gods, and is replete with Hindu pilgrimage sites: Gangotri, near the source of the sacred Ganges river; Yamunotri, at the head of the Yamuna river, where pilgrims boil rice in the hot springs below the temple to the goddess Yamunotri so that they may eat the "food of the gods;" Kenarnath, the divine resting place of the god Shiva, and Badrinath, the home of the god Vishnu. The Garhwal is the holiest and most sacred area in all of India.

I had been rafting the Tons, one of the innumerable glacier fed rivers of the Garhwal. It is a little known tributary of the Ganges and at its source are the snowfields of the 20,720 foot high mountain called Bandarpunch, the monkey's tail. The Tons is considered holy to Shiva, one of the most complex of the Hindu gods. Shiva blows hot and cold: he is at once Shiva the Beneficent and Shiva the Avenger. In the homes along the Tons, there are small altars where candles burn below bright printed posters of the ambiguous god. Here is Shiva carrying, in his four hands, a trident, a deerskin, a drum, and a club with a skull at the end; Shiva with a serpent around his neck; Shiva wearing a necklace of skulls. The streak of blue in his hair represents the Ganges, for it is Shiva who brought the Holy River to earth, breaking its fall from heaven by allowing it to trickle through his matted hair. Shiva is usually depicted as having a third eye in the middle of his forehead. When the extraneous eye is closed, Shiva is pacific and the figure symbolizes a search for inward vision. When the third eye is open, Shiva the Wrathful rains fire and destruction upon the earth.

N. N. said that these tales of the gods weren't necessarily the literal truth of creation. They were a way of thinking about creation, life, and the meaning thereof.

It is a commonplace observation that India, and northern India in particular, has been a hotbed of innovative spirituality since the dawn of civilization. Hindus, Moslems, Jainists,

"MAIN SQUEEZE"—THE FIRST REALLY NASTY RAPID.
(STEVE CURTIS)

Sikhs, Buddhists, Christians exist side by side and all react one upon the other so that, over the centuries, it has become religion—colorful, earnest, variegated—that defines the country. Indians as a people are intoxicated with religion, and even a visitor of sharp and jaundiced opinions is likely to be tumbled willy-nilly in the torrent of spiritual concerns.

N. N. was right, of course. My little swim in the Tons was an exercise in perceived mortality. Food for compulsive thought. I couldn't, for instance, shake this terrifying religious image. It is Shiva as I had seen him in the posters, Shiva the Pacific, the inward looking. Suddenly, the third eye snaps open and there is piercing fire, nuclear white and final.

I thanked N. N. for the beer and the conversation then hobbled off to my room. When you begin to imagine strange three-eyed gods winking at you, it's time to regroup, reconsider, change your religion, even finish the last beer and go to bed.

Delhi is the capital of India and its administrative center, New Delhi, is often described as a city of gardens. Unfortunately, I had come to this otherwise graceful city in the worst of times, which is to say during the month of May. Afternoon temperatures rose to 110 degrees and would hold there for another month until the cooling rains of the monsoon. Dust, fine as talc, floated over everything and colored the sky a dull whiskey brown. In the countryside, whirlwinds swept over the baking plain and, at a distance, it was impossible to tell the sky from the earth.

Delhi's heat, in the month of May, tries men's souls. In 1986, on May 13th, a man named Gupta killed his wife because he believed she was sleeping with another man named Gupta. Eight persons—members of a wedding party who had asked for some water at a temple—

were injured in a fracas with the temple keepers who believed the water would be used to mix alcoholic drinks. A civil servant who had not been promoted at the dairy board killed himself and left a note excoriating his superiors. There was a Santa Ana tension in the still burning air of the city, but May and June are also the months of snow melt in the Himalayas, the months the foothills erupt in wildflowers, the months most auspicious for a pilgrimage to the cool beauty of the sacred Garhwal.

Sixteen of us were camped in a lush meadow, by a wide eddy on the Tons river, in the Abode of the Gods. There was a scent of rhododendron in the air and the temperature, at four in the afternoon, stood just shy of eighty degrees. The river valley was narrow, four hundred yards across, and the hills rose steep and spire-like on either side, obscuring a glittering ridge of the high Himalaya to the north. There were leafy alders on the meadow. Deodar pines, like lodgepole pines, forested the higher slopes. It was a young river valley, recently cut in geological terms, and the Tons, fed by spring snowmelt, was running high and fast.

It was our first day on the river, and Jack Morison laid it out for his nine paying passengers. Jack had been a boatman for Sobek Expeditions for a full decade, running rivers from California to Chile and back again. Now he is the president and chief guide of White Magic Unlimited, a rafting and trekking outfitting business out of Mill Valley, California. He had made a first descent of the river five years ago. The original plan had been to raft the better-known Yamuna River, of which the Hindu scriptures say: "No mortal mocks her fury; no mortal stops her onward flow." But the Yamuna had struck Morison as a pretty tame ribbon of water—about Class II whitewater: "rapids of medium difficulty with clear, wide passages"—and he didn't think American mortals would be willing to travel all the way to India for a gentle float trip. Hiking east, over an icy ridge, he came upon the Tons. It was his dream river, the river he could build his company around.

As Jack spoke, local people from the nearby village of Mori gathered about. The children came first, followed by old men, and finally men who seemed to hold positions of authority in the village. They wore clean western-style clothes in subdued colors. The women did not come into our camp; they sat on the ridges in tight little groups and occasionally the wind would carry the tinkle of giggles down into the meadow where we sat.

This would be the fourth time the river had ever been run, Jack said. The trip was really "a commercial exploratory" which meant there would be a lot of time spent scouting the rapids ahead and deciding on strategy.

There was plenty of big water, but what set the Tons apart from other big water rivers Jack knew—he mentioned the Bio Bio in Chile and the Zambezi in Zambia—was the "consistency" of the white water. "It is one rapid after another," he said, "almost eighty miles of Class III and IV and even Class V rapids. The whitewater sections are separated by a hundred yards or less of flat water, which are probably moving at five to seven miles an hour." Class V rapids are defined as "having extremely long, difficult and violent rapids that follow each other almost without interruption ... plenty of obstacles, big drops, violent current and very steep gradient...." The obstacles and drops on the Tons meant the rafts would have to do a lot of evasive maneuvering in heavy water. It was a very "technical" river.

The major danger, of course, was being thrown from one of the rubber rafts or having it flip. A person might be held down for some time in a big hole, might be thumped up and down in a circular motion—"Maytagged"—but the more deadly situation would be to be swept through several consecutive rapids. "On most rafting rivers," Jack said, "there will be a quiet pool at the end of a rapid." On the Tons, however, the rapids were "closely linked,"

"Mr. Rana smiled and asked if our rubber rafts were inflated with helium. 'Just air,' I said. My friend seemed disappointed by the technological poverty of this arrangement."

and even the strongest swimmer could be swept from one rapid to another. "The water is cold," Jack said, "it's all spring snow melt now and the longer you're in it, the more it saps your strength. Swim too many rapids, and you'll be too weak to make it to the bank. If you go in, do everything possible to get out after the first rapid."

Such was the nature of our pilgrimage.

A man feels a fool. Here I was, sitting under one of the alders trying to read a book entitled *Hindus of the Himalayas* and getting absolutely nowhere because I was surrounded by a hundred or so Hindus of the Himalayas who wanted to know what I was reading.

The book, an ethnography of the region by Gerald Berreman, said that the plains Brahmins considered the people of the hills to be rude bumpkins. They live in this most religiously significant area of India, but according to Berreman, they engage in "frequent meat and liquor parties . . . are unfamiliar with scripture, largely ignore the great gods of Hinduism, marry across caste lines," and do other things that made me think I'd enjoy their company.

I read that passage to a man named Ajaypal Rana who declared it "blasphemy." His tone was mild, unconcerned. He might just as well have said the passage was "interesting" for all the passion in his voice. I read on. "Says here that people 'conceal these activities' and they 'project behavior indicating adherence to the accredited values of society.' "

Mr. Rana smiled and asked if our rubber rafts were inflated with helium. "Just air," I said. My friend seemed disappointed by the technological poverty of this arrangement.

The night was just cool enough for the thinnest of sleeping bags, and I had laid mine out under one of the leafy alders, in a field of calf-high marijuana and mint. The breeze felt like velvet, and the stars swirled above in the clear mountain air. Far to the south, the sky flickered electric blue as heat lightning shimmered over the baking plain of the Ganges River.

We had talked for several hours, the Hindus of the Himalayas and I. There were men with obvious physical handicaps among the villagers, but they had been teachers or farmers or tailors. There were no beggars among the hill people.

Which had not been the case in Delhi. On the streets, the heat pounding down from above, then rising up off the concrete, kept battalions of beggars working feverishly. There was no shade, no place to sit, and so the horribly mutilated hopped or rolled or lurched along, hands (or what passed for hands) out, beseeching looks on their faces. The novelist and travel writer, V. S. Naipaul, a West Indian Hindu who wrote two brilliant books about his travels in India, the land of his grandfather, found the sheer numbers of beggars particularly distressing. In *India: a Wounded Civilization* he wrote: "The very idea of beggary, precious to Hindus as religious theater, a demonstration of the workings of karma, a reminder of one's duty to oneself and one's future, has been devalued. And the Bombay beggar, displaying his usual mutilations (inflicted in childhood by the beggar-master who had acquired him, as proof of the young beggar's sins in a previous life) now finds, unfairly, that he provokes annoyance rather than awe. The beggars themselves, forgetting their Hindu function, also pester tourists; and the tourists misinterpret the whole business, seeing in the beggary of the few the beggary of all."

There had been, in Delhi, a young man, nearly naked but for a white loin cloth. He was lean and dark, starkly muscled, and his right leg had been amputated just above the knee. He saw me—an obvious tourist—across a wide boulevard choked with the chaotic late afternoon traffic that, in India, is a form of population control: that day, in Delhi alone, three died in accidents and seventeen were injured. The man came for me, threading his way nimbly through the cars, hopping on one bare foot and a crutch fashioned from the branch of a tree. I was amazed at his dexterity, the athletic fluidity of his movements.

The beggar hit the sidewalk and just for a moment I saw triumph in his face, and a kind of joy. But, as he fell into hop step beside me, the light died in his eyes and he stared fixedly with a wet and pathetic spaniel-eyed beggar's gaze. "Alms," he said.

I am a man who habitually doles out spare change to winos, seeing, I suppose, the possibility that I might, one day, total my karma and find myself sitting in an alley behind a tattoo parlor swigging muscatel from a bottle in a paper bag. But this idea of the sins of the previous life resulting in the mutilation of children by beggar-masters and misery pimps: I would not, I decided, perpetuate this system. I would not, as a matter of principle, give money to beggars.

"Alms," the one-legged athlete moaned.

I stared through him and silently chanted the mantra that makes beggars disappear. "You are invisible. . . ."

He hopped along by my side for three city blocks—"you are invisible"—then peeled off and made for the other side of the street, playing picador with the taxis.

I kept replaying the encounter in my mind and it was keeping me awake. His misfortune wasn't his fault. Giving him money: the penny or so he wanted, would it be such a sin? I thought: it would be like standing on the brink of hell and tossing in a wet sponge.

T he first day out of Mori was the easiest. There were rapids without a lot of rocks. The people had gathered by the hundreds to see us off. It is a romantic conceit, but I had rather hoped they might regard us with awe. "Crazy brave fools risking watery death for naught but glory. . . ." That sort of thing.

As it was, we had severe competition from a band of Gujars, semi-nomadic Muslim herdsmen, who had come in that morning. I heard them driving their cattle along the trail above our meadow, and saw them in the pale light of false dawn: fine tall people with aquiline features shouting and laughing on the hillside above. The women wore intricately patterned

STARTING OUT—THE FIRST DAY WAS THE EASIEST. (STEVE CURTIS)

pant and tunic combinations and covered their heads with colorful scarves of bright red or green. The older men dyed their beards red. All the males, men and boys, wore red skull caps embroidered with golden thread and topped by a red pompon on a braided stalk.

There had been Gujars among the Hindus the night before, but this was a special group. Their clothes were finer, brighter, the women wore more bangles, their cattle were fatter, and their dogs were bright-eyed and well fed. They were, I learned later, show biz Gujars.

The group, about eighteen of them, set up in a meadow not far from us and the people of Mori abandoned us for the Gujar show, which was undoubtedly more interesting than watching people load rafts all morning. The Gujars had with them several dusty black Himalayan bears, sometimes called moon bears for the white or orange-yellow crescent on their chests. The bears were controlled by a long rope that ran through the nose and out the mouth, but they seemed to respond to verbal commands. There was "sleeping bear" who lay on his back with his paws in the air, "smoking bear" who sucked on a six-foot-long stick of bamboo, "disco bear" who danced, and "hugging bear" who gently embraced a local child. The people of Mori laughed, threw coins to the Gujars, and strolled back to watch us cast off.

And so we paddled out of the eddy, caught the current, and went spinning down the Tons, crazy brave fools who would risk watery death but who were, demonstrably, no more interesting than your basic dancing bear. The Gujars had stolen our thunder and destroyed a romance. "Stupid damn hats," a man paddling beside me said. "Makes 'em look like nitwits."

Two days later, we hit "Main Squeeze," the first really nasty rapid. It was hellishly technical. The river narrowed down to thirty feet, and, naturally, a bridge spanned the Tons at the point of its greatest fury. The water thundered between rock walls in wildly irregular waves that clashed, one against the other, throwing spray ten feet into the air. Just before the bridge, the river rose up over a rock—a domer—then dropped four feet into a hole. The hole was six feet long, and at its downstream end, a wave four feet high curled back upstream.

We wanted to hit the hole dead on, power paddle into the curling wave, punch through, jog right to avoid the tree trunk pylon for the bridge, duck under the bridge—Jack Morison said he'd never seen the Tons so high—then hit hard to the right. Ten feet past the bridge, the river widened to fifty feet, but a rock thirty feet wide cut it into two ten foot channels. The left channel was shallow and rock strewn. We would need to pull hard right as soon as we passed under the bridge.

There were seven of us in the paddle boat: three of us on each tube with paddles and Jack Morison manning the oars from the frame in the back. Jack called out orders—"paddle right"—and muscled the bow into the line we'd chosen. We had spent two hours scouting Main Squeeze and we ran it in thirty seconds.

Those of us in the paddle boat were getting cocky, impatient with all the scouting Jack thought necessary. We were a strong team and we worked well together. Why couldn't we just R and R: read the river and run? There was some grumbling about this matter.

A tributary I couldn't find on the map—local people called it the Pauer—emptied into the Tons, effectively doubling its volume, just before the town of Tiuni. The river below gathered force and the gradient steepened until the Tons was dropping a hundred feet every mile. It was a wild ride, the Tons below Tiuni. There were, for instance, five major rapids just below the town, with no more than twenty yards of flat water in the whole run.

Occasionally we hit a hole out of position and people were thrown from the boat—"swimmer!"—but we managed to right ourselves and scoop them out of the water without stopping.

A mile downstream from the town, we passed a dozen or so men sitting on the rocks beside a six foot high pile of burning sticks. We were paddling hard, dodging rocks and punching through curlers, but there was time enough to see the body on top of the funeral pyre. A yellow sheet covered the torso to the shins and flames licked at the bare feet.

The ashes would be dumped into the Tons and they'd flow into the Yamuna, which empties into the sacred Ganges. There, in those holy waters, the soul of the departed might achieve "moksha": liberation from the cycle of being, from the necessity of being reborn.

At the moment, however, the physical body was being consumed in the burning flame of Shiva's open third eye.

On the second to last day, the river entered a long narrow gorge. The cliff walls that rose on either side were an oddly striated travertine that looked like decorations on some alien and inhuman temple. We had come seventy miles, dropped almost three thousand feet, and the river had spent much of its power. There were long flat water floats where it was so quiet we could hear the chatter of monkeys and the calls of cuckoos. The land, which had looked like a steeper version of the northern Rockies upstream now took a more gentle, tropical rhythm. Palm trees grew at the edge of the cliffs and their roots dropped eighty feet into the nourishing water of the Tons.

There were waterfalls here and there, and once, floating languidly under cobalt skies, we passed through a falling curtain of mist that stretched one hundred feet along a mossy green cliff wall. It was warmer here, eighty-five degrees, and I raised my face to the cooling water. The sunlight was scattered in that silver curtain—each drop a prism—so that for a moment what I saw was a falling wall of color that shifted and danced in the breeze. The mist had the odor of orchids to it, and I wondered then why it was that anyone would want to be liberated from the cycle of being.

There was big trouble the last day. The Tons had lately been so flat and friendly that the last series of rapids were a major surprise and are, in fact, called Major Surprise. I followed Jack and his boatmen as they scouted the noisy water: there was a hole, a pretty good curling wave, a house-sized rock, and a small waterfall called a pour-over. We needed to skirt the rock, punch through the hole and pull left in order to hit the pour-over at its shallow end, which would give us a drop of about four feet.

Major Surprise ate us alive.

I recall hitting the hole and punching cleanly through the curler. But we didn't get left, not even a little bit, and the boat rose up over a domer so high that I found myself looking directly into the sky. We tipped forward—the drop was eight feet—and the boat seemed to hesitate momentarily, like a roller coaster at the summit of the first rise. This, I told myself, does not bode well.

The first thing a person notices underwater in the turbulence of a big hole is the sound. It's loud: a grinding, growling jackhammer of unrelenting thunder. You do not register temperature, and, if you are being Maytagged, you have no idea where you are. It's like catching a big ocean wave a bit low: there's a lot of tumbling involved, not to mention a sense of forces beyond human control.

The river took my swimming trunks. It ripped the tennis shoe off one of my feet; it sent me thudding against unseen rocks, shot me to the surface dead center in the middle of the hole, sucked me down again and batted me around for a period of time I was never able to calibrate. It didn't seem fair. I couldn't even recall falling out of the boat: the entire situation was unacceptable.

Some time later I came to the surface and the hole was behind me. The river ran right, between a large rock and a canyon wall. A person could get wedged in there, underwater. I swam left, and suddenly felt myself being hurtled down a smooth tongue of water toward a series of peaked waves of the type boatmen call haystacks. It was like being sick, like vomiting. After the first painful eruption you think, good, that's all over. But almost instantly your stomach begins to rise—oh God, not again—and that is the way I felt being sucked breathless into the second rapid.

While I was zipping along underwater, trying to get my feet downstream to ward off rocks, the other members of the paddle boat team were enjoying their own immediate problems and proving Jack Morison's contention that we were taking the river entirely too lightly. John Rowan and Martha Freeman had been sucked to the right and managed to pull themselves out after the first rapid. Jack and Billy Anderson held on to the boat, which was still stuck in the hole and being battered by the upstream curler wave. Sue Wilson and Douglas Gow were somewhere out ahead of me in the second rapid.

I surfaced and spotted Gow in the flat water between that second and third rapid. He was ten yards downstream and he didn't seem to be swimming at all. His helmet was missing. I thought he might have been Maytagged rather badly, that he might be unconscious, and I am proud to say that I swam to the man who needed help. (In point of fact, Gow had taken off his helmet because it had slipped down over his eyes and he couldn't see).

"You okay?" I called when I was within arm's reach. Gow practices emergency medicine in Australia and is used to reacting calmly in tense situations. "Fine, thanks," he said, and then—oh God, not again—I was pulled down into the third rapid.

There was, in time, a sense of water moving more slowly. Sunlight shimmered on the flat surface, which seemed to recede even as I swam toward it, but then there was air and a handhold on the rocky canyon wall. Presently, Morison and Anderson came by in the boat and fished me out of the river. I lay on my belly on the floor of the raft and spit up a quart of yellow water.

We were somewhere else then, pulled up onto the sand at the left side of the river. Sue Wilson and Doug Gow were gasping on the bank. Someone gave me a pair of swimming trunks to wear. This did not seem to be an important matter. I lay on my back, on the floor of the raft, looking at the sun, and there was a moment when it seemed to darken slightly, but I did not lose consciousness. I thought of Shiva's blinding third eye, of a long lewd wink.

CAHILL CONSIDERS HIS DESTINY. (STEVE CURTIS)

I went to Rishikesh, the holy city on the banks of the sacred Ganges, just in case.

The river runs through a wide, rocky gorge there, and every day pilgrims by the thousands cross over a suspension bridge that spans the Ganges and leads to the temples and ashrams of Rishikesh, to what the guidebooks call "the abode of saints and sages." To get to the bridge, you have to walk down a wide staircase set against a white cement wall. There are large rectangular boxes sculpted into the wall, and sitting in these boxes are the most unfortunate, the most horribly mutilated beggars in all of India.

Either they lived in those boxes, or they were carried there each morning, because it was clear that none of them could walk. As I passed, they called out to me in the most theatrically pathetic and heart rending tones: "alms, alms, ALMS...." I made them invisible and passed on to the abode of saints and sages.

A wide cement walkway ran along the ridge top, and, in the formal gardens on either side, sacred cows grazed on a variety of colorful flowers. Beggars didn't seem to be allowed here, near the temples, but holy men lined the walkway. There were more sadhus and gurus and anandas and babas and bhagwans and rishis and maharishis than a guy could shake a stick at. A man in a white loincloth with yellow sandalwood paste on his forehead offered to bless me for a rupee. I gave him the eight cents, just in case, and he held out his palm to me, like a police man stopping traffic.

Under a tree set in the center of the walkway, a thin dark man lay on a bed of nails, a collection bowl for donations by his side. He wore a skimpy loin cloth that revealed a thin appendectomy scar angling up from his groin. Nailed to the tree was a large frame containing four photographs. The first three showed the same man lying on his bed of nails in front of what I took to be various holy places. The fourth was him reclining in a pile of thorns.

Further down toward the main concentration of temples I stopped into an herbal medicine shop where, according to a leaflet I was given, they sold "chandra prabhavati," which was said to "cure piles ... rheumatic pains, gonorrhea, syphilis and spleen complaints." I asked to buy some mahavrinraf oil, which "checks the fallings of hair, invigorates the nerves, and removes brain fag." They were fresh out of mahavrinraf oil.

Some earnest young people—three or four Indians and a like number of Westerners—urged me to follow them to their ashram. "Let's go," I said brightly, but something in my attitude—brain fag maybe—put them off.

There were steps that led down to the holy river, and places along the bank to bathe. A bath in the Ganges is said to wash away a pilgrim's worldly sins. The river was swift and cold, hard to swim. I got myself out into the teeth of the current and let it carry me several yards. It felt good, going with the flow like that.

Passing back over the bridge, I stopped in front of the boxes in the wall and allowed myself finally to see the beggars. "Alms," they cried and I gave them alms. I stood there tossing wet sponges into the fires of hell, just in case.

Later that night, in Dehra Dun, I met N. N. Badoni. He told me that the soul seeks its master. I told him about the Tons River.

AN ISLAND OF PEACE IN A NOISY, MODERN CITY (JIM SLADE)

James Salter

▼

ROADS SELDOM TRAVELLED

As children we were not taught to love Japan. In the newsreels little men were raising their rifles exultantly in the air in conquered Chinese cities, and cheap toys made in Japan always broke. Set against this were two thrilling tributes, *The Mikado* and *Madame Butterfly*, romantic and of the past.

Then came the war.

I remember going for the first time. We flew up from Okinawa —it was in 1946, eight months after the surrender. The country was in ruins. We landed at Atsugi, the airfield near Yokohama that MacArthur himself had flown into when he arrived as proconsul, and drove to Tokyo on roads empty of all traffic except an occasional army truck. The city itself was shabby and smelled of excrement. At night everything was dark. We were warned to eat nothing that had not been peeled or cooked, and a carton of cigarettes would buy a weekend. It was utter defeat.

Decades passed.

Together with my grown son, who had not been born when I was a fighter pilot—the envy, as I thought, of all who were not—I found myself in Japan once more. The old Imperial Hotel was gone. Every trace of exhaustion and war had vanished. When we arrived in Tokyo, having flown all day across the Pacific, it was evening. The traffic was heavy, it might have been Los Angeles or Queens. We were on our way to Kyushu, the second smallest and southernmost of the four main islands. We were joining a bicycle tour of Australians. I had packed, as if for a journey to the Pole, every item listed in the advisories received from the organizers of the tour. My son confidently took only about a fifth of what was recommended. It turned out he was right.

We slept that night in an airport hotel. It was too late for dinner and we were tired. The Tokyo Giants were playing on television. The first thing one notices about Japan, returning after long absence or arriving for the first time, is staggering expense. The hotel cost about ten times more than a hotel on my last visit and twice as much as New York. Early the next morning we caught a flight to Kyushu. We were the only non-Japanese on the plane, on which an obliging stewardess was taking pictures of several pairs of passengers with the passengers' cameras. After a couple of hours we let down for landing at an airfield by the sea, the city of Miyazaki just to the north. We were coming in over the water, with palm trees and steel light structures painted the familiar orange and white. There was a clear, empty feeling of the tropics.

One of the guides had driven up to meet us. The group, which had already been on the road for several days, was about forty miles away, resting its legs near a little town called Nichinan. We drove south on a beautiful sunny morning. Yasuhiro was the guide's name. He had a bronzed face and a brilliant white smile. "Call me Yas," he said, using up a good part of his English. The road hugged the shore. There was blue sea on our left, and a Sunday concert on the radio was playing a spirited arrangement of "Anchors Aweigh."

After some fifty minutes we pulled off the road and drove down a narrow track half hidden by vegetation. Set back from the beach in a small clearing was a nondescript building with screened porches. It was a small Japanese inn, a *minshuku*. In such places the rooms are simple and nearly bare, separated only by screens or sliding paper walls. No English is spoken and two meals come with the price. Shoes, of course, are left at the door. The host was watching television, which he wordlessly interrupted to bring us tea. We sat on the floor and sipped it. Barely visible in other rooms and scattered outside, alone and in two's and three's, the Australians were lying about. The introductions were casual. There were five men and five women, including an older married couple. They ranged from their mid-twenties to fifty years old. If you've been on a tour you've met them all. There was a teacher, a male and a female nurse, a pharmacist, a secretary, an engineer. It was Chaucer. The chief guide, whose name was Keiichi, was called Kay—he was about forty, tanned and wiry, firmly in command. He could have been the leader of a platoon that fought its way down through Malaya in 1942. My impression was that he never slept.

Outside we were given our bicycles—ten speed tourers, well used, without saddlebags or encumbrances of any kind. We got the two that were left. There had been a misunderstanding. For some reason it had been assumed that my son was a mere child and a smaller bike had been brought for him, but one of the guides obligingly agreed to ride it while the other drove the van that carried all the luggage. Off we went.

Kyushu runs north and south; about 250 miles long, 100 miles wide, and shaped like an

FEVERISHLY PURSUING
WESTERN IDEAS, JAPAN
REMAINS A COUNTRY OF
ANCIENT TRADITIONS.
(JIM SLADE)

upside-down J. At the curved northern tip is Nagasaki, for centuries the sole port open to foreigners. At the southern end a great body of water enters, and near its apex is Kagoshima. Like all of Japan the island is mountainous. The big cities and main roads lie along the shore.

Our route covered the southernmost part, the two long arms of land that form the sides of Kagoshima Bay. It was late May and the weather was hot. The rainy season was only a few weeks away. For the most part we stayed close to the sea. Unknown towns, roads without names. Japanese villages are very much like those in Sicily, another island of dark eyes. Architecturally they are undistinguished and often crudely commercial, signs and advertisements over everything. The predominant color is gray. Still, there is a sense of tranquility and order. The open seacoast itself is unspoiled. Between the road and the sea there is only the rare house and almost never a restaurant or hotel. In the towns, of course, it's different.

We usually rode in the morning for three hours or so, stopped for lunch, and went on for three or four hours more in the afternoon, stopping frequently for cold drinks, which are sold everywhere along the road in vending machines. Coca-Cola—no two words in the world are more widespread—fruit juice, and a native restorative called Pocari Sweat which I never felt desperate enough to try. Depending on the terrain, we covered between thirty-five and seventy kilometers a day. The pace was moderate although there was a kind of understanding that it was not good form to dismount and walk up even the steepest of hills—and some of them were steep. There were some of first category difficulty and there were some, as they say in the European bike races, beyond category. Sun beating down on the hard road, eyebrows soaked with sweat, the route going up and up endlessly, past quarries, past forests, past everything, with no indication of where or even if it would end —these were some of the daily pleasures. You are standing on the pedals and even then they barely move. The bike is practically motionless. No one in sight. Above you the road turns. Perhaps it's the last turn before the crest. If not, perhaps the next to last. Is this a description of touring? Partly. By now I have nearly forgotten the burning legs and a muttered command to yourself for just twenty more strokes. What remains is the glorious feeling of finally reaching the destination, pulling out the bedding and lying down for half an hour or so without speaking.

In the country inns there is calm and serenity. Perhaps you have not come to Japan for these things. Usually there is not much choice. In the spare, harmonious rooms there is a low table with a tea service, hot water in a large thermos, and boxes of tea. Nothing else. Out the window there are palm trees and an empty beach, or rice fields, or the back of a nameless hotel and a train. The principal entertainment is the bath.

Every foreigner knows about these—Japan is famous for them. The Japanese, a friend of mine who knows them says, have a genetic advantage which keeps them from getting hangovers. They are apparently also resistent to second-degree burns, which is what you will get if you ill-advisedly step into the water without the intervention of a maid or whoever is around to make it cooler. For some reason you are not supposed to do it yourself, but this is serious and you cannot bother with propriety. The bath is for soaking, of course, not washing. Soaping and rinsing are done beside the bath, and the cleansed body is then gently boiled. The Japanese endure this for a long time. Until recently the sexes commingled in the bath but the custom is disappearing.

"Did you go to the Jungle Bath in Ibusuki?" another friend who had been on a celebrated—for him—trip to Japan in the 1970s asked.

"Yes."

"And bathe with all the women?" he asked eagerly.

"The women's bath was separate," I said. The room had been very large, about the size of a basketball court, with a high wall of river stones completely separating the men's and women's sides, though you could hear them laughing over there and talking.

"A wall?" my friend said. Dismay was on his face. Not even a decade and the fabled Japan he had known was vanishing.

In the baths the men held a small towel, like a bouquet, in front of their genitals as they entered. They brought their small sons with them, sometimes their very young daughters. One man had his two little girls, one of them about four, the other seven or eight. They showed no embarrassment or curiosity. They swam in the hot pool, limbs gleaming, wet black hair framing their lovely faces.

The food is Japanese, the hotels and inns are Japanese, the sea and sky are Japanese. We are sleeping on *futons*, the slender sheaf of bedding that is made up on top of the *tatami* floor, and sometimes on regular beds. Nevertheless, for us, speaking only a few words of Japanese and strangely clad, gliding through landscape and lodgings, not part of either, it is impossible to know the people. The wife of the married couple, who is the teacher, has brought along and is reading a novel by Soseki Natsume, the first great modern writer of Japan, who had a profound influence on writers who came after like Tanizaki, Kawabata, and Mishima. My son is reading Lafcadio Hearn, the most important of the foreign writers to illuminate Japan for us. Hearn, insofar as an outsider can, became Japanese, lived there, taught at the Imperial University in Tokyo, and married a Japanese woman, the daughter of a samurai family. One of his stories, of the life and death of a cricket, *Kusa-Hibari*, is as

"For us, speaking only a few words of Japanese and strangely clad, gliding through landscape and lodgings, not part of either, it is impossible to know the people."

pure and haunting as anything I know. The country he wrote of is already no more but its spirit has not changed.

To a large extent I was drawn back to Japan by the quality and elegance of its writers, of whose existence I was not even aware when I was younger. Sympathy and admiration, however, are not sufficient to bring one to a real understanding of Japan. The obvious barriers, language and custom, are too wide. Feverishly pursuing western ideas and fashions in clothes, music, sports, eating, almost everything one's eye falls on, the Japanese are nevertheless separated from the West by a formidable gulf. Theirs is a unified, blood-shared culture. It is a culture that declines to be known. What is happening on the other side of the curtain we try to divine by arranging the details of a journey into some kind of coherence, but the arrangement is our own and hastily put together. The true pattern and depth eludes us. The stunning final act of Mishima's life we are able to describe and even in a sense to understand but its impulse remains incomprehensible.

Kagoshima, where we spent several days, is the city where Japanese navy pilots trained for the attack on Pearl Harbor. They came out of the mountains to the west, dropped down to rooftop level and roared over the houses and department stores on the way to the docks and blue water of the bay. In one of these department stores, Mitsukoshi, I glimpsed the new Japan: gleaming decor, fashionable boutiques, and a basement that was a combination of Macy's and the first floor at Harrod's, with food and drink of every kind and description brilliantly lit and handsomely displayed. The only things I saw that were American were Famous Amos Cookies and a handful of California wines. Whatever you bought was quickly and beautifully wrapped, which is typical of Japan. In Tokyo even the department managers know how to wrap and willingly do so. I preserved the paper in a number of cases, hoping to be able to duplicate the wrapping, but although I marked the folds with sequence numbers I still couldn't do it.

We stayed in a modern hotel in Kagoshima, commercial and with extremely small rooms. We had breakfast in a dining room on the top floor. It might have been Naples with the sun-silvered bay and its own Vesuvius, an active volcano named Mount Sakurajima, above. Japanese breakfasts are meals of some consequence, *miso* soup, several kinds of fish, rice,

A "REGIMENT" OF SCHOOL
CHILDREN
(JONATHAN E. PITE)

raw eggs (which the Japanese break into their bowl of rice), salad, pressed seaweed, fruit juice, tea, toast, pickled vegetables, and five or six other things.

The city reminded me of Italy in other ways—the crowds, narrow streets impossible to find again, countless small restaurants and shops. There are arcades and long, covered galleries as in Bologna or Milan, streetcars, and here and there a slightly garish, pastel building called a "love" hotel with awnings discreetly hung to conceal the parking places.

Japanese homes in certain cities can be visited through a kind of cultural exchange program, and this had been arranged. The two of us were picked up at the hotel the second night by a young couple in their twenties. They had a new car and a two-year-old child who was whining and attempting to get into the back seat with us. There were two other children at home, the wife informed us. Her name was Mayumi. "Do you like children?" she asked.

"Who doesn't?" I said.

Their house was in a residential district of the city called Hiyamizu, which means cold water. It was already dark. The streets were narrow and serpentine. We parked in a small space in front of the entrance, a space exactly the size of the car. The children, a girl of seven and a boy of five, were waiting inside. I had vaguely expected them to bow and retire shyly to another part of the household, although travelling with their younger sister should have given me a more realistic idea. We sat in a small living room decorated with inexpensive western-style furniture while the children crawled over our legs, across the back of the sofa, spilled things on the linoleum floor, and brought out books and favorite toys in an effort to gain attention.

The husband, Kenichi, worked for a bank. It was one of the largest in Kagoshima, with many branches. He was in a junior managerial position and got, as I remember, one day a week off and half of Saturday twice a month. He had one week of vacation a year. We made an attempt in the confusion to eat some of the dinner the wife had prepared and finally set off for a visit to her parents, who lived not far away. The thing that struck me was that we left the house unlocked and the children by themselves with instructions to wash and go to bed. Strangely enough, I had the impression this was what they would do. I thought of my own country which seemed violent and dangerous by comparison. In Kagoshima, in the morning, little children of five and six walk unattended in their school uniforms along the streets and alleys, and on suburban roads girls in white blouses glide by on their bicycles, flooding to class like flocks of cranes. It is a different world. The buses and trolleys are undefaced, the people friendly and polite. There are few drugs. Families are tightly formed.

The next day at the hotel there were gifts for us from the family, including a child's grammar I had admired and a note saying that the daughter wanted us to have it. *Now we wish you good health and happiness forever*, the note ended.

The bikes were left behind in Kagoshima beneath the layer of ash, fine as pumice dust, that spreads over the city from Sakurajima day and night. From there we took the train. There is a poem of Kipling's, burningly romantic, about a galley slave who is finally freed and who watches in sorrow as his galley beats out to sea without him. *I am paid in full for service. Would that service still were mine!* It was something like that. I looked at the bicycles lined up outside the hotel—I would not be seeing them again or riding through sunshine and rain. On one of those days near the end I had found myself for some reason all alone. I didn't know where the others were, either far ahead or far behind. It was cloudy and cool. There was occasional very light rain. It was one of the most beautiful mornings of my life, unhurried, smooth, going along the shore. I had no past, no future, I had surrendered it all to the empty road. On the rocks below, the sea was clear and green. There were small rice paddies between the road and the shore, weatherbeaten houses, quiet villages. I was singing as I went, euphoric, at peace with earth and heaven.

The train, modern and solidly built, left Kagoshima at six in the evening. Suburban stations with their hundreds of waiting bicycles flowed by. The lights of small houses began to come on. There were rooms by the tracks with clothes drying in them, men in undershirts watching television on *tatami* mats as their wives prepared the evening meal. The roadbed was exceptionally smooth and the cars well-lit and clean. We slept four to a compartment with a freshly ironed *yukaza*, a printed cotton robe, folded on the pillow for each passenger, and sometime during the night we passed through the tunnel beneath Shimonoseki Strait that separates Kyushu from Honshu, the main island, on which Tokyo and Osaka are situated. That night also, sleeping, we passed through Hiroshima.

CLOSE TO THE SEA, THE
PACE WAS MODERATE,
THOUGH IT WAS NOT REALLY
GOOD FORM TO DISMOUNT
AND WALK. (COURTESY OF
WORLD EXPEDITIONS)

From Osaka, where we got off, we went directly to Nara, an historic town that was once, twelve hundred years ago, the capital of Japan. It is a town of magnificent wooden temples, the heritage of Buddhism's entry into Japan here. One of the temples, Todai-ji, is said to possess the largest wooden structure in the world. There are two parallel religions in Japan, Buddhism and Shintoism, but they are not mutually exclusive—some aspects of life fall under one, some under the other. There are Shinto shrines and Buddhist temples. The temples and pagodas of Nara have been built and rebuilt over the centuries as they have been damaged or destroyed by wars, fires, and natural disasters. Apart from statues, nothing is quite original but nothing is new.

Regiments of schoolchildren were touring the temple buildings on cultural visits. They were in uniform, the girls generally in some kind of middy blouse and skirt, the boys in white shirt and pants. The students wanted to try their English. Urged by classmates, the nerviest came forth. "Excuse me," they said as their companions burst into giggles, "what time is it?" My son by this time was a hardened case. He found the Australians uninteresting and being herded around by a group leader oppressive. On the second day of the tour—I should have realized what it meant—he had cut the sleeves off his T-shirt and began battling for the lead on the road. He missed climbing, which is what he would have been doing if he were back home. At every opportunity he did pull-ups to build his arm strength, on the doorjambs of hotels, the awnings of ferries, wherever he could find a hold. He kept to himself and read climbing magazines on the bus while the guide described the things we were on the way to see. But the unforgettable image I have of him is surrounded by Japanese schoolchildren who were magically drawn to him and who squealed and tried to talk while he responded, his goodness betrayed by the expression on his face and the warmth of his smile. Perhaps some day he will return, under circumstances as different from these as those of my two visits, and see the country with different eyes. There are things here that simply touch the soul. We were near the grave of Ganjin, the Chinese priest who was perhaps the most important figure in the introduction of Buddhism to Japan and who supervised the building of the first temples. The graves of many of the famous figures of Buddhism are lost or unknown, but this one has survived for more than twelve hundred years. There was a greenish pond nearby with a few leaves floating serenely in it, and as we were standing there a big carp lazed up and put a leaf on his head.

Our guide in Nara was a woman in her mid-thirties, the wife of a university professor. The story of her life came out as we toured the temples. She had eloped in Nara. She and her husband were both teachers at the time and very young. Her husband's father had just gone bankrupt, so there was no money. They lived in a small room, six *tatami* large (*tatami* mats are about three by six feet), with a very small kitchen and no bath—they used the public baths. That was long ago. She had been married a long time. Too long, she said.

"The wives of Japan are so busy," she later explained. "Dry out *futon*, wash their clothes every day, go to market *every* day, clean house. Very busy. I'm not that kind. I'm very bad wife."

The day we left for Kyoto I walked out by myself very early in the morning. There was the sound of birds and the low, smooth rumble of a train beyond the fields in which a woman was already at work, almost hidden in the dense cucumber vines. At the end of a narrow street were the train tracks. In the upstairs window of one of the houses overlooking them was a lone woman smoking a cigarette. She did this with sudden, decisive movements, her black hair swinging as she looked one way and then the other as if examining the morning and finding it the same. Then abruptly she disappeared. "Woman is to keep," our guide had said—I think she meant preserve—"and man is to destroy. Japanese man is always fighting and killing. Japanese woman is very good at keeping."

Kyoto, about an hour away from Nara, is the spiritual center of Japan, with beautiful shrines, temples, and palaces like quiet islands in the noisy, modern city. We stayed at a small *ryokan* in a lively district called Gion. It was on a crowded side street opposite a shrine. All day we walked the endless, rectilinear streets to shrines, Zen gardens, palaces. At night the trains let off thousands of passengers coming home from work, and the restaurants along the Kamo River were lighted like countless boats. When we came in late there was the click of tiles, the aroma of tobacco smoke, and the murmur of voices from the office behind the reception desk where the owner, who was a woman, was gambling with three or four men.

The *ryokan* was four stories high and relatively modern. There was one woman of all work, good-natured and accommodating. She had gold teeth in her smile and laughed readily. When we were bathing she seemed to pass by the open window frequently and occasionally to call out something. In the morning while the Japanese guests were eating breakfast in silence and watching the news on television, she would serve, coming into the small dining room and asking us, "Toast-o? Toast-o?" I don't know where they got the bread but it was cut in slices an inch or more thick. Somehow she learned I was the father of the athlete I was sharing a room with and this seemed to amuse her greatly.

I still didn't know her name but the morning we were leaving she came out of the kitchen as I walked down the hallway in my *yukaza* after breakfast and, grinning, said something to me. I didn't understand what it was. She began to pat my stomach and rub it, saying *toast-o* several times, *papa-san*, and various other things. She hugged me. The owner came out of the kitchen and was embracing me, too, rubbing my stomach and patting me familiarly on the backside, laughing, talking to me and to the other. My son passed by. "What's going on?" he asked.

"I don't know," I said.

Could they be from the old days, I suddenly thought? Do they know me? From Tokyo, the gray city, the pilot's city, days that were, the brilliance of nightclubs, debris in the streets, the mornings of waking in strange rooms? Unlikely. Even at their age they were far too young.

We took the Bullet Train to Tokyo along with hordes of schoolchildren. Fuji was in clouds, we didn't see it. That night there was a farewell dinner in an Italian restaurant in the hotel. Some of the group had bicycled through China for three or four weeks before coming to Japan and were now going home. The married couple was heading north, perhaps to Hokkaido. A few were going to Vladivostok to take the trans-Siberian railroad to Moscow, then to England. In the morning they were gone.

The name of the *ryokan* in Kyoto, incidentally, is Masuya. The address is Minami-iru, Higashi Yama-ku, Kyoto, telephone 075-561-2253. No English is spoken and it costs about twenty dollars a night. The rooms are small but very clean, the front ones overlook the shrine. I don't think they know my name but if you go there, tell them I may be coming back.

"BETWEEN THE RAPIDS THE WATER SEEMED ALMOST BENIGN." (CHRISTIAN KALLEN)

Jay McInerney

▼

DEADLY HAZARDS, MINOR HASSLES

On the road between Hwange and Victoria Falls in Zimbabwe stand several road signs that read Deadly Hazard! We never determined the exact identity of these hazards, though there were several serious candidates: wild animals, armed Matabele guerillas, land mines left over from the recent war of independence. For people like myself, risk was an aspect of the lure of travel in this part of the world. If safety and comfort were unqualified blessings I'd have stayed home. Certainly my wife, Merry, would have preferred Bermuda.

Despite the dire warnings, the zebra-striped minibus eventually deposited us at the Victoria Falls Hotel, a stately, sprawling mint-green relic of British Colonialism that would look right at home in Bermuda. The present queen of the Commonwealth had spent her honeymoon here, and it appeared to have survived the transition to majority rule more or less intact. We arrived just in time to catch the buffet lunch on the terrace. Waiting in line we witnessed a reunion of two jungly wallahs, hearty white Africans in matching tans and khakis.

"Quite a season," said one, after inquiries about wife and kids. "You probably heard about that rhino that rammed one of our vans. Gored an American. Died before we could fly him out. My God, you've no idea how difficult and expensive it is sending a body back to the States. A bloody fortune and no end of paperwork."

"Americans are a walk in the park," the other said, dipping for the curry. "We get a lot of Arab clients. Had one chewed up by a lioness last year, and Muslim law dictates burial within forty-eight hours. Well, if you don't think we were at wit's end trying to get the pieces back to Yemen or wherever the hell it was."

"Get the boy to carve you a slice of that roast. It's rather good."

That night I slept poorly, in spite of the luxury of a recent shower and a real bed after many nights of camping in the bush. Somewhat handicapped, it is true, by a bottle of Zimbabwean red wine, consumed with dinner, which the wine steward had assured me was "very fresh, sir," as if in this part of the world youth were a great virtue in a wine. I was thinking about water hazards. The proximate thunder of Victoria Falls echoed in my ears, nearly as disconcerting as the roar of a lion stalking outside a tent in which one is trying to sleep—something I had recently experienced. I rolled and tumbled within the sheets, imagining vast cataracts of whitewater. Merry slept soundly, which hardly seemed fair, since she was the one who from the start had questioned the sanity of this expedition. That afternoon, we had seen Victoria Falls for the first time, and beneath it the enraged waters of the Zambezi, which we would shortly descend in rubber rafts.

To reach the falls from the hotel of the same name you descend a path flanked by a gauntlet of curio sellers—"I trade big rhino for your American jeans, sir"—but these distractions recede as the sound of the falls rises, the temperature cools, the mist begins to glisten on your skin and on the vegetation, which in the space of fifty yards changes from arid mopane scrub to tropical rain forest. This island of thick greenery extends to the verge of a deep, narrow gorge, so that a pedestrian view of the falls is inevitably dramatic and abrupt.

The paradox of travel in the era of television and photography is that wherever we go we have already been there, our eyes trained by lenses till our direct encounters with reality seem second-hand. We carry stick-on graffiti around in our heads: "Johnny Weismuller was here," or "Mutual of Omaha's Wild Kingdom presents...." In recent weeks I had been often reminded of this condition: I recognized most of the wild animals I spotted in the savannas and forests of Zimbabwe as stars of public television; and in every airport we passed through someone was reading the movie tie-in edition of *Out of Africa*, the one with Redford and Streep on the cover. But the Upper Zambezi and Victoria Falls restored much of my faith in travel.

The Falls are on such a scale that no camera angle is comprehensive, a scale almost commensurate with our diminishing capacity for wonder. From our vantage on the Zimbabwean side we first looked out on Devil's Cataract and the Main Falls, across a series of shuddering ramparts of whitewater disappearing in their own mists toward Zambia, more than a mile away. A rainbow rose out of the white spray at the invisible bottom of the gorge, more distinct than any I'd ever seen, appearing as solid as Cecil Rhodes' steel bridge further along the gorge. Looking down this sheer rift in the earth's crust into which a broad, solemn

UPPER MOWIMBA FALLS—
EVEN THE NAME SOUNDED
OMINOUS.
(CHRISTIAN KALLEN)

river abruptly disappears, you sense you are peering into the interior of the earth; you hear thunder that might echo the big bang of creation, feel the aftershock in the form of a continuous tremor underfoot, and in this interval of hypnosis, experience a fleeting grasp of the vastness of geologic time.

The Zambezi river is almost a mile and a half across when it falls into a gorge only twenty yards wide at some points; the result may be something like stampeding a few million buffalo through a railroad tunnel. I've never been particularly afraid of water, but the sound and fury of that river disturbed my sleep.

At breakfast on the terrace we ran into Wayne and Rick, who were terrorizing the waiters with double entendres and orders for stimulants that did not appear on the breakfast menu. We had met them the previous night in the dining room. They introduced themselves as "two assholes from Texas."

"We're on a quest. We're looking for deepest, darkest Africa," Wayne had confided, as the dance band plunged recklessly into "New York, New York." In more specific terms, they were here, like us, for the whitewater expedition down the Zambezi. Wayne was a sex therapist, Rick a child psychologist, both professors at the University of Texas at Arlington, both married, with a daughter apiece. One of the things we liked about them was that they loved the dance band, the quasi-French menu, the Edwardian dining room. The average American traveller is too often indignant to find that the surface of Africa has changed somewhat since the time of Livingstone. A traveller from Zimbabwe might just as reasonably expect to fly to the London of Dickens or the California of Twain. On the other hand, we *had* come looking for deepest, darkest Africa: something pristine and primitive and dangerous.

After breakfast we all shared a cab to the Zimbabwean border, each of us toting black rubber bags holding the possessions he would need for the next week. Here we commmenced the border shuffle, which occupied us for the next couple of hours, and which reminded me of several passages in Livingstone's journals where he describes the mandarin negotiations during his transit from the domain of one tribe to that of the next.

We checked out of Zimbabwe without incident and took the cab onto the bridge, a kilometer-long no man's land spanning the gorge. Zambian women with huge bundles on their heads walked beside the road. A terror-stricken man suddenly appeared through our windshield, running toward us and waving his arms, a huge baboon snapping at his butt. Two Zimbabwean soldiers armed with submachine guns slapped their knees and laughed appreciatively. The baboon suddenly broke off pursuit, sat up and started grooming his chest. Wayne informed us that the AIDS virus was believed to have originated with baboons in northeastern Zambia, which gave us something to think about.

At the Zambian border we were greeted by Mike Grant, a sunny, bearded Californian who was in charge of our expedition. He told us we had to return to Zimbabwe and check back into the country, which didn't seem to make a great deal of sense. A man of action rather than words, Mike was at a loss to explain, saying, "Believe me, this is the way we have to do it." I later concluded that in going down the river we would be alternately in two countries, and unless we were officially in both countries at the same time we would be illegal aliens in one or the other. We piled into a Sobek Land Rover and drove back to Zimbabwe, where there were new sets of forms to fill out. Merry did ours, in deference to my fear and loathing of documents, and of any kind of writing in which you can be punished for lying. She foolishly listed my occupation as "Writer," which is something of a red flag to Third World officialdom.

"What is your purpose in Zimbabwe?" demanded the alarmed clerk.

"He's going to float down the river in a rubber raft," Rick explained.

"And write about it," Wayne added. "He's a famous pornographer. He *loves* rubber."

I was detained for twenty minutes and made to fill out additional forms promising to surrender myself and explain my movements at the time of my departure from Zimbabwe, which was going to be tricky since I wasn't planning to enter Zimbabwe, but to turn around here and go back to Zambia. Mike hovered nervously at a discreet distance. Merry was upset that as my wife she didn't even rate her own visa, and it was with some difficulty that I dissuaded her from complaining to the Comrade Immigration Officer.

"Report to Customs," the comrade demanded after he had made me fill out every dusty form he could fish out of his desk, several of them printed up by Ian Smith's White Rhodesian government for use against potential black subversives. The Customs window was right next to the Immigration window and the Immigration Officer was watching me, but Mike waved us away from the desk.

"Walk out the door and get in the Land Rover quick," he whispered. We made it out the door and across the tarmac without drawing any gunfire. A few minutes later we were back at the Zambian border, where we might have been arms dealers or even yellow journalists for all they cared. The Immigration folks waved in friendly greeting as we drove right through. Zambia seemed to have a kind of Caribbean ambience. "No problem," is the one English phrase that everyone commands. Though God help you if you want to change money, run a business, or get a spare part for your Land Rover.

F our hours later we were on the Zambezi floating towards the first set of rapids, having pushed an ailing Land Rover several kilometers, passed a ragged village of grass huts marking one of the oldest continuously inhabited settlements on the planet and descended a steep, rocky path into the Songwe gorge. Along the way, Mike had briefed us on whitewater technique in general and the Zambezi in particular. On the first point, the rule was to work against your instincts. As you approach a wave, those in front of the raft dive forward onto the front tube, more or less headfirst into the maelstrom. This strategy, called

VICTORIA FALLS, WHOSE SCALE NO CAMERA ANGLE CAN ENCOMPASS. (GARY LEMMER)

"A terror-stricken man suddenly appeared through our windshield, running toward us and waving his arms, a huge baboon snapping at his butt. Two Zimbabwean soldiers armed with submachine guns slapped their knees and laughed appreciatively."

tube-crashing, tends to prevent the boat from flipping over backwards. The corollary of this is high-siding—moving toward the wave. Specific local hazards include crocodiles, hippos, and whirlpools, and here one's natural instincts can be trusted. If you fall out of the boat or if it flips over, you are well-advised to get out of the river as soon as possible. On the other hand, you want to be careful where you step getting out of the water, since both shores of the Zambezi were sown with landmines during the recent war. Here, it seemed, were the Deadly Hazards we'd been warned about.

Wayne, Rick, Merry and I were up in the front of a raft piloted by Jib Ellison, a reticent, naturalized Californian who despite his nickname and his Upper East Side birth certificate, denied having been to prep school in the East. Jib manned the oars. He had us rehearse the basics of high-siding as we drifted slowly through the black water above the rapids. The river was higher than on any previously attempted run, and we had put in below the Tenth rapid, some miles downstream from the Falls, with the plan of returning to the Falls at the end of the week, if possible, to do the first day last.

The three rafts hovered along the edge of an eddy line. Jib waited for the thumbs up from Mike Grant, and then turned us into the current. "See you downstairs," Mike called, as our raft was sucked into what looked like a violently descending escalator. At the brink of our descent, looking down a slick forty-five degree slope that culminated in a violent white backwash, I thought, "This isn't a rapid—it's a fucking waterfall." Jib whooped, Indian warrior fashion. Then we dropped into the hole and Wayne landed on top of my back and Merry screamed, or maybe it was Rick, and then I was underwater for quite a while.

We pounded through three big waves and I thought we had capsized, but there came a moment when I realized we'd made it, and after learning to breathe again we all started whooping in the manner of our guide.

Wayne lifted himself from my back and said, "Was it good for you, Jay?"

"The earth definitely moved for me," said Rick, still on top of Merry.

The last rapid of the day, Number Eighteen, was the wildest, a long train of waves with one central monster that crests and breaks at regular intervals, although whether it breaks on top of you or harmlessly behind is pretty much a matter of luck, according to Jib. We hit it somewhere between. The second boat down, piloted by Mike Grant, lost a rider. Laura, a senior at Andover, was swept out of the stern, but she turned up at the bottom of the chute relatively intact.

Shortly after the sun had disappeared below the western edge of the gorge, we pulled into shore drenched and shivering, and it was only after the fire had been started that I began to notice the campsite. All day we had been floating between sheer walls of black basalt. This broad sloping beach of white sand originated in the Kalahari desert, was wind-swept across the Zambezi watershed, carried downstream in high water and finally precip-itated out here as the river crested and dropped back from flood stage. It may be larger next year or it may disappear after the rainy season. This was the first expedition of the year and the guides were glad to find it intact. They unloaded the boats while we chose campsites and the Zambian support crew, known collectively as the high-siders, set to work on our dinner in the fading light.

Rick and Wayne unveiled their bar, Duty Free vodka and Scotch in plastic containers. I had a flask of single malt. We would be on the river six more days. Suddenly it didn't seem like enough.

"We may have to fall back on the pharmacy," Wayne said. He dug a giant Ziploc bag out of his gear and listed the contents: "erythromycin, tetracycline, Ampicillin, chloroquine,

Demerol, Seconal, Valium, Halcion, assorted muscle relaxers." Rick fished out his own supply. He had additional analgesics, including an exotic new synthetic barbiturate that couldn't be mixed with alcohol, or it would result in bladder explosion. I couldn't match this Texas chemical wealth, although I had one ace: tincture of opium, a specific for dysentery, the very stuff on which Coleridge had composed "Kubla Khan." Rick and Wayne were really impressed. They wanted to try some immediately but I suggested we wait for an occasion.

That night we slept under a sky that was huge despite the brackets of the canyon walls, dense and brilliant with stars. The Southern Cross migrated sideways over the rim of the gorge.

In the morning the sun didn't appear until long after first light and it was much too cold to get out of the sleeping bags. The river was swift, steely gray and uninviting beyond the beach. Plumped, brightly colored sleeping bags were scattered across the sand. Smoke rose from the kitchen—an alcove of basalt where the high-siders huddled around a driftwood fire shivering in their hand-me-down gym shorts and shredded T-shirts. Two mangy and emaciated bush dogs ate the sand on which last night's dishwater had been dumped. Thin strains of Bob Marley's "I Shot the Sheriff," drifted up the hill from the kitchen.

We lost three of our party that morning. This camp was the last point from which it was possible to hike out, with a guide, there being no way out but down the river for the next six days, and a family from Connecticut decided to take the dry road.

Fortunately, after breakfast preparations, eating, washing up, packing, waterproofing and securing of gear into the rafts, it was after ten and the sun, which appeared over Zimbabwe about 9:30, was beginning to thaw us out. Almost immediately we plunged into a long rapid called Morning Shower that opened everyone's eyes. Merry had discovered it was drier in the back of the raft, and our new tube crashing companion was Joseph, one of the high-siders. The youngest Zambian on the trip, he spoke the best English, and clearly enjoyed running the rapids, whereas his two companions seemed to feel it was a weird way to make a living, although better than unemployment and malnutrition.

Most of the Zambians I talked to could not understand why people rich enough to afford luxury hotel rooms and exotic forms of leisure would want to compromise their comfort and even risk their lives in this manner. The simple problem of survival was still real to them, and they were baffled by our nostalgia for it, our need to flirt with danger.

We negotiated seven or eight major rapids over the course of the day without flipping, although Jib didn't think much of our performance. Between the rapids the water seemed almost benign. We loosened our life jackets and lay on the sides of the tube. The walls of the canyon did not seem negotiable to anything without wings, but during the morning we saw several klipspringers—small, whippet-like antelope that rocketed up the basalt cliffs at our approach. Wayne and Rick were not impressed. They scanned the banks for major wildlife. They would be skeptical about this being deepest darkest Africa until they saw a hippo or a croc. Merry and I were already convinced.

Our first days in Zimbabwe had been spent at Chikwenya, a remote bush camp on the lower Zambezi. Despite the abundant wildlife, including a family of cheetahs, we had felt that the injunction against walking to supper without an armed escort was excessively cautious. Then, our last day there, a tanned, bearded young Englishman floated into camp in a canoe. Tim, a doctor with a passion for Zimbabwe, was trying to navigate the entire length of the Zambezi as a means of raising money for a six-year-old girl named Briar Stevens, whose father had run Chikwenya till she was severely mauled by a lion a few feet from the

SCOUTING DEEP THROAT
(CHRISTIAN KALLEN)

supper table. Briar was now a parapalegic, and in the past three years she had outgrown most of her orthopedic equipment. As we left Chikwenya, Tim had told me to expect him on the Sobek whitewater expedition, which would be one leg of his journey. I was sorry he hadn't made it. He had an earnest glow in his eyes when he spoke about Briar Stevens, about how cheerful and bright she was, and I would have been glad to be along for part of his campaign. Tim, his friends told me, kept returning to Africa, while insisting that each trip was his last, that his medical career in England would finally claim all of his attention. But Africa was under his skin, as was Briar Stevens, and I suspect he will keep coming back.

At lunch—tinned-corned-beef sandwiches—I talked to Mike Speaks, the third guide, an Alabaman whose Daddy had told him they were descended from Speke the great English explorer, companion and rival of Burton, and the white man with the best claim on discovering the source of the Nile. The latter day, American Speaks [*sic*] is a man whom it is hard to imagine indoors. He lives half the year here in Zambia, the other half in a log cabin near Mount McKinley. Like many river guides, he runs the other kind of whitewater in the winter—that is, he's a cross-country skier.

"I guess when we're not on the rivers we like to go to where they come from—the snow in the mountains," Mike says. Apparently Mike's idea of a good time is to venture alone out into the wilderness for a few weeks in the dead of winter with a pack on his back and skis on his feet.

The final rapid of the day was called Upper Mowimba Falls. This sounded ominous. "Why don't they just call it Upper Mowimba Rapid?" I asked Jib as we drifted downstream in the failing light.

"You'll see," Jib said. Jib, Orientally laconic, reminded me of a karate teacher I had studied with in Japan.

Although it was nearly dark, and we were all eager to hit the camp below the Falls, we pulled over to scout the rapid, walking downstream to a promontory from which we could check it out.

"Gnarly," said Jib, looking down at the series of cliffs over which the water thunders. Gnarly is an important word in the limited vocabulary of whitewater rafting. It is a word of broad application for the guides—a term of approbation for people, for instance—though it's also with a very apt observation of what a river looks like when it gets compressed and twisted and dropped over rocks. Upper Mowimba Falls was gnarly.

We stayed up on the rocks to watch Mike Speaks take his boat through. Speaks pulled frantically on his oars trying to get the right line through the rapid while his passengers clutched the rope wearing heartbreaking expressions of fear and regret. The boat dropped straight down the first big chute and then stood up almost straight on the first big wave. The raft seesawed this way several times through the rapid, almost disappearing from sight into one gnarly hole, and those of us on shore, with our excellent seats, were secretly hoping for a disaster. Maybe I'm perverse, but I think having overcome the ignorant fear of the first day, we had reached the point in the trip where we wanted confirmation of the sense that this was risky business. We wanted a close-up of a deadly hazard. Seeing *another* boat flip, or get attacked by a croc, for instance. On the first expedition down this stretch of the Zambezi, a trip organized by Sobek in 1982, a big croc had chomped one of the gray rafts, perhaps mistaking it for a dead hippo.

That night we camped on a plateau of flat topped basalt rocks and had spaghetti for dinner. Wayne and Rick shared what was left of their Scotch, and we came close to exhausting my own supply. With dinner we had some very decent South African red wine, billed as a 1979 estate-bottled claret.

"There won't be much more of that," said Brian, a Brit who'd been resident in Zambia for some years, "once these sanctions start flying." In New York and London, the front pages had been full of South Africa, and here, a matter of miles from the border, the subject kept coming up. Wayne and Rick had been on a flight from London with Robert Mugabe, fresh from an unsatisfactory meeting with Thatcher. Merry and I had experienced the anger of a white Zimbabwean couple who felt that the troubles in this part of the world were mostly the fault of American liberals. Something seemed about to explode, on the one hand, and on the other hand, we met vacationing white South Africans who didn't acknowledge that anything had changed, or that anything would change.

The next day brought two major portages. Just below camp we had to haul the three rafts over the basalt to avoid Lower Mowimba Falls, a violent chute of silver water. Like road cuts that lay open the geologic complexity beneath a landscape, these falls and rapids illustrated the power and volume of the river just when you'd started to fall asleep. I shirked porter's duties for a few minutes to assemble my fishing rod and cast it into a likely-looking pool. My spinner was hit hard, and for the next ten minutes I played a tiger fish to a growing audience. As I brought the fish toward shore the three high-siders leaped on it, avoiding the barracuda-style teeth as they hauled on the six-pound test monofilament, wrestling the fish up onto the rocks. After a violent struggle, the fish rolled down the rocks and dropped into the river whence it came.

I spent the day mourning my tiger fish and hauling rubber rafts and cargo over hot, sharp

"Like road cuts that lay open the geologic complexity beneath a landscape, these falls and rapids illustrated the power and volume of the river just when you'd started to fall asleep."

rocks. Rick and Wayne concurred with my feeling that we would rather go over Victoria Falls than do another portage.

That night we camped just above Ghostrider, a long and legendary rapid that had flipped two rafts on the exploratory trip and many since then. On that first trip, Richard Bangs, the expedition leader, having watched his companions flounder, had pushed his own raft into the current and let it float down empty of passengers. The riderless raft made it through, giving the rapid its name. Since then, Mike Grant and others had taken the big swim in Ghostrider. Jib and the two Mikes spent more than an hour examining the rapid, looking for its weak points, while the high-siders cooked dinner and Rick, Wayne, Brian and I had a contest to see who could drink the most Zambian gin.

That night, or morning, I woke up thirsty and stiff, sand in my hair and in my mouth. A rosy glow flickered in the sky. I rolled over just in time to see the crescent moon setting at the far end of the gorge, dropping swiftly like a luminous scythe towards the earth.

All boats and riders made it through Ghostrider, to the secret disappointment of a few of us. Each new rapid was raising my threshold of adrenalin. I wanted to stick my head into the foaming jaws of Deadly Hazard and pull it out at the very last second. The problem is, of course, that the last second, or the last inch, is best defined beyond the verge. Before that, the threshold seems infinitely elastic and unreal. I tried to explain my desire for disaster, which seemed to be the core impulse for this trip, to Merry, who didn't have a shred of patience or sympathy for the idea. Rick and Wayne were on my side. Men tend to be more romantic than women, though clearly the borders of safety were real and determinate enough for our guides, who came up against them frequently.

Deep Throat, which we confronted around noon, seemed like it might be the border between Good Clean Fun and Russian Roulette. All morning the guides had warned us, making it sound like a liquid mine field. They became tense and terse as they watched for the bend preceding the rapid. In our boat the passengers were fairly giddy. "No way I'm going to portage this one," Wayne said.

Rick said, "Don't be a wimp, Jib."

"Go for it."

"We'll see," said Jib.

The rafts were beached in an eddy above the rapid. We climbed the rocks to find a vantage point. The view was impressive, and daunting. The river, which was more than a mile wide upstream, was here compressed into a chute some fifteen or twenty yards across. The water between the basalt cliffs resembled a ski trail in a state of avalanche; further down, whirlpools boiled. The main current threw itself against the far cliff and ricocheted down into a hole. Mike Grant said, "I've never seen it this high. This is bad." With the water so high, the usual portage was flooded. The cliffs here were steep. To portage safely might have taken six or eight hours, and for this reason they decided to run the rapid on a voluntary basis. The sensible folks could hike out to the first eddy.

To chasten the more vocal among us, who were brandishing the concept of *cojones*, Mike told us the story of Gary Lemmer, a guide who had flipped the year before. He had been sucked down with the current to a depth where the water was silent and pitch black, then ascended until sound and light began to return, only to be pulled down again. When he surfaced, a couple of hundred yards downstream, Lemmer was unconscious, bleeding from the ears and nose, and for weeks afterward suffered severe headaches.

Mike pointed out the spot where he'd gone under, the big hole beneath the wall.

"I guess he found it," Wayne said.

"Found what?"

"Deepest, darkest Africa."

Mike Grant went through first with two of the high-siders in the front of the boat and Brian in the back. We watched Mike struggle with his oars as he failed to get the high line he was looking for, and we watched from a cliff fifteen or twenty feet away the expressions of the four as they glanced off of the wall of water and dropped into the big hole; the raft stopped cold so that the high-siders almost went over the front and Brian fell over backwards, just managing to hang on to the guide rope and struggle back into the boat, which hung in the current for seconds before it was picked up and carried off safely.

I made it, too, and I was glad, not relishing the picture of myself bleeding from the ears. That night we consumed the remaining stock of liquor and wine, and Joseph asked Wayne if he and the rest of the high-siders could try some of those nice pills he had in his pack. Joseph, being a hustler, had an inventory of the personal possessions of everyone on the trip, and made a habit of requesting the donation of items that particularly appealed to him, including our sleeping bags, "which would be so heavy to carry home to America." Hilarity reigned into the night. Wayne taught the high-siders how to sing "Kumbaya," which seemed strange but somehow appropriate at the time. The next morning Joseph and his companions were slow in getting breakfast going. He said the muscle relaxers were powerful medicine. "I sleep like a big stone."

The river became increasingly tame and broad from that point on, as if it were tranquilized, too, coming up on the expanse of Lake Kariba, into which it disappeared for many miles, although the crocodile population increased in inverse proportion to the gradient, and one after another of us got sick from all the river water we'd swallowed. I didn't get sick right away. I waited until my last night in Africa to come down with a big fever that wiped out most of the memory of my last days.

The last thing I really remember before the fever kicked in was flipping over and plunging, with a curious feeling of fulfillment, into the Zambezi.

It was with an unusual sense of completing a circular river trip that we arrived, at the end of the last day, at the point where we had started. That morning we had put the rafts in where we had intended to start the trip, in the spray of Victoria Falls—a foaming pool called the Boiling Pot. The water was still extremely high, higher than on any previously attempted descent. As Jib pushed the boat off I saw the skull and horns of a big waterbuck lodged in the rocks just above the pool, the relic of an animal swept live over the falls during the rainy season, an omen or a charm.

The third rapid was not supposed to be a bad one but we entered it slightly askew and hit the first wave at a bad angle. I felt the boat go over backwards and stand perfectly upright before pivoting. For a moment we could have gone either way. I was trying to keep the boat upright but hoping it would go over, and just for that moment I was exactly where I wanted to be in the world, looking down into the whitewater, having discovered at last my destination, imagining that waterbuck with his big horns going over the edge of the falls and drifting slowly, endlessly down the arc of the rainbow into the spray.

MIKE SPEAKS, "A MAN WHOM IT IS HARD TO IMAGINE INDOORS."
(CHRISTIAN KALLEN)

"WE COULD SEE THE HUTS ON PILINGS BEHIND THE PALMS." (BENOIT QUERSIN)

Alex Shoumatoff

NOSY KOMBA

(At the invitation of Sobek, Shoumatoff, his sons Andre and Nicky, aged eight and six, and his frequent travelling companion, the Belgian ethnomusicologist Benoît Quersin, spent two weeks on Madagascar—a place Shoumatoff had been longing to get to. The travel arrangements were deftly handled by Lemur Tours, a Malagasy outfit based in San Francisco. The expedition reached Nosy Komba, a delectable island off the northwest coast of the Grande Île, on January 11th).

Late in the morning we dropped anchor off Nosy Komba and rowed ashore to the largest of the island's villages, Ampangorina, nestled in a sandy cove lined with coco palms. We could see the huts on pilings behind the palms, and under the palms beached outriggers, naked children playing, half a dozen women in colorful sarongs sitting before the shells and pottery they had set out on sheets for us to buy. The villagers, who were sitting on porches sewing, cleaning fish, nursing children, had a lot more Bantu blood than the predominantly Indonesian people we had been meeting on the Grande Île. Some looked up and smiled, some ignored us.

The first order of business was to pay our respects to the lemurs —primitive primates that have been outcompeted by monkeys and are extinct everywhere in the world but on Madagascar. Nosy

Komba has several troops of *koumba,* or black lemur, which are revered by the villagers. The lemurs were waiting for us in a pasture behind the village, which we had to pay an old woman four hundred francs to enter. One of our Comoran crew had brought some bananas, and the females mobbed us as we held them out. The females were golden-furred, fox-faced, with white beards and ear tufts, while the males, who hung back, were black; so "black" lemur is a sexist name, especially inappropriate since the females are dominant. Among lemurs, unlike all other primates, females get to eat first.

I struck up a conversation with a young man in the village who had a sarong wrapped around the lower half of his body, the same as the women wore, but higher up. His name was Robert. He spoke French, having studied with Catholic missionaries on the Grande Île. The schooling on Nosy Komba only goes up through the primary years, and it is in Malagasy. Few speak French. I asked Robert why the lemurs were sacred, and why it was *fady,* or taboo, to eat or kill them or to remove them from the island. *"Avant,"* he said, "we were ruled by a king called Ampanga, who raised lemurs. His tomb is in the forest outside the village. When he died there was nobody to command the lemurs. Half of them went wild. The other half stayed around the village. They are considered sacred because they are the king's animals."

I asked Robert if there was somewhere in the village where we could stay for a few days. He said his aunt Madiu had two extra rooms and the only bar and restaurant in the village, so we went to see her. Madiu was a slender, soft-spoken, very black woman of thirty-nine. One of her upper left teeth was capped with gold—a mark of status, a fashion started by the Indian dentists on Nosy Be, a larger, more cosmopolitan island nearby. Her French was limited. She showed us her extra rooms. They were neat and cozy. The beds were canopied with mosquito netting. "This is great," I said. "How about some lunch?" she asked, and fed us a relative of barracuda called *kiko* cooked in coconut milk with lemon juice and curry. It was superb.

Wondering why there was no man in the house, I asked Madiu why such a good-looking woman and an accomplished cook as she wasn't married. *"Madiu pas bon pour le mariage,"* she said, shaking her finger vehemently. She had already lived with two men, she explained. *"Maintenant le chef c' est moi."* She was making out fine on her own. The restaurant and the rooms were slow, but she had customers for her rum and beer coming to her door at all hours of the day. She hung beer and soft drinks in the shade, in colorful stockings, to cool in the breeze. Her last guests had also been *externes*—two Japanese entomologists who had come the year before to study the mosquitoes on the island. They had eaten with their fingers and claimed to be able to converse with the lemurs. "That's not possible, is it?" she asked.

In the afternoon we went in Robert's outrigger canoe to a small island a few miles away called Nosy Ambariube, which he said meant *L'Île de ne casse pas le bois.* "There is a tree there whose branches it is *fady* to break," he explained. (Madagascar may have more marvelous local taboos than anywhere in the world.) The canoe was narrow, deep, and sharp-prowed, and it moved quickly through the water as we paddled out of the cove. There was an outrigger on one side, which Robert said in heavy seas you always kept downwind, so you wouldn't flip. On the other side a rack, with a harpoon and two masts wrapped in a sail resting on it, extended over the water, counterbalancing the outrigger. The design is probably derived from the Indonesian *praho.* After ten minutes Robert lashed the masts to a crosspiece in front of the canoe and raised the sail—a triangle of patched canvas, and we went with the wind, Robert holding the paddle at the stern as a rudder.

We passed several styrofoam buoys, below which traps baited with bananas, sea-urchin

ROBERT'S OUTRIGGER
CANOE—NARROW, DEEP,
AND SHARP-PROWED. (BENOIT
QUERSIN)

guts, shellfish, and hermit crabs were waiting for lobsters or fish to wander into them. The fishermen went out from seven in the evening until four in the morning, Robert told us; then they took their catch to the market on Nosy Be. They usually came home with a thousand francs—a dollar fifty—and slept for the rest of the day. Robert steered the outrigger into some sea grass flats, then we got out and dragged it up over rocks encrusted with small purple-edged oysters and went to see the tree whose branches it was forbidden to break. It was a legume of some kind, with paired fleshy leaflets and strings of twelve to twenty beaded pods. (I forwarded Quersin's slide of it to Peter Lowrie at the Missouri Botanical Garden, who identified it as *Sophora tomentosa*, a seaside plant common throughout the Indian Ocean). "Ça ne touche pas," Robert warned us. "Ça reste tranquille." I asked him if he knew the origin of the *fady*. "The ancestors of Antinturna, another village on Nosy Komba, are buried on this island," he said. "When there is a death everybody comes over here and gets drunk. *Devient fou.* One time they started to tear apart this tree. Suddenly a strong wind, a cyclone, came up and they couldn't get back to the village for several days. The chief said they were being punished for what they had done to the tree, and from then on, it was *fady* to touch it."

We walked down the beach, and Robert said, indicating some woods with his eyes, "Look quickly in there and you will see the tombs." There were two cement sepulchres in the woods with crosses on them. "Is everybody from Antinturna buried here?" I asked. "No. Only the kings. It is *fady* to visit the tombs except when there has been a death. We can only look at them quickly and from a distance. The people of Antinturna would be angry if they knew we were doing even that."

Several hundred yards off the island there was a group of rocks called the Three Brothers, and just below the surface in the water before them lay acres of coral gardens—some of the most colorful and complex reefs on earth. I had snorkeled in the Caribbean and off Brazil, and Quersin had once supported himself for a winter skin-diving off Corsica, but neither of us were prepared for this reef. *"Quelle panache! Quelle folie! Quelle invention! Quelles couleurs éclatantes!"* Quersin kept sputtering as we cruised around with our masked faces in the water.

We saw corals that looked like brains or cauliflower, others that branched in green, orange, blue, or lavender pastel-colored antlers. I poked the tip of one of my rubber fins at a giant clam wedged in a coral canyon; its sinuous blue jaws contracted in spasms like a climaxing *vagina dentata.*

The boys, meanwhile, were collecting shells in the shallows—gold-ringer cowries, olives, murexes, sundials. Five hundred of Madagascar's mollusc species are unique to the island.

Life in Ampangorina was extremely laid back. There were four hundred and ten people in the village, belonging to three families, each of which traced its descent from a different *dady,* or dead king, and was headed by a different old man, or *papa.* You weren't supposed to sleep with a member of your family, but that was about the only restriction on whom you could sleep with. "The population is very pacific and intelligent," the representative of the *pouvoir révolutionnaire* on the island, a Monsieur Tombo, told Quersin and me when we called on him one morning. On the cane wall behind him was a photograph of Madagascar's president, Didier Ratsiraka, in full regalia. "There is no crime, no jealousy, no marriage," he went on. "I've been here four years and there have only been four marriages in the whole *circonscription.*" The *circonscription* took in the entire island, with nine villages on the coast and four in the interior. "Here there is *union libre.* The couples trust each other."

The day began at around 5:30, with roosters crowing, babies crying, laughter, conversation. The sounds of the village stirring to life were joined by the sounds of other activities, blending into a continuous happy hum that lasted through the morning: women pounding rice in mortars (or "smush bowls," as Andre called them), hanging wash to dry on rocks, making glossy graphite-glazed mugs, turtles, and ashtrays to sell to the tourists, men sharpening axes on stones, a carpenter nailing down the floor of a new hut, children playing prison ball in the schoolyard, or a game with old flashlight batteries that had been painted different colors,

**A MASTER VALIHA PLAYER
DEMONSTRATES HIS SKILL.**
(BENOIT QUERSIN)

a boy sitting in the dirt paddling an imaginary outrigger, a girl kissing a plastic doll. The hum died down in the heat of the afternoon, as the women lay dozing or nursing babies under the palms, then toward evening it picked up again. By 9:30 the village was dead to the world.

The chief usually sat under an ancient spreading mimosa at the far end of the village, with several other old men, whittling model outriggers from rosewood that were accurate to the last detail. I had seen their work for sale at the airport on Nosy Be. Quersin bought one "for political reasons." One of the old men, the chief told us, was a master *valiha* player. The *valiha* is a sitar-like instrument of Indonesian origin, with metal strings stretched around a bamboo cylinder, and the national instrument.

Quersin prevailed on the old man to play, but he protested through Robert that "my joints are swollen. My fingers won't move any more. I'm retired." So Quersin placed headphones on the old man's ears and switched on his tape recorder—the latest portable, professional-quality Sony, a WA-8000 autoreverse that fit into his sidebag and even had a nine-band shortwave. Quersin kept on the cutting edge of audio-visual technology. He had started as an ethnomusicologist lugging a forty-pound Uhr into the field. The old man listened—it was the blind rummie *valiha* player, whom Quersin had recorded the day before, playing at the entrance to the lemur pasture—and perhaps taking it as a challenge, wanting to show how the instrument is really played, or realizing that this might be his only chance to lay down his music for posterity, he excused himself and went for his *valiha*.

When he returned, a chair had been brought for him, Quersin had hung his external stereo microphone from a stick in front of it, and several dozen of the villagers were sitting at a respectful distance. Quersin asked him to sit down and play a few notes while he listened through the headphones and adjusted the mike for wind interference. Then he nodded, and the old man began to pluck octaves in a marching rhythm with his thumbs, while his long, graceful fingers picked cross rhythms and interlacing riffs in sixths. After a few minutes he broke into a falsetto wail. It was like the music of spheres, harmonically rich and subtle. Time seemed to be suspended during the hour or so he went on. But the audience was more fascinated by Quersin, who was filming the recital with his Sony 8 video-cassette camera and shooting stills with his Pentax. At one point an outrigger sailed into the cove and nosed up on the curved white beach. The water was like turquoise glass. In the foreground a group of young women stood against a new rosewood outrigger that three of the men had just taken a month to build. It was a work of art. The young women were lush and innocent. The whole scene was like a Gauguin.

Robert took me twice to see his grandfather, Besimoa, who was "over a hundred years old," Robert claimed, and was the interpreter of *la loi des rois*, the traditional laws of the village. The meetings took place in the evening, in Besimoa's tin-roofed hut. *La loi des rois* wasn't something one talked about *en plein air, devant le peuple*, Robert explained. The second time, the chief was present. The four of us sat on small stools, his grandmother lighted a kerosene lamp and brought us bowls of warm banana gruel, Besimoa tapped some snuff from a medicine canister onto the back of his hand and inhaled it, and the interview began. I started by asking the same questions I had asked the time before, rephrasing them slightly, and Besimoa gave me slightly different answers, with new details, but still not the full answers. One of the answers contradicted something that Robert had told me. Robert said sheepishly, "*C'est ça la différence des réponses.*" The problem, I realize now, was that I had stumbled on a very complicated belief system, and didn't know the right questions to ask, and also that Robert was editing Besimoa heavily. Lengthy, eloquent paragraphs were being reduced to a few sentences.

"The chief usually sat under an ancient spreading mimosa at the far end of the village, with several other old men, whittling model outriggers from rosewood that were accurate to the last detail."

THE BEACH AT NOSY KOMBA
—A SANDY COVE LINED WITH
COCO PALMS (BENOIT
QUERSIN)

The people of Ampangorina, like most of the inhabitants of the west coast of Madagascar, belong to an ethnic group called the Sakalava. (Much of what follows has been gleaned from conversations with the anthropologist Gillian Feeley-Harnik, who studies the Sakalava, and from an article by the anthropologist Jacques Lombard entitled "Le Temps et l'escape dans l'idéologie politique de la royauté Sakalava-menabe," an exercise in Levi-Straussian structuralism that was over my head, and undoubtedly over the Sakalava's heads as well.) Originally the Sakalava were from the South. Robert understood Sakalava to mean "*qui est parti de loin*," which wasn't true; it means "people of the long valleys." At the end of the seventeenth century the Sakalava expanded all the way up the western coast to the northern tip of the island, subjugating the local people, the Vazimba, and even making raids in boats along the eastern coast of Africa, where they picked up a lot of African blood and practices, including *tromba*, spirit possession, and the cult of the dead kings, the *dady*. One of the important Sakalava dynasties, the Maroserana, may not even be biologically Sakalava, but an offshoot of the emperors of Zimbabwe. Ancestor worship among the Sakalava is almost mystical in its pervasiveness and complexity. Besides the *dady*, they recognize three other categories of ancestors: the *tsiny*, who are human ancestors in general; the *raza*, a hierarchical group organized by the *dady*; and the *koko*, the seventy-seven errant spirits of the forest, who are the souls of the Vazimba, the original occupants of the areas the Sakalava moved into. Some of these, according to Lombard, inhabit actual, historical space, others "ideological space." The most important ancestors are the *dady*. The Sakalava believe that their lives are still governed by them, by all their previous monarchs who ever lived—and particularly by their local monarch (living or dead) and his recent ancestors. They have an expression "*ampanjaka tsy ampody avelo*", which means "the king never dies."

There is still a king of Nosy Be; he operates the telephone switchboard at the police station in Hellville. The last king of Ampangorina was Ampanga, the man who raised lemurs. Robert said that Ampangorina means "do not forget the king." Ampanga died around 1850, and his son moved to the Grand Île. Although there is no longer a king on Nosy Komba, a Fête de Tous les Rois is celebrated for three days in July, with "clapping, dancing and drums," Besimoa told me, and up until about forty years ago the celebrants used to make tails and walk like the lemurs, the king's animals. There is still a "queen," a descendant of Ampanga, who comes each year from the Grand Île for the festival. *La loi des rois* is taught to the young through songs. It consists of ten *fady*. We went over them twice, to make sure I had them all.

1. do not kill, eat, or remove the lemurs
2. do not visit the tombs except in the event of a death
3. do not eat pork
4. no dogs in the village
5. no guinea fowl
6. do not sleep with your brother, sister, or cousin
7. do not bathe in the ocean at night
8. women cannot work in the rice fields on Thursday
9. do not whistle in the village at night
10. do not carry fire or a lantern through the village at night.

On the whole, they seemed a pretty reasonable set of commandments. I could understand the one against bathing in the ocean at night—a shark might get you—but what about the one against whistling in the village at night, I asked Besimoa. How had that come about? A long time ago, he explained, a sickness was going around, and the *homme imagineur*, the priest who advised the king on spiritual matters, figured out that it had been caused by a nocturnal whistler.

"When are you coming back?" Robert asked as we slid the new dugout into the water and hopped aboard; the chief had said we could take the new dugout to Nosy Be; it had never been in the water. "I don't know," I said. "Next year, I hope." "Will you bring me some paper, and an English-French dictionary, and a dialogue book?" Such hunger for the written word! I thought. In my world the written word was dying. There was a glut of printed matter. The average reader's attitude was "damn—another page."

With the money we had paid him for his services, Robert was going back to the missionaries on the Grande Île for a few months; one of them was an American who had said he would teach Robert English. His sister Tsuakumbu was also coming along to visit their mother, who lived on another island. Tsuakumbu was sixteen and already a buxom woman. She was a *tsekimawangi*, a *petite soeur*, as girls from fifteen to twenty-five are known in the village. So there were six of us in the outrigger.

An old woman I had made friends with the day before waved from shore as we pulled out of the cove. She had been making pottery. I had asked if I could take her picture. What will you give me, she had asked. A kiss. "*Ça ne m'intéresse pas*," she had said. "*Je suis vieille.*" As we passed the rocky point a huge sea turtle, probably a green turtle, came up for air, then went down again, and a series of widening rings spread out over the glassy water from where it had disappeared. Then we were in the open sea. Robert raised the sail, and we tacked toward Nosy Be.

The boat hadn't been caulked, and it was leaking pretty badly, so Tsuakumbu climbed over me and began to bail water with a halved gourd from the space between me and Quersin, who was paddling at the bow. As she scooped up the water quickly and flicked it over the side, squatting with her head down in front of me with one hand on my knee, she began to sing a soft, beautiful tune, with a subtle flat Quersin could hear but I couldn't. The chorus went "*andenossa tariadiamu.*" For a moment she looked up. Our eyes met and she gave me a radiant smile.

"What's she singing?" I asked Robert. "We must have the sail cords tight, so we can move fast." And we all began to sing.

A LEMUR—EXTINCT EVERY-
WHERE IN THE WORLD EX-
CEPT ON MADAGASCAR
(BENOIT QUERSIN)

"IT IS AT ETOSHA PAN THAT I FINALLY COMPREHEND WHY THE ROMANS WERE SO FLABBERGASTED BY AFRICAN ANIMALS."
(M. STILES)

Barry Lopez

▼

THE RESPLENDENT ORYX

It would be a hard trip. The plan was to drive west from Johannesburg across the foot of the Kalahari Desert, and then out onto the stone plains of the Namib, a desert where one might hear the voice of God as easily as in the Negev. From there back east and farther to the north, to Etosha Pan, a bare shield of blistering light, ringed by grasslands and bushveld, where, if fortune blessed us, we might find one or two black rhino. From there farther east into a nether region along the Angolan border called the Caprivi Strip, occupied by South African troops. From there south into Botswana, the spectacular game parks that harbor the Okavango Delta and the country south of the Chobe River, which teem with elephant and zebra, with giraffe and wildebeest, with impala, waterbuck, and half a dozen other antelope; and through which, like veins of

"I lay alone in my room on the seventh floor of the Park Lane Hotel in the Hillbrow district of Johannesburg with Roberts' Birds of Southern Africa *spine up on my chest and my eyes closed in a daydream."*

silver in a granite boulder, move lion and leopard, wild dog, hyena, and cheetah, the killing business of life.

I lay alone in my room on the seventh floor of the Park Lane Hotel in the Hillbrow district of Johannesburg with *Roberts' Birds of Southern Africa* spine up on my chest and my eyes closed in a daydream. Would we see the firecrowned bishop, the lilacbreasted roller, the steelblue widowfinch? Would we be dazzled speechless by the unearthly blue shoulders of the malachite kingfisher; see marabou storks, heads bowed in ministerial gravity before the hyena-cracked bones of a fallen kudu? Of the melodious lark's threescore songs, would we hear one? Would we see the saurian ostrich plunging across the desert like a beast from the Mesozoic, gunshot bursts of dust rising at its stride, quiet hazel eyes searching the country ahead for a way out?

We would see all this. I would see birds I'd never heard of—apalises, eremomelas—and birds whose names I stumbled over—cisticola (sis-TIK-ohla), hoopoe (WHO-pooh). Some of what lay ahead I could not at that moment have imagined. Six of us and a guide were to spend nearly four weeks on the road, five thousand miles in a Land Rover, all that country and its myriad denizens from elephant grass to puff adder before us. The journey would be exhilarating. I would feel come-to-life in the presence of wild animals, uplifted by the days with them in their own country. What would make the trip hard, I thought, opening my eyes and staring into the sheet of glare from the white stucco wall of the balcony, was the memory of Johannesburg.

I rose to shower. An American newspaper correspondent had offered to take me for a drive through the wealthy northern suburbs of the city and possibly into Alexandra, a black township adjacent to Johannesburg, if we could get past the military barricades. I had no illusion that, in the few days I had set aside for this, I would stumble on some insight into the South African rationale for apartheid; nor did I expect to emerge from my interviews and experiences with a clear grasp of the trouble that seethes here, a fundamental racism, a terrible violence against human beings skimmed daily, like business news, in the local papers, both black and white. I merely wanted to see, to know briefly the strangeness of it, like a man at the gates of a zoo. I wanted never again to see a wild landscape without this knowledge at my core.

I walked miles in Johannesburg. It is a city of banal architecture and storefront businesses, wary and ham-fisted. Nadine Gordimer, who lives here, has called it "foreboding and fascinating." With even the slightest reading background—Joseph Lelyveld's *Move Your Shadow,* William Finnegan's *Crossing the Line,* Gordimer's short stories, the writings of Steve Biko and Breyten Breytenbach, J.M. Coetzee's *Waiting for the Barbarians* (a book that reverberates wildly here)—with but a simple grasp of the oppression, the wretchedness of black life in this oddly retrograde nation, one is astonished by the look of oblivion in white faces in the streets. Lelyveld, who lived in Johannesburg in the mid-sixties and early eighties, writes of the "willful obtuseness" of the white populace, that so many appear "deliberately numb to obvious moral issues."

The correspondent I contacted took me first into the northern suburbs—Houghton, Parkwood, Sandton—and then to Alexandra. The patrician homes and the fastidiously manicured grounds of the northern suburbs remind Americans most often of southern California, of Bel Air or Westwood. Alexandra is a warren of garbage-bag yurts and ramshackle sheds, a squalid settlement in which even the rudest amenities—running water, electricity, bald-tire cars—are barely in evidence.

I took my correspondent friend to lunch. He volunteers, from a position that seems calm

and detached rather than inured, that what amazes him most in South Africa is the resilience of blacks who are repeatedly jailed and tortured. When I ask, with some apprehension, how conscientious the Bureau of Information is in controlling what writers report, he says, of course, to have nothing to do with them and that their vigilance is not constant, leaving a certain gray area, in which he endeavors to work. It is this capriciousness in law enforcement, he says, that keeps everyone off balance here. Just so had the young soldiers at the entrance to Alexandra allowed us to pass without acknowledgment, no word of admonition or greeting. When I ask my companion if he thinks that at any time soon blacks will be able to vote, to travel freely in the country, he says, with a slight note of forbearance, "This is not civil rights. This is revolution."

The following day, with another acquaintance, I drive out to a farming town called Delmas, some forty miles east of Johannesburg. Arguably one of the most important political trials in South Africa has been going on here for over a year, though a Wall Street Journal reporter found that local people were largely unaware of it. Nineteen middle-aged black men are on trial for murder, treason, and related charges—in short, the prosecution argues, for attempting the violent overthrow of the government of South Africa.

On the face of it, the state's charges seem grandly paranoid; in the view of the foreign correspondents I spoke with, the merits of the case are specious. The men on trial were present at a violent township protest triggered by the implementation of a new system of repressive taxation. A board of black town councilors, elected with virtually no popular support and allegedly controlled by Pretoria, imposed the taxes. Five of the councilors were killed in a riot widely believed to have been provoked and encouraged by the South African police.

The courtroom benches can accommodate about a hundred spectators. There are about eighty here, all black, mostly elderly. My acquaintance and I are the only whites. (Delmas was chosen as a venue partly because it would be easier to secure against demonstrations than a Johannesburg courtroom. It is also so far off in the countryside as to be inconvenient to reporters and beyond the travel means of most blacks. The Lutheran Council of Churches buses parents and relatives of the defendants here every day, a seven-hour round trip.)

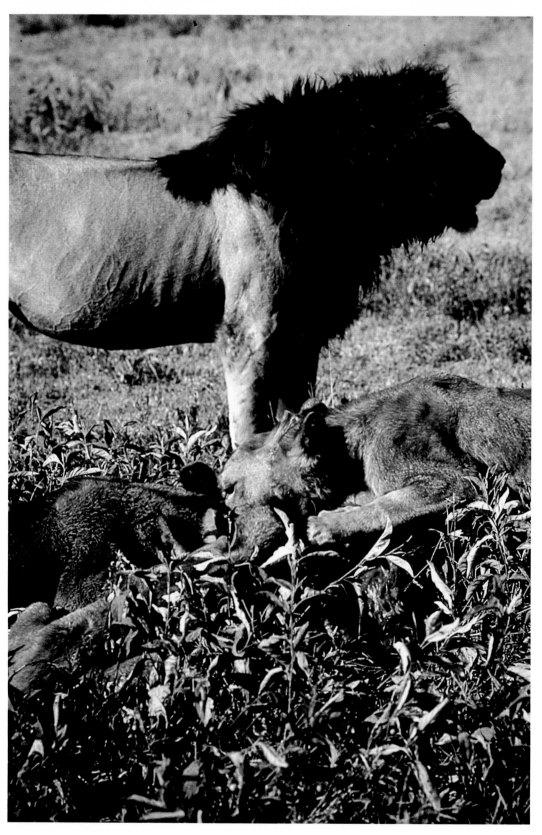

I am hardly seated before I am fixed by the rigid and accusatory finger of a South African policeman, sitting before the bench. He rises from his chair and with a snap of his wrist motions for me to leave the room. In the outer hallway he says I am not permitted in the courtroom without a coat and tie. It is obvious to him that I am a visitor, come out from the city, and that I have no coat and tie. It is clear he regards my presence as a show of support for the defendants and he seems pleased that I am foiled. He departs with a summary nod and a self-satisfied smirk.

There are four or five people in the hallway, among them a black man sitting with his wife in front of another courtroom. I ask if he will be here for a while and he says yes. Can I possibly borrow his coat and tie for a few hours? Yes, certainly. The policemen on duty at the doors I have just come through gawk at each other in disbelief like callow adolescents. I nod sharply to them as I pass, to let them know all is now in order. The officer who asked me to leave offers me a blank stare that hardly disguises his disgust.

To an outsider the proceedings seem arch and sinister. The entire process of adjudication is in the hands of whites; the defendants are all black. The presiding judge, his pale hands moving with foppish annoyance among his documents, glowers balefully, as though he senses insurrection. There is something unmistakably menacing here, but it is derived more from strains of patriotism in the room, the undercurrent of state paranoia, than from any threat of revolution. The defendants sit together quietly, seemingly at ease in the room, smiling occasionally. One of them is testifying in Sotho, through a translator. A ceiling fan turns weakly above the bench. The trial, I am told, is likely to go on another year.

The day before we leave for the desert I go downtown to Khotso House, on De Villiers Street. Six or eight human-rights and resistance groups that help blacks deal with the problems of living in South Africa are housed here, including the South African Council of Churches, the Congress of South African Trade Unions, and the Detainees' Parents Support Committee. My conversations with these people merely confirm the plight, the abject dismal existence of the majority of men, women and children in South Africa. I carry the bewildering reality of this away with me, wondering why I had to confirm it. It is because, like a thousand other visitors to South Africa, I cannot fathom the reality.

On the way back to the hotel, I pass through Joubert Park and stop to watch a chess game. The pieces are half the size of the players; the board, perhaps twenty feet square, is laid out on the pavement. Observers lounge on benches to three sides. The players are two or three moves into the game and one is contemplating his next move. In the distance I can see a tide of blacks streaming toward the railway station and surging around a phalanx of buses that will remove them like a blight from Johannesburg before dusk. Here a black man—one who apparently has permission to stay the night—mulls his strategy. He finally makes his move, king's bishop to queen's bishop four. Immediately he loses the piece to queen's knight on the other side. The opposing player, a straining irony, is white. I watch the black's next move. It is clear he is going to be soundly thrashed.

I sat in my hotel room that night, reading a long technical paper on black rhino, and remembered something that Joseph Lelyveld had written in *Move Your Shadow*. He stated that people opposed to apartheid in South Africa are compromised by "the comforts and golden climate" of the country. The door to the balcony was open. I could see a thunderstorm moving across the horizon to the north, eastward toward the high veld. It is, I reflected, a sublime landscape. You could become lost in its beauty.

It is late afternoon. The Angelus light of dusk shimmers on the hills of Kalahari Gemsbok National Park, between Namibia and Botswana. We are two days out of Johannesburg, sitting in the Land Rover in the middle of a shallow, arid basin, watching springbok graze. They are alert but not alarmed. Under these circumstances I can begin to dismantle the image of springbok in my mind, to penetrate the surface of the name. Springbok, diminutive antelope, stand about thirty inches at the shoulder. (The name comes from their habit of bolting in a series of prodigious five-foot vertical leaps when they are threatened). The upper part of its body is a bright cinnamon brown, its underbelly and slender legs a nearly pure

THE RESPLENDENT ORYX
(M. STILES)

white, the two colors separated by a dark reddish-brown band along the flanks. The horns are lyre-shaped.

With binoculars and this opportunity to sit quietly with them, I begin to see that the shading is not uniform: the band on the flanks is browner in the females, redder in the males; and it seems to pale in older animals. The younger animals are distinguished by a greater angularity in the line of each horn. The horns of the females are more slender, less massive toward the base. I try to commit these details to memory. I put the binoculars aside and try to distinguish these nuances at a distance with my naked eye. The attempt to do so is an exercise, the desire to do so part of the wish to make a respectful entry into new country.

On the way back to camp we see small herds of blue wildebeest and an animal I feel inexplicably drawn to, a type of oryx called a gemsbok, a large fawn-colored desert antelope. Something I had not pictured to myself, and which would emerge clearly in the days ahead, is the exquisitely complex symmetry of an antelope's head. Look into the face of springbok, male impala, tsessebe, red hartebeest, kudu, roan and sable antelope and you see an often subtle chiaroscuro, a pattern of shade and light that carries upward into the graceful curvature of the horns. Do young mathematicians, I muse, still find their dissertations in the development of such symmetries?

Several days later we are in the Namib Desert, in western Namibia. I have known about this desert since childhood, but there is no way to adequately prepare for such a place. The aplomb that may come with a reading knowledge of it, from a book of photographs, or a documentary film, the feeling that one has a reasonable grasp, is simply undermined. The land is too immense, too intricate always, too resistant to the imposition of boundaries to be glossed, a characteristic so salient in some landscapes as to be both amusing and intimidating.

The sense that the Namib was suddenly before us came at the western edge of a dry, scrubland plateau called the Namaland. We rose out of a bleak basin, drowsy with the afternoon heat, to find mountain ranges anchored like a convoy of warships on an improbable stone plain. The proportions of the land changed so abruptly the gray mountains seemed not only twice as high but twice as far away as was plausible. The earth gleamed with metallic light, bare-boned, utterly silent. In a gap between two ranges I saw a horizon so far off I felt giddy.

We drove across the black stone desert, a landscape like foundry slag sheathed in bronze light. No color, no blade of grass softened it. And then at the foot of a stone hill we found gemsbok. Eight of them, including one but a few months old. They riveted us with stares. Where were they bound? And from where on this iron plain had they come? Their robust health seemed incongruous, the wordless stance eloquent.

We camped that evening beneath a large camel thorn tree at a place called Sesriem ("six oxen"), where there was water. The next morning we were up long before sunrise. Our plan was to drive to a place called Sossusvlei, far out in the Namib, a vlei, or oasis, where grasses and trees grow in a valley beneath dunes that tower more than a thousand feet, the highest sand dunes in the world. Occasionally huge flocks of flamingos gather here.

We break an axle in the Land Rover on the way out, so have some hours to walk. Where the stone plains give way to the dunes I find the footprints of gemsbok and at one point a few dark hairs from a gemsbok's tail. I lift the shells of lizard eggs from the sand. They are so delicate they shatter, no matter the gentleness of my hands.

O ne hundred miles northeast of Swakopmund, a town on the Namibian coast where we have the axle repaired, lies an isolated range of mountains called the Brandberg. In the Tsisab Valley here in 1918 a German surveyor named Reinhard Maack found a mural that had been painted, it is generally assumed, several hundred years before by Bushmen. The most famous feature of this rock drawing is the dominating figure of a person called the White Lady. She has a white torso and white legs and is carrying a bow and arrow in her left hand. The mural is painted on a half hemisphere of granite, and the woman, in the middle at the bottom, is surrounded by zebra, a few eland, antelope with human legs behind, and two sorts of people, the diminutive Bushmen and the taller Himba people with long, mud-caked hair and clay-smeared bodies.

There are many stories about the mural, its meaning and origin, but I am satisfied to feel its vitality and imagination, to let it provoke rather than verify anything I think. It occurs to me, sitting before it, that I know virtually nothing of the human history of the landscapes we have been travelling through, save, vaguely, that Bushmen (or San people, as they are more respectfully called now) were once here and that the historical tribes include Damara, Ovambo, and Herero people. This strikes me as odd, my lack of knowledge, until I reflect that much of the country we have been moving through still belongs to the animals.

My companions hike the mile or so back to camp on the south side of the dry Tsisab riverbed. I have discovered leopard tracks at a small water hole and follow them with difficulty across to the north side. I finally lose the spoor but not the feeling of a faint electric current in the air, perhaps days old, that tells of the leopard's passage. On the way back to camp I find the exoskeleton of an enormous ground beetle, nearly three inches long, and the footprints of a small antelope called a klipspringer and of large rodents called rock dassies. Hyena and red-rock rabbit scats. I am delighted with these scraps of intelligence, an occasional bird song, the development of a sense of intimacy here. At one point I find thousands of stone flakes exposed on an eroded hillside. I examine a dozen or so carefully,

"We rose out of a bleak basin, drowsy with the afternoon heat, to find mountain ranges anchored like a convoy of warships on an improbable stone plain."

looking for telltale marks, until I am satisfied this is the work of human beings. Unbelievably, I have stumbled into what archaeologists call a lithic site, a place where people once made stone tools and weapons.

I course the dry riverbed on the way back to camp, studying it closely. I bend down for the bone of a creature I can't identify—a small mammal. I squat there in the last light, feeling a pervasive satisfaction. This detritus is evidence of the passage of creatures—a hyena's chalky scat, knapped stone, the faint spoor of the leopard.

In the mural, the zebra, the Himba, and the others are striding over the land, in the timeless time.

It is at Etosha Pan that I finally comprehend why the Romans were so flabbergasted by African animals; we have our first long look at giraffe and elephant, and the black rhino. To eyes that know only the animals of the northern hemisphere these creatures seem, indeed, outlandish, behemoths with articulating noses, cartoon necks, the last with a face like a triceratops. And the zebra looks as though someone had given Przewalski's horse to a child to decorate. These thoughts, I know, are rude; but human history is full of such ridicule for all that seems different, beyond the refuge of the familiar. It is a frame of mind, I think, that dominates when what is different ceases to be astonishing and becomes banal, or opaque.

On the far-stretched savannas at Etosha one or two animals found grazing in the distance become, as you draw closer, a dozen animals; the dozen become hundreds, and so on, until you realize you have drawn up on the shores of a sea of them, that there is no "other side." You are on the verge of something different from the human; and the twentieth-century mind knows that what is here is all that is left. It is these animals, here, that must be queried if we are to fathom the divisions of life: springhare, kori bustard, duiker, bat-eared fox, wildebeest, cheetah.

A lioness rests under a small acacia tree with the gutted and half-eaten carcass of a springbok. Her belly is round with the meal, and head erect, she is dozing on haunches and chest, her right front paw cupped before her sedately. We are but twenty feet away in the Land Rover; with my binoculars it is as if I were standing beside her. Her yellow eyes have the mottled texture of gooseberries. A fly rises from her paw, lands on the muzzle of the springbok. A red-billed francolin feather rests against the left foreleg of the springbok. A zebra white butterfly flutters past. Within a half mile, herds of zebra, springbok, and wildebeest graze. I have been looking at the lioness for about fifteen minutes before it dawns on me that the closest animal to her, about two hundred yards away, is another springbok, which has been facing her, staring at her all this time, motionless. We drive on.

It had taken some considerable bureaucratic wrangling with the Namibian police to get permission to travel farther to the east, to enter and pass through a militarized zone along the Angolan border. (Namibia is illegally controlled and administered by the Republic of South Africa. South African troops skirmish regularly with members of an independence movement, the South-West Africa People's Organization, and regularly invade Marxist Angola on the pretext of attacking alleged SWAPO training bases there.)

We wish to travel east along the Okavango River, which forms the border with Angola, then, where it turns south, we want to carry on through a virtually uninhabited area called the Caprivi Strip until we reach the Kwando River, at which point we will be south of Zambia and no longer of concern to the authorities. From there we can enter Botswana and the game parks east of the Okavango Delta, which are our destination.

We do finally obtain the necessary papers and clear the roadblocks and checkpoints along the way with little difficulty. It is a somewhat surreal part of the journey. The native settlements we pass do not seem so much impoverished but rather human enterprises at the periphery of a terrific storm. More than a few people I see have eye infections or show signs of kwashiorkor, a protein deficiency. The feeling that emanates from those who turn to stare at us is of an enfeebled and besieged people, bewildered by the military vehicles that roar up and down the road, and by people like ourselves, travellers drifting through these corridors like Cleopatra on the Nile. The children laugh and clap and spin wildly in the dust. The adolescents stare with sheepish grins. The older people look on with blank faces or glance up with exasperation and disapproval from whatever business they have at hand. Some do not even look up as we lumber through.

You can feel the calculation, the strategies for survival being weighed. The breadth of my ignorance, which leaves only these feelings to imagine and decipher, makes me shiver. It is from settlements like these that black men depart with dreams of wealth, to work in the gold mines of South Africa. I feel as if I am looking backward from another century, but I know it is like this almost everywhere in the world, a sad, heroic, and strange indenture.

The days in Botswana's Chobe National Park are the most idyllic of the journey. We camp for three nights at the edge of Savuti Channel, a stream bed that in wet years carries water from the Linyanti swamps in the north southward into Savuti Marsh. Water has not flowed in the channel for six years. It is thick with grasses, through which hyena approach our camp each night. The first evening they make off with several shoes before we are the wiser. They are not amusing, like the easily frightened vervet monkeys who have visited our camps. They are not belligerent and scoffing like baboons. They are eerie—formidable, curious, big-shouldered beasts waiting in silence at the edge of the fire's light. When we retire to our tents they enter camp. They are looking for food, but the young ones may snatch anything; people who've gone to sleep negligent, with their tent flaps open, have been badly bitten on the foot or head. The sound of hyena laughter in the darkness is terrorizing. They are one of the few animals in all the domains humans have occupied to have struck back, lightly, like this.

Out on Savuti Marsh are shoals of animals: impala, blue wildebeest, Burchell's zebra, elephant, giraffe, cape hunting dog, lion, water buffalo. Early each morning and each evening we drive out among them. To view them from the roof of the Land-Rover, to have that completely unimpeded vision, and to drift slowly across the roadless marsh and through the fringing woodlands from clearing to clearing, water hole to water hole, to do this during the most benign and lucent hours of the day, is to feel an intense sense of pleasure, of appreciation and privilege.

Roberts' Birds of Southern Africa lists nearly nine hundred species. In the first two weeks of the trip I have seen seventy or eighty of them, all new to me. Here on the marsh were great flocks of Abdim's stork and cattle egrets, and five kinds of eagles: tawny, martial, bateleur, brown snake, African hawk. At an impala carcass I watched that many species of vulture at work: whitebacked, hooded, whiteheaded, cape, and several huge (eight-foot wingspans) lappetfaced vultures. These marvelous variations on the straightforward theme of large raptor and vulture were unanticipated.

The most startling moments at Savuti Channel for me were those in which I glimpsed lions. I had never really understood lions. They were not an animal I was drawn to or for which I felt any special admiration. This all changed one morning in the space of less than ten minutes. We encountered two males in open country north of the marsh just after sunrise. They had the bearing of animals early at a rendezvous. They walked short distances slowly and sat, or stood staring at the horizon. Their manes were full; they were limber, lean-muscled, fully mature animals. At one point the one with a darker mane stood up and walked deliberately toward a herd of impala. In that stillness we heard the impala snort, the evacuation of their bowels. He had their undivided attention.

But he was not interested in impala. The air of both cats was insouciant, becalmed. It was so quiet we could hear one of them breathing. With my binoculars I stared at the scars on their faces and forelegs, at the pattern of color along the rim of the ear, at the sheave and cord of muscle in haunch and shoulder. I began to sketch their heads in my notebook, the bold thrust of the chin, the outsize muzzle.

In the days that followed we met these same two lions again and, in separate groups, the others in this Beach Boys pride (named for white beaches along Savuti Channel): another mature male, as imposing as these two; six females, one nursing a month-old cub; and two sets of cubs, three of them about sixteen months old and three about eight months old. We saw a pair of adults mate; we watched the cubs wrestle, chase, ambush, and bash one another. By meeting them under different circumstances at different times over four days, we came to some appreciation of the complex social dimensions of their lives. Staying in one place for a while permitted this. Each morning or evening when we found them, or some trace of them, I understood more clearly the way they fit into this country, into this particular landscape. I felt the first glimmer of an understanding of the African bush.

We moved from Savuti south to an area called Moremi Wildlife Reserve, on the eastern edge of the vast Okavango Delta, an unusual, inland delta that carries the Okavango River out onto the northern edge of the Kalahari Desert, where it disappears.

We set up our camp on the south bank of the Kwaai River. It is dusk and sprinkling rain lightly when we arrive. After making some tea I sit down in the makeshift shelter of a tarp and finish the day's notes. A stunningly beautiful woodland kingfisher perches on a limb of the huge sycamore fig tree at the foot of which we have set up our kitchen. Bats begin to flit about. Vervet monkeys arrive and sit shyly at the periphery of our activities. Burchell's starlings and crested barbets and a single redbilled woodhoopoe cleared from the trees as we arrived; now I hear the voices of two owls, scops and pearlspotted, both quite small.

In a notebook in my lap, in the last light, I can see a set of outlines I have drawn that day to suggest the same four-square pattern in the face of hippo, elephant, and warthog. The last thing I see clearly is a small bird on the railing of the single-lane, wooden bridge over the river, hawking the air for insects. Then, suddenly, fireflies are winking, tens of thousands of them, over the reeds.

From a native settlement on the other side of the river come the sounds of children fretting dogs, the timbre of human voices but no clear word, the sharp, desultory tympani of human life. (In the morning I will move about in the dimness making breakfast, stoking the fire, thinking again these are the voices I hear. Ian, the young guide, will smile wryly and incline his head, indicating I should listen more closely. It is, in fact, the muttering of large birds called ground hornbills, scouring the grass for insects.)

We are a long way out. It has taken seven hours to make the eighty or so miles here, in four-wheel drive over a one-lane, two-track road. Another week lies ahead of us, in the Okavango Delta itself and in the Kalahari before we return to Johannesburg. Sitting here in the darkness—the bellowing of hippos, now, comes downriver—and feeling the slight weight of my notebooks in my lap, I am acutely aware of the sense we wish to derive from the meager bits of information about life that are our lot.

I recall a line from a poem I read before leaving for Africa: "We are filled with affection

"Sitting here in the darkness— the bellowing of hippos, now, comes downriver— and feeling the slight weight of my notebooks in my lap, I am acutely aware of the sense we wish to derive from the meager bits of information about life that are our lot."

for things dying." I reflect that the wild animals are really only safe anymore within these refuges, Moremi and Chobe and Etosha. Even there the pressure of poachers can be murderous—and has been for rhino and large elephant. We are to assume, I suppose, that all things will go better if the animals remain here, do not wander. I am saddened by this endless compression of life in the modern world, the steady elimination of possibilities, the sequestering of things for their own good, to protect them from the wrath and desire of others, to hold them away from exploitation, to protect the economies they might threaten.

The owls no longer call. The fireflies continue to wink. I hear a splash and a brief thrashing and turn after a moment to see Ian shift his eyes, extend his chin in the firelight toward me, to acknowledge the mystery. Perhaps a Pel's fishing owl, throttling a young crocodile.

In papers I left in a suitcase back in Johannesburg is an interview with a young South African writer named Njabulo Ndebele. In the words of one reviewer, Ndebele explores in his fiction "the destructive nature of the obsession with injustice," and he himself speaks of the need for a literature "that will outlast the anger."

At this remove from Johannesburg I have the memory of my own sadness and anger, walking the streets of that town; but I am suffused at this moment with the tension and sound of crepuscular life along the edge of the Kwaai River in northern Botswana. I think I know, I am that arrogant to think I know, what Ndebele means by outlasting anger. It is an anger I feel toward anything that stifles other life, that stifles personality.

I rise from the roots of the sycamore fig and stare out over the water. Once, only a few days ago, I saw a flock of birds rise into low angles of morning light from beneath the hooves of a herd of zebra. They were carmine bee-eaters, rose-colored birds with deep blue crowns and muted green rumps. For a split second the sun froze them in a metallic flash against the striped and heavily muscled flanks of the zebra. This image alone, I thought, if you could remember it in its fullness, would carry you beyond anger. With that, or the image of gemsbok, lithe, resplendent in their stone deserts, you could return to Delmas. I had no idea how those men on trial, as composed, as eminent, as dignified in that other stone desert, would survive; but I understood how they could. Without even asking, it is what you are given out here. These gifts, the healing.

"A FEW MILES DOWNSTREAM, THE RUFIGI TAKES ITS FOOT OFF THE ACCELERATOR, NEVER TO SPEED AGAIN." (STAN BOOR)

Tom Robbins

▼

AN ADVENTURE IN MEAT

The first time that I was bitten by a tsetse fly (Ouch! Son of a bitch! Those suckers *hurt*!), I was convinced that in days, if not hours, I would be nodding out, snoring on the job, dreaming at the switch, yawning like a playboy stranded in Salt Lake City, another droopy victim of the dreaded and sorrowful "sleeping sickness."

During my two weeks in the Selous, my tender flesh subsequently was stabbed, my vintage blood swilled by at least forty tsetse flies, so far without dire consequence—although I must confess that as I begin this report, I'm starting to feel a little drowsy.

Should I doze off in the middle of a sentence (an experience probably not uncommon to some of my readers), I want it known there's no regrets. The lethal lullaby of an infected tsetse (the most romantically named of all the flies) is preferable to the anesthetic drone of computers, compact cars and television sets, and the wild, hot beauty of the Selous is worth almost any risk.

The Selous is the largest uninhabited game reserve in the world. Located in central Tanzania, a couple of hundred miles south of Mount Kilimanjaro, the Selous is no national park where tourists sprawl on rattan sofas, sipping gin and listening to the BBC as, from the air-conditioned safety of posh lodges, they spy shamelessly on mating lions. In the Selous, one doesn't catch a safari bus to the corner of Giraffe and Warthog. To see the Selous, one hikes and one paddles. And when an aggravated hippopotamus is charging one's rubber raft, one paddles very hard, indeed.

When I announced to family and friends that I was going hiking and river-rafting through a vast patch of African cabbage, they didn't ask why. They must have realized that after three years bent over an idling and backfiring novel, skinning my knuckles on every bolt and wrench in the literary toolbox, I needed to blow a little carbon out of my own exhaust. Perhaps they also sensed that after my recent dealings with editors, agents, lawyers, producers and reviewers, I might be primed for the company of crocodiles.

Nobody was particularly concerned that I was off to walk with the animals, talk with the animals, squawk with the animals. After all, I once turned down an offer of zebra steak in a weird restaurant in Hawaii, and have made it a lifelong practice never to date women who wear leopard-skin pillbox hats. My beast karma was pretty good.

Nevertheless, having heard AMA terror stories of schistosomiasis and malaria, of elephantiasis-enlarged scrotums the size of beachbags, and, yes, of the languid legacy of tsetse flies, they fretted one and all about tropical disease.

Well, not to worry. First, I was inoculated against most tropical diseases (there's no [yawn] serum to ward off "sleeping sickness"), and second, the very fact that the Selous is unoccupied by humans or farm animals means disease is rarely contracted there. In the Selous, the tsetse is all pester and no siesta. Ah, but I'd overlooked one thing. The Selous itself is a tropical disease: feverish, lethargic, exotic, achey, sweaty, hallucinogenic and, as I've learned since coming home, recurrent.

Just when I think that I am over it, that rush-hour traffic, income tax forms and two viewings of *Amadeus* have worked their civilizing cures, I suffer yet another attack of Selous. It comes on with a humid vapor, with a vibration of membrane, with howls and hoofbeats that nobody else in the room can hear, and although I might be in the midst of something truly important, such as choosing which brand of burglar alarm to install on my newly violated door, it never fails to distract me with memories of a sweeter, if less comfortable place; a place where even time is honest, and primitive equalities prevail. . . .

It's our first day in the bush. At this point, I'm still a tsetse virgin. From the port city of Dar es Salaam, we have travelled into the interior on a toy railroad: one locomotive, one car, and narrow-gauge track, all three built by the Chinese. It was definitely not a main line. It was a chow mein line.

Okay, okay, but the chow on the train *was* pretty good. We bought it through our windows at brief village stops. There were cashew nuts, absolute state-of-the-art mangoes, and thumb-sized bananas that melted in our mouths. Prices were so cheap they made us feel like muggers.

During the five-hour rail trip, we had gotten acquainted with our leaders, employees of Sobek Expeditions, a company of, well, reasonably sane adventurers from Angels Camp, California. These Sobek people had chased thrills, chills and spills all over the globe, but they were as excited as the rest of us when, halfway into the ride, we began to spot a few animals. A baboon here, a warthog there, a small herd of distant bushbuck, and in the ponds and marshes (lavendered with water lilies the color of Oscar Wilde's hankies), yellow-bill storks taller than most Little League second basemen, poised there among the lily pads as if waiting for a throw from centerfield.

Yes, it was exciting, but there was a bit of a theme-park atmosphere about it, as well; as if those random creatures had been placed in our field of vision by a San Diego entrepreneur. Then, suddenly, a pair of giraffes bounced into view. When the engineer mischievously sounded his whistle, the giraffes panicked. Stiff stilts churning, necks waving like rubber bands, they bolted toward, rather than away from us—and in their confusion very nearly crashed into the side of our car. One wheeling giraffe was so close I could have flipped a cashew into its terrified muzzle.

Oh Boy! Oh Tarzan and Jane! This certainly was Africa. But it was not yet the Selous.

Our first day in the bush finds us up at dawn. Having only seen dawn from the other side of the clock, I never imagined daybreak might actually be pleasant. The tsetse-like sting of 5:00 A.M. is softened by the sight of an elephant family, Mom, Dad, Bud and Sis, carelessly mashing a million dewdrops as they Vachel Lindsay down a green valley to a waterhole.

We watch the elephants from the veranda of the Stiegler's Gorge camp, the last outpost of humanity we'll enjoy before we venture into the Selous. We had slept at the camp, or tried to sleep, for an all-night newsboy choir of hyenas periodically sang us awake. Late the previous afternoon, the train had deposited us at a village called Fuga, the end of the line, where we—eighteen of us, including the Sobek guides—were met by a trio of Land Rovers and driven for a couple of battering hours down an Armageddon of a road, a moonscape of a lane to Stiegler's Gorge. By the time our gear was stowed in our respective huts, it was dark and a rusty gong had summoned us to a dinner of green beans and steak.

Dave, a Sobek veteran, had hoisted a morsel of steak aloft in the lanternshine. "Impala," he had said, studying his fork. "At first, I thought it might be sable. Africa is an adventure in meat."

At any rate, it's our first morning in the bush, and a detachment of us hike for three hours from the Stiegler's Gorge complex, beneath a sun that already is hissing like a blowtorch. Down in Tanzania, it's July in January, and if the sun has anything to say about it, there are fireworks every day.

The savanna grass is green but dry and it crunches underfoot. J'nanga, our native game guide, steps noiselessly on the bare patches between clumps of grass, but we cement-footed Americans sound as if we're breakdancing in a silo of Rice Krispies. Our gauche sneakers scuff at fresh cheetah tracks, at shiny licorice drops of wildebeest dung, at impala skulls as bleached as a surfer's eyebrows, short wildflowers and a mega-Manhattan of ants.

Scattered about the plain are trees that resemble huge stone jars, trees that resemble delicatessens festooned with salami and pepperoni, trees that appear to be growing upside down, trees that look like fifties haircuts, their foliage barbered into Sha-Na-Na flattops; and, most prevalent, leafless trees bristling with thorns so long and sharp they could pierce the heart of a bureaucrat.

The trees, the flowers, even the piles of gnu poo are attended by butterflies, some as tiny and yellow as buttercup petals, others as big as pie tins and colored like Shanghai silk. There are also many bees. No, although they're built like Belushi, they're not killer bees, but we

haven't learned that yet, and it is while fending off one of these buzzers that Flo falls, cameras and all, into a warthog burrow.

Warthogs aren't killers, either, except maybe when cornered, but with their curved tusks and flat-iron faces, they look like the nightmares of a lapsed Jew who's just had his first bite of ham. The steelwool warthog, not pink Porky, is the pig that ought to have the job of announcing "That's all, folks." Who'd argue? On another game walk, a week later, seven of these swine came barreling, one by one, out of a deep burrow that we were innocently passing, nearly knocking the pins from under a startled Yvonne and planting the fear of the Ultimate Sausage in each of us. On our calendars, that day became known as "The Day the Earth Spit Warthogs," and Yvonne, for one, will probably devote January 21st to prayer and fasting for the rest of her life.

On this, our first day in the bush, there are no pigs at home, however, and nothing is bruised except Flo's dignity. It is while she's brushing herself off that J'nanga sights a herd of buffalo.

There are about two hundred of them, weighing in at three tons each, and it doesn't take Ray Kroc's calculator to figure that that's a whole lot of McBuffalo burgers. Fortunately, we're downwind from the herd, so we're able to move within forty yards of it before we're noticed.

There's a large fallen tree in our vicinity and J'nanga directs us into its dead branches. We watch the buffalo and they watch us. It's difficult to tell who's more nervous. The mature bulls station themselves at the perimeters of the herd, glowering with almost tangible menace. They paw the ground and snort short Hemingway sentences, resonant with ill will.

J'nanga is thinking he might have made a mistake. The Cape buffalo, rotten-tempered, heavy of hoof and horn, is among Africa's most dangerous animals, and here he's gone and got a half-dozen honkies treed by a herd that could reduce Grand Central Station to gravel. The buffalo are indisposed to retreat, and we seem to have lost that option.

Jim, an environmentalist cowboy attorney accustomed to stalking Sierra sheep, grinds happily away with his video camera while J'nanga ponders the situation. In Jim's ear, I whisper, *"Hatari!"* I suspect Jim has seen more John Wayne movies than I, but if he recognizes the Swahili word for "danger," he doesn't let on. "Big *hatari!*" I whisper. He goes on videoing.

It's hot enough in our tree to broil escargot, and even the hardy Sobek daredevils are beginning to see mirages. Over there to the left: is that a grove of thorn trees or a Club Med pool? Perhaps J'nanga is getting lightheaded, too. He commences to whistle, shrilly, through his fingers, as if at a bathing beauty. At the sound, the buffalo stage a semi-stampede. They thunder to a spot beyond Club Med, a good eighty yards away, before stopping to resume their cold-war diplomacy.

Taking immediate advantage of this partial withdrawal, J'nanga hustles us out of the tree and, covering us with his rifle, dispatches us toward a low hill—on the opposite side of which, a few minutes later, we are charged by an adolescent elephant.

Between meals, as well as at table, Africa is, indeed, an adventure in meat.

The next morning, the real fun begins. Bleary-eyed from the insomnolent effects of hyena serenade, we put our rafts in the water and paddle into the Selous. For the next two weeks, we'll see no other humans, just animals, birds, fang-snapping reptiles—and, of course, the gods of the river.

Sobek employees are quite familiar with river gods. Running rivers is what Sobek is predominantly about. Anybody who does much river-rafting gets to recognize the invisible deities who rule each particular river, sometimes each particular rapid in a river. The very word "Sobek" is borrowed from the crocodile god of the Nile. It was chosen both as a charm and an homage.

Rivers are the true highways of life. They transport the ancient tears of disappeared races, they propel the foams that will impregnate the millennium. In flood or in sullen repose, the river's power cannot be overestimated, and only men modernized to the point of moronity will be surprised when rivers eventually take their revenge on those who dam and defile them. River gods, some muddy, others transparent, ride those highways, singing the world's inexhaustible song.

In terms of whitewater (a Sobek rafter's plasma), the Rufiji, the river that drains the Selous, is a pussycat. Once free of the confines of Stiegler's Gorge, it hums a barely audible refrain. Ah, but though the gods of the Rufiji are fairly silent gods, we are soon to learn that their mouths are open wide.

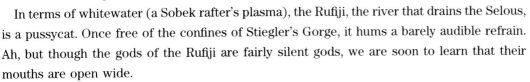

Actually, the Rufiji is a river *system*. As it approaches the Indian Ocean, it separates into channel after channel, forming a plexus of waterways so confusing no explorer has quite been able to map it. At one point, it vanishes into the palm swamps of Lake Tagalala, only to slither out on the eastern side like a many-headed serpent.

Through Stiegler's Gorge, the Rufiji gives us a fine fast spin, comparable, say, to the waves of the Rogue, if not the Colorado. One rapid, in fact, is so rowdy that our cargo-rigged Avon rafts dare not challenge it; thus, less than an hour after we've put in, we're involved in a laborious portage.

A few miles downstream, the Rufiji takes its foot off the accelerator, never to speed again. It just grows lazier and slower until there's virtually no current at all. Deprived of the luxury of drift, we're forced to paddle the entire distance—forty-five steamy miles—to our take-out point. Moreover, the rafts are so heavily loaded with equipment (including Jim's four video cameras) and supplies (including Chicago Eddie's gold jewelry), that it requires a marathon of muscling to move them along.

None of us passengers is an Olympic paddler, exactly, and the Sobek crew might have had to provide more than its share of the locomotion were it not for the impetus of hippopotamus. Every languorous labyrinth of the Rufiji is choked with hippos, and for a full fortnight those lardy torpedoes were to dominate our lives.

There're plenty of crocodiles, chartreuse and ravenous, in the Rufiji, as well, but like the CIA, the crocs are funded for covert operations only. Crocs are masters of the sneak attack. The nastiness of hippos is magnificently blatant.

Apparently, among animals as among human beings, we entertain misconceptions about who are the good guys and who are the villains. The horned rhinocerous, for example, enjoys a public reputation equivalent to that, say, of a black biker. "Lock up the children, Elizabeth! Big *hatari*!" The hippo, on the other hand, having been filmed in frilly tutus by Disney, its gross grin having been cutey-pied by a thousand greeting-card artists, is regarded as affectionately as a plump old ward boss.

Basically, however, the rhino is a quiet, shy, gentle creature. Sure, it will half-heartedly charge a Land Rover, but that's because its eyesight is so poor it mistakes the vehicle for another rhino, with whom it would mate or spar. Like many a biker, the rhino is mainly just out for a good time. The hippo, on the other hand, is loud, hostile and aggressive. Extremely territorial, it pursues with fury anything audacious enough to move into its neighborhood. Ward boss, all the way. Nothing, neither lion nor leopard, python nor crocodile, will tangle with a hippo. The unattractive rhino is the victim of a bad press. The cherubic hippo kills more people every year than any other animal in Africa.

When we discover rhino tracks one day, on a plain a few miles from Lake Tagalala, our native guides literally jump for joy. They had believed all rhinos gone from the Selous, destroyed by poachers, who market the powdered horn to Oriental ward bosses with waning sex drives. Conversely, we paddle past a hundred hippos daily, not one of whom offers us anything but trouble.

Cries of "Hippo right!" or "Hippo left!" ring out every few minutes from the Sobek guides. Should one of the surprisingly swift monsters prove particularly threatening, a guide slaps the water with his paddle, making a resounding *Swak!* that frequently will halt a charge, at least temporarily. Meanwhile, everybody else in the raft paddles as if his or her life depends upon it.

When we put into shore for lunch or to camp for the night, we're exhausted. Panting, arms aching, stewing in our own perspiration, we stumble from the rafts and flop down in the nearest shade. It's Miller time, right? Wrong. No beer, no ice. The refreshment we're served is Rufiji punch: raspberry Kool-Aid made with river water that has been purified via medicine kit. The water is eighty degrees, buzzing with silt, stinking of iodine and no doubt heavily laced with crocodile drool and hippo pee. We welcome it as if it were French champagne.

Characteristically, hippopotamuses make a noise that is a cross between scales being run on an out-of-tune bassoon and the chortling of a mad Roman emperor. Throughout the night, we are treated to their ruckus. The guides say that the hippos, being nocturnal feeders, are protesting because we've set up our tents in their dining room. Personally, I think they're making fun of us for the way we guzzle that punch.

Our food is a James Beard-sized improvement over our beverage. Under crude conditions, the Sobek guides manage to turn out delicious spaghetti, chop suey and, amazingly, banana crêpes flambé. (Have the native guides any doubt that we Americans are crazy, it vanishes as they watch, eyes wide with horror, as Dave sets fire to a quantity of perfectly good rum.) True, toward the end of the journey, supplies running thin, we might fantasize about one of those little *osterie* where, with a smear of garlic and a squirt of wine, an Italian can make a dead fish sing like a nightingale. But we haven't come to the Selous to eat and drink.

Even were there restaurants in the Selous, the cuisine of the Tanzanian interior consists primarily of *ugali*, a pasty dough that is torn into pieces with the fingers and dunked in sauce. Sauce de impala, sauce de sable, sauce de dik-dik, sauce de flying termite. An adventure in meat. And although there are sweltering moments when I'd gladly trade my first-born child for a frosty bottle of Safari Lager, that brand of beer, the only one available in Tanzania, is no gold-medal winner.

We haven't come to the Selous to wine and dine, nor to sightsee and shop. We've come to seek an audience with the river gods, to show ourselves to them and accept their banishment or their boons. We've come to test ourselves against water dragons with ears like wads of hairy bubblegum, with the bulging eyes of a drunken ward boss and the gaping yawn of a million cases of "sleeping sickness" rolled into one. We've come to the Selous to outrace the hippos.

Did I say that we are exhausted at the conclusion of our morning and afternoon paddles? True, we're tired, but we're also exhilarated. We're so elated our bones are practically celebrating in their weary sockets, and, narrow escapes or not, it is with *eagerness* that we wrap ourselves against the homicidal sun and go out on the river again.

Because of the naughty habits of the crocodiles, we're forced to bathe on shore, showering with buckets of muddy water drawn cautiously from the stream. Now, Chicago Eddie might

whine that he'd rather be soaking in a tub in some fancy hotel, but nobody believes him. The Rufiji pantheon, lurid of feather, strong of tooth, has wired an ancient tingle in Eddie's cells, and, like the other seventeen of us, he broadcasts secret signals of ecstasy—Radio Eden—as he penetrates ever deeper into the Selous.

Perhaps it would be helpful could I inform you that the Selous is the size of Rhode Island with a crust of Connecticut tossed in. Unfortunately, such facts are not at my disposal. My East African guidebook contained that sort of information, but I loaned it to a fellow rafter and it was never returned. She hinted that when our supplies ran low, she boiled it for breakfast, talk about your adventure in meat. That same woman also claims to be watched over by the ghost of her deceased dog Juliet, and that it's this phantom poodle, rather than guides and gods, who are steering us safely through the hippos. That is the kind of lady she is, and I, for one, am happy she's along.

All I can report is that the Selous is extensive, its wildlife density is amazing, and if its heart (a heart of brightness, to contradict Conrad) is invaded by other than scattered poachers, the annual Sobek expedition, and an infrequent government inspection team, the evidence is missing. We meet strange insects here, including a sort of miniature science-fiction flying fortress, as glossy black as Darth Vader's stovepipe, with long, thick, schoolbus-yellow antennae, but there isn't a trace of litterbug.

The Selous is savanna: short grass, middle grass and tall grass savanna. Some of the plains seem almost manicured, so meticulously have they been mowed by the mouths of munching herds. The green hills roll like surf into a distance, where they turn slowly to purple. From Tagalala on to the sea, elegant palms line the various banks of the river. Occasionally, we come upon a Tarzanesque glade, complete with pool and vines.

Johnny Weismuller, the consummate movie Tarzan, was the tallest hero of my boyhood, and more often during my life than is socially acceptable, I've been moved to imitate his famous yell. To some, the Tarzan yodel is corny, campy, childish and vulgar. To me, it's more stirring than the bravest battle cry, more glorious than the loftiest operatic aria, more profound than the most golden outpouring of oratory. The Tarzan yell is the exultant cry of man the innocent, man the free. It warbles back and forth across the boundary between human and

beast, expressing in its extremes and convolutions all the unrestrained and holy joy of
ultimate aliveness.

In the past, unfortunately, I've usually bounced my Tarzan yells off the insensitive ears of
cocktail-lounge commandos. Here, at last, in the glades of the Selous, it is released in proper
context. It gives me that old Weismuller Saturday matinee primal chill as it comes quavering
out of my throat to mix in the Selous twilight with the smoker's coughs of a distant pride
of lions, the spooky erotic murmurs of a treeful of waking bats; and that ceaseless pulsebeat
of body Africana, the echoing hoot of the emerald-throated wood dove.

Our last day in the Selous is structured much like the others: up at dawn for a game
walk into the bush, breakfast, break camp, two hours on the river, lunch, rest, two
more hours playing Dodgem-car with the hippos, set up camp, another game walk before
dark, dinner, bed. At the end of such a day, one requires no tsetse injection to speed one's
slumber. On this final eve, however, many of us lie conscious, listening, holding onto every
note of the ninety-piece orchestra of the African night. It is as if we dread the morning and
our return to what we call civilization.

I'll bet that Bob, in the adjacent tent, is recalling the impalas we had seen that dusk,
crossing a narrow ridge single file, so that we could count them the way a child at a crossing
will count boxcars: there were exactly sixty-five silhouetted against the setting sun.

And I venture that Kathy, an erudite woman with a library of wildlife manuals in her
knapsack, is still puzzling over the blank stare the aging guide M'sengala had given her when
she'd asked whether the rare hartebeest we'd spotted was *Lichtenstein's* hartebeest. After
that, M'sengala, whom we'd nicknamed Eddie Murphy, Senior, cracked up every time I
inquired if we were looking at Rauschenberg's wildebeest, Rosenquist's bushbuck, Wessel-
mann's waterbuck, or Zabar's borschbuck. Even though he doesn't understand a word of
English, M'sengala got the point.

Certainly, M'sengala, with his goofy, infectious laugh, is in *my* thoughts. I'm remembering
how shocked he looked when Curt slipped the Sony Walkman headset over his leathery
ears and turned up Huey Lewis and the News, and how quickly he began to grin and then

*"On this final
eve, many of us
lie conscious,
listening,
holding onto
every note of the
ninety-piece
orchestra of the
African night. It
is as if we
dread the
morning and
our return to
what we call
civilization."*

to dance, as if he could not stop himself from dancing. M'sengala got down! The Selous, itself, gets down. Down to basics, to the curious if natural rhythms of life.

And death. For if there's abundant life in the Selous, there's abundant death as well. We'd seen a pack of wild dogs cripple and devour an impala; a bloated hippo corpse being ripped to shreads by twenty crocodiles; the remains of a feline-butchered wildebeest, black clouds of flies buzzing like *paparazzi* around its instant celebrity of blood. We could hear those flies from thirty yards away.

Yes, there're ongoing dramas of death in the Selous, but except for the small amount imported by poachers, there's no unnecessary violence, or greed, no cruelty. Nor is there politics, religion, trendiness, ambition, hype or sales pitch. Perhaps it's the very purity of the Selous that makes us cling to it, reluctant to let go.

For two weeks, we have travelled in the realm of the eternal. There is escape from the prison of the past, disinterest in the uncertainties of the future. There is no other place. The Selous is *here*. There is no other time. The Selous is *now*.

And as we lie in our tents on the grassy plain of eternity, it must occur to each and every one of us that the Selous is the way the world was meant to be—and everything else is a mistake.

Nonetheless, we do return to civilization, and I have to tell you, now that I'm back, I'm ready for a nap. If it should prove that a tsetse has, indeed, drugged my juices, then, O river gods, grant me a graceful fall into the sleep of the Selous. The bright slumber of Africa. The snooze of Kilimanjaro.

HIPPO! "IT PURSUES WITH FURY ANYTHING AUDACIOUS ENOUGH TO MOVE INTO ITS NEIGHBORHOOD." (CURT SMITH)

LLAMA ARE NO LONGER SACRIFICED BUT STILL ROAM THE SQUARE IN CUZCO. (COURTESY OF SOBEK EXPEDITIONS)

Max Apple

ANDEAN ODYSSEY
SCREENPLAY FOR TRAVELOG

CAST

JESSICA: 13, curly-haired Cindy Lauperite—just wants to have fun.

MAR: 13, Jessica's best friend. Dark Argentinian turned Texan, hungry for her homeland but a stranger to Peru.

SAM: 10, Jessica's brother, Max's son. Baseball fan trying to follow Houston Astros season while caught in the Andes with father and sister.

MAX AND SUZANNE: lovers.

JOHN AND BINDY: lovers.

MARIELLA: Peruvian tour guide. River specialist and careful observer of Yankees in Peru.

FIDEL CASTRO: aging dictator. He portrays himself.

"The Museum of Gold, a clutter of riches that should cure anyone's desire for jewelry."

SETTINGS

1. Lima: capital of Peru. Dry and ugly. Roofs are common luxury here, the way swimming pools are in Southern California. Exudes Third World gloom. Ragged children live in the streets. There is a notable absence of joggers. The Museum of Gold, a clutter of riches that should cure anyone's desire for jewelry. Lima is a one-day stop before the mountain trip.

2. Cuzco: as exotic as Lima is mundane. Almost 14,000 feet in the Andes, ancient Inca capital; the pre-Pizarro capital of the world.

3. The Sacred Valley of the Incas: breadbasket of Peru. Rich farmland along the Urubamba River. Site of Camp David retreat for Inca emperors.

4. Machu Picchu: city of unknown Inca origin and use. Built in late 15th century, abandoned by late 16th century. Discovered beneath the jungle by Hiram Bingham in 1911 as he sought the lost city of Vilcabamba. Probably the Spaniards never knew of Machu Picchu. In its mystery it is the perfect background for this cast of children and lovers.

5. Urubamba River: a tributary of the Amazon.

TIME

Late June 1986. The World Cup finals are in progress in Mexico City. The roar of the crowds through many staticky radios is the background hum of this era.

LOCAL COLOR

In Lima: prison riot in progress. Police kill more than 200 prisoners.

In Lima: international conference. Leaders of world's Socialist countries have taken over the downtown hotels. The streets are closed to tourists.

In Cuzco: the Festival of the Sun is about to begin. The modern version of the ancient rites of sacrifice, human perhaps, llama for sure.

In the mountains: Sendero Luminoso guerrillas plan revenge for the murders during the prison riot.

PLOTS

1. Trade and commerce

Jessica, Sam, and Mar understand that the world is in part a gravity-stricken shopping mall. Mar discovers that her fluent Spanish makes her able to trade efficiently with the natives. She interprets for Jessica and Sam. As they barter with the Indians, the K-Mart objects that the children own seem as wondrous to the natives as the Peruvian earrings, whistles and shawls seem to Jessica and Mar and Sam. The children decide to trade everything they own except their portable electronic games. They establish values quickly. A pair of running shoes equals a small tapestry, a vinyl raincoat begets a wool sweater. Without money the purity of goods emerge. Items are either useful or beautiful. As the children jabber and touch, they are increasingly surrounded by native children until it is finally not the goods they look at but the young Indians. By the end of the trip the three American children are dressed in Indian shawls, capes, and hats, and wave goodbye to Indian children wearing running shoes and sunglasses.

Musical Themes: "Material Girl," "If I Had a Hammer."

2. Love

A. John and Bindy: he a real estate developer, she an airline flight attendant. Peru is a warm-up for their appointment with happily ever after. They will go from here to the great Statue of Liberty celebration in New York on the 4th of July. They look only at one another.

Peru is a dreamscape around them, a necessary setting. It could be Nepal or Key West or Hawaii, anyplace that looks appropriately romantic in the background.

Musical themes: "We Are The World," "Be My Urubamba Baby."

B. Suzanne and Max: she, former geology student, he, writer. He, father, she, young adventurer. She reads history in the rocks around them, he wavers between adventure and worry. They look at one another as much as John and Bindy do, but sing less. These are the more troubled lovers. The world that John and Bindy have reduced to romantic background sits on their shoulders. In their sighs, the mountains groan.

Dramatic themes: Othello, Antony and Cleopatra.

SCENE: Jessica, Sam and Max in a one-story suburban house in Houston, Texas. The Sobek adventure book is in front of them. "Wheel of Fortune" is on TV. The scraps of a pizza are on the table. The children are taking turns spinning the globe just as on TV the contestants spin the Wheel of Fortune. Sam, blindfolded, has stopped the world with his index finger.

SAM: Here.

JESSICA: It's the Pacific Ocean. You've got to pick a real place.

SAM: Every time it's my turn I get the Pacific Ocean.

MAX: Try spinning it counter-clockwise.

JESSICA: Very funny. My turn.

Her well-groomed fingernail alights near Oklahoma City.

Max is listing all the places as the children select them in their random world-spinning. While the children play with the globe, his mind is on South America. His father came to the United States on a merchant ship from Eastern Europe along the South American coast. He remembers his father talking about Montevideo and Rio and Buenos Aires. These are his first choices. He is also remembering the perverse delight on the face of his fourth-grade teacher as she told him that the Panama hat was made in Ecuador, not in Panama. This fact still haunts him, still seems wrong.

SAM: If we don't go to the Pacific Ocean then I'm not going.

MAX: How about Hawaii?

SAM: Is it in the Pacific Ocean?

MAX: Yes.

Mar, Jessica's friend, joins them. She spins the world too.

MAR: If you go anywhere near Argentina, I'll come along.

SAM: Is it in the Pacific Ocean?

MAR: The Atlantic Ocean.

SAM (*thoughtfully*): OK.

SCENE: *Exterior. Downtown Lima.*

The streets are blocked off because of the international meeting. Outside the government buildings guards in civilian clothes carry machine guns and crowd around car radios to listen to the World Cup games. The static from the radios sounds ominous because it comes from a cluster of men carrying guns.

On the steps of the President's house, Suzanne leans back, relaxing. Max reads the newspaper.

SAM: Did the Astros win?

MAX (*looking in the paper but knowing it's hopeless*): You're in Peru. Nobody here cares about the Astros.

SAM: I care.

MAX: I'll look for the Miami paper when we go back to the hotel.

SAM: There's scores right on the front.

Max and Suzanne look.

SAM: Fronton Island 260. It must have been a runaway.

MAX: That's the number of people killed in a prison riot.

SAM: Where?

MAX: Here.

SAM: In Lima?

MAX: Yes. But far from here. It has nothing to do with us.

Fidel Castro walks onto the set. He is dressed in his usual army fatigues, but speaks with slow dignity. He looks like Fidel but sounds more like Abraham Lincoln. Fidel directly addresses the audience:

FIDEL: You see, my friends, that colonialism and tourism are kissing cousins. 260 prisoners murdered by the police a few miles from where they are sitting and these tourists think it has happened on the moon. Look at them.

He points to John and Bindy and Max and Suzanne. He sings "Love Makes the World Go Round," but substitutes "Revolution" for "Love."

When the voice of the staticky radio screams Goal! Goal! Fidel stops singing and runs toward the security men to find out who scored.

FADE to an Aeroperu 707 rising above the roofless houses of gray, dingy Lima. The plane climbs toward Cuzco. A long shot shows the spectacular view of Cuzco from the air. It does look like the belly button of the world as it sits in the middle of the surrounding mountains. Zoom in for a close-up, making the city look more like a football stadium, its terraces bleachers, the players, Quechua Indians dressed in bright fabrics, squatting everywhere before piles of sweaters, shawls, earrings and ponchos. The Indian women wear high straw hats and carry their babies in bright shawls wrapped around their shoulders. The infants are so silent that they are almost indistinguishable from the bundles of straw and twigs that the women also carry on their backs.

SCENE: *A close-up of the cast entering the Hotel Royal Inca. They are all slightly wobbly from the altitude and lack of sleep. They are in the hotel courtyard surrounded by tropical birds as they sip coca leaf tea. In this moment Cuzco seems to be the most serene city on earth.*

CUT to Interior. The main church in the Plaza des Armas, a 17th-century building atop an ancient Inca temple. Move in for a close-up of the Last Supper, Inca version. In this one there is no sky radiating behind the Savior, but there is a large table; some disciples, some mugs of corn beer. Jesus contemplates the main course, a roasted guinea pig spreadeagled before him.

CUT to panning shots of the Plaza des Armas, the main square of Cuzco. There are 17 churches in Cuzco, all former Inca temples. The temple that once reflected the sun throughout Cuzco still has the stone hooks that once held the gold plates the Conquistadores stripped and sent home as evidence that the new world was worth a few tropical diseases and an occasional war.

SCENE: *A local guide is talking about the history of the Conquistadores in Cuzco. As she drones on and tourists snap photographs, Fidel Castro once more enters to offer his opinions to the audience.*

FIDEL: It's very simple. Wherever there was gold, the Conquerer took it and gave the people God. It's just a difference of one letter, and a bit of decoration here and there, just a civilization destroyed.

SCENE: *In the courtyard of one of the churches young army recruits are lined up. They are learning to be comfortable with rifles but they stand awkwardly on the sides of their feet. Their boots are new. One of the soldiers laughs and points to them. Before they get used to guns they will have to become accustomed to wearing shoes.*

SCENE: *Twilight, exterior. The steps of the cathedral in the Plaza des Armas. The Plaza is now filled with Indians from the countryside who have come to Cuzco for the summer solstice, the Festival of the Sun. The children are roaming through the crowd. Suzanne and Max are trying to keep up with them.*

MAX (*in awkward Spanish to a Cuzco resident*): Is it true that they still sacrifice a llama at this festival? Is it a substitute for a human sacrifice?

CUZCO RESIDENT: The head man of the village acts like the priest used to act. They used to cut out the heart of a llama. Now they just make it bleed a little.

Versions of American high school bands are drowning out the conversation. There are also native dancers in the square. Indian families cook corn and soup and chicken. Wherever there is no cooking, there is selling, mostly sweaters of alpaca wool. The cast mingles with the crowd. Even outdoors in the festive atmosphere you can still feel the gloominess of the 17 churches built upon the Incan ruins.

SCENE: *Exterior, 4 A.M. The main square still has a few revelers. In the small park in front of the Royal Inca Hotel three young men sing, "Will The Fat Lady Please Come Out?"*

SCENE: *Interior, hotel room. While the noise goes on and the sun rises, Jessica, Sam and Mar sit in their beds playing their portable electronic games. They are too tired to talk. The beeping noises of the games seem to have replaced language. Those electronic noises accompany the sun as it rises over Cuzco, its capital, on this day of the sun festival. No one in the cast has slept. Max and Suzanne are reading in bed. Mariella is preparing a menu for lunch on their rafting trip. John and Bindy are trying on one another's wool sweaters.*

SCENE: *Cuzco Railroad station. The sun, still accompanied by the sounds of electronic games, illuminates the railroad station. The Indian merchants crowd up even onto the train. The train's steep climb and then the descent to Machu Picchu begins. In the noise and motion of the train we still hear the electronic beeping. The sun has now risen for its festival day.*

SCENE: *Exterior, morning. The ruins of Machu Picchu. Max and Suzanne watch the sun burn away the clouds. The terraced hills and carefully built stone houses seem to play hide and seek with the sky. The day tourists have not yet arrived. Machu Picchu feels as deserted as it was for hundreds of years. A fortress perhaps, clearly a place that only the desperate or the driven would choose. It reminds Max of Masada, another shrine of the hopeless. He tries to dissipate his feeling of loneliness by playing with the children.*

SCENE: *Suzanne, Max, Jessica, Sam and Mar are playing hide and seek in Machu Picchu. The safe place is a big rock shaped like a playground slide.*
Now begins a series of cuts between the cast playing hide and seek at Machu Picchu and the proceedings at the Festival of the Sun in Cuzco. The tempo becomes much faster, the choral echo is the voice of the children running in Machu Picchu and yelling "safe" when they come to the smooth rock. The word "safe" carries over into the scenes in Cuzco.

SCENE: *Cuzco, exterior. From a group of Indians in travel dance the chief emerges wearing a tall impressive headdress. An assistant leads a llama towards the place of sacrifice. The bands play.*
CUT to Machu Picchu. Suzanne chases Sam and Jessica through the ruins as they run for the safe rock.
CUT to Cuzco, the train station. The same scene as the day before. The tourists are on the train. The Indian market is crowded up against the train.
An explosion. The last car on the train begins to blow glass and steel through the crowded market.
CUT to Plaza des Armas: the Indian headman, in imitation of the Inca rite, has cut into the llama. The llama bleeds over its white breast and onto the steps of the cathedral.
CUT to railway station: chaos. Tatters of woven fabric and pieces of pottery are mingled with glass and steel and luggage. It looks as if disaster, too, is for sale.
CUT to Machu Picchu: Sam reaches the main rock a step ahead of Suzanne. They are both breathless and laughing.
SAM: Safe.
CUT back to the bombed railroad station. We still hear the echo of Sam's "safe" and the noise of radios blaring out the World Cup games.
CUT to Machu Picchu: Night: exterior: John and Bindy are embracing. They are stretched out in a tiny stone hut. A misty rain begins to fall.
JOHN: You know a whole family probably lived in a place this size.
BINDY: I thought only virgins or priests lived here.
JOHN: Then probably whole families of virgins and priests lived in this tiny space.
They kiss. It rains harder.

CUT to exterior, John and Bindy about an hour later. They are at the gates of Machu Picchu looking toward the hotel but unable to get out. It is hours past closing. John yells for help. Only Pancho, the hotel's pet alpaca, wanders towards them.

JOHN: We're locked in here, Pedro.

BINDY: His name is Pancho.

JOHN: O.K., Pancho, Pedro, whoever, go for help. Get Mariella.

The alpaca looks at the stranded couple, raises his lip slowly and spits.

CUT to the cast leaving the train at a deserted spot in the Sacred Valley. A white van with a rubber raft atop it is awaiting them. Mariella stands near the tracks talking to a man. It is clear from the way he puts his arm around her that he is her husband, George. When tears come to Mariella's eyes Max knows something is wrong. He looks for his children who are throwing a ball beside the railroad tracks.

CUT to Mariella, and her husband George telling the cast that the Machu Picchu train has been bombed.

JOHN: Can we go back to Cuzco?

GEORGE: I don't know if it's safe.

BINDY: Is it a revolution?

GEORGE: It is the guerrillas. They are crazy but they never did this before. This is the first time they ever killed tourists. As soon as the news came out our next groups canceled.

BINDY: How many were killed?

GEORGE: Nobody is sure yet. Six or seven and many wounded. There are Americans dead too. Only the last car exploded.

Fidel Castro walks onstage to address the audience.

FIDEL: You see, it makes more sense to visit a mature revolution. In Havana there are no bombs.

He begins to dance and click his fingers to the Carmen Miranda song, "Yes, We Have No Bananas," only he says, "Yes, We Have No Bombs." He stops, and sounding as if he is an actor in a Merrill Lynch commercial, he says very solemnly, "And Cuba, an island paradise in the balmy Caribbean, is also a safe place for your excess capital."

A PERUVIAN CHILD WHO HAS NOT TRADED HER NATIVE CLOTHES
(JACK HOLLINGSWORTH)

SCENE: *Exterior. Yucay: a village in the Sacred Valley. A white 17th-century convent converted into a hotel. The cast are the only guests. Interior: the bar. A fireplace, couches. Only the young bartender's white jacket distinguishes him from the 14-year-olds outside the hotel who are driving the cattle home from grazing.*

John and Bindy enter.

JOHN (*to the non-English-speaking bartender*): Two Pisco sours and run a tab for room 12.

The boy understands nothing, and continues to rub the glasses that are already clean and dry.

SCENE: *Suzanne and Max walking among the farm animals in front of the converted convent. In the courtyard is a 500-year-old tree. A few hundred yards past the tree is the ruin of the summer home of the Emperor Manco. Barefoot children lead their cattle home. A dog barks at everyone. The children are in rags but their happiness is evident as they run among the livestock. The animals are fat and the children too seem well fed. A man pulls a baby lamb along on a thin leash. Suzanne and Max lean against the ancient tree. Although there is none of the dramatic beauty of Machu Picchu or Cuzco in this courtyard, the bliss of daily life is unmistakable.*

SUZANNE: It's terrible about the bomb. I hope George can get through to our families.

Suzanne and Max hug one another beside the ancient tree. While they kiss, the dog barks at them and the children stare. A farmer walks past carrying an ancient wooden plough.

SCENE: *Night, in front of the convent. The entire cast looks up. The stars are popcorn that has just exploded onto the darkness.*

MAX (*to John and Bindy*): It's so beautiful, maybe you should get married here.

JOHN: Not a chance. We're going to do it at the Grand Canyon.

SCENE: *The Urubamba River. The group is doing surprisingly well through the sometimes difficult rapids. Four Indian boys are running along the bank of the river waving to them. Sam has a bag of marbles. The cast rows to the shore where Sam distributes some marbles and some jacks to the Indian boys. After the raft is again in the middle of the river a ragged little boy, about 3, catches up with the older boys. He is crying because he didn't get any marbles. The group goes back to the shore, gives him his marbles. The Indian boys, friends now, accompany the raft, running as far as they can along the bank of the river. As the land ends they sing out in Quechua: "ay lee le ami." Mariella teaches the cast how to answer in Quechua: "ay lee lee anchu." The greetings and partings continue. The sounds of their friendship: ay lee le ami, ay lee lee anchu, echo as the raft moves through the Sacred Valley.*

SCENE: *Exterior, high in the mountains above the Sacred Valley. The voice of Mariella narrating as the camera pans the area.*

MARIELLA: The Indians call this place Pachu Teca, the spine of the universe. There are still holy men here in these mountains who know things. People go to ask them questions.

BINDY: Oh, let's go, I loved seeing the mystics in Nepal. I'll ask them to tell our future.

John snaps pictures of the brown mountains.

SUZANNE: Don't the guerrillas have their bases in the mountains, too?

Mariella nods sadly.

SCENE: *The Cuzco airport. There is now heavy security here. The cast has to open their baggage and then identify their luggage on the tarmac. The plane is delayed for hours because the President of Peru, Alan Garcia, is coming to Cuzco to visit victims of the bombing and meet with the area mayors. Tourists and Indians sit on the benches and on the floor of the small airport terminal. As they wait, Bindy dreams.*

She is in the mountains at the Spine of the Universe. She looks at her compass to make sure she is in exactly the right place. A holy man squats before her. He is wearing a T-shirt that says "Magnetic Center of the Planet."

Bindy is dressed as a bride. Her long white dress descends like clouds into the Sacred Valley.

BINDY: We're here on a pre-honeymoon. We got engaged at Machu Picchu. I came to ask you our future.

She hands the holy man a packet.

BINDY: This is what they said I should give you.

HOLY MAN: Thank you.

BINDY: What's my future going to be like?

HOLY MAN: Are you sure you want to know this?

BINDY: I am a little scared. But being scared is part of the adventure, isn't it? I don't like being scared about things like bombings, though. Why do the guerrillas do things like that?

HOLY MAN: Are you a stewardess?

BINDY: Yes, how did you know?

HOLY MAN (*points to the wings she wears on her bosom*): Your airline is in danger.

BINDY: A bomb?

HOLY MAN: A merger. Your airline will be absorbed.

BINDY: And me?

HOLY MAN: You too.

He points to John who appears beside her, and begins to take snapshots of his bride standing next to the holy man. Suzanne, Max, Jessica, Sam, and Mar now appear before the holy man. Suzanne is wearing a headdress of purple wildflowers and a bright colored dress of native cotton. She is an Indian princess. Max is beside her in a Panama hat made in Ecuador. He carries his children as the Indian women do, little bundles of life around his shoulders.

John snaps their photograph too.

SUZANNE: Now tell us.

HOLY MAN: Photography is the language of travel. There are no words to tell.

SUZANNE: Specifics, please. Save the universals for the next crowd.

She points behind her. There, awaiting their turn with the holy man, are Fidel Castro, Alan Garcia, and the entire Argentinian soccer team.

HOLY MAN: You're not a usual group. I see some character in you, but still you're not immune.

MAX: We came to the Andes for adventure, not for prophecy. Let's go.

HOLY MAN: All adventure is prophecy. I could have told you before you were born that you would go in your father's footsteps. And you, young princess, you would go anywhere.

SUZANNE: With the right company, yes.

Fidel Castro joins them.

FIDEL (*in the voice of a salesman*): Well, come to Havana, then. In Havana there are no bombs, not even much propaganda. Havana is becoming safe for comedy, safe for art. I hope we'll have a major-league baseball team by the turn of the century.

The roar of the crowd from Mexico City's soccer stadium shakes the mountains. The Argentinian soccer players leap into the air and hug one another. An announcer repeats hysterically, "Goal, goal, goal."

FIDEL (*above the noise*): Anyone can predict soccer. Tell us about the world, about politics, revolution, love, death, tell us the truth.

The holy man rises. All the noise stops. The soccer players look foolish in mid-embrace.

HOLY MAN (*to Fidel*): Silly dictator. For the price of a tour you expect the truth.

BINDY: You told me.

HOLY MAN: Then I will tell everyone. I advise all of you to go home, save your money, and take another trip next year.

BINDY: Is that all?

HOLY MAN: You can do it lots of times. Experience is cumulative.

Mariella strums a guitar, Jessica, Sam, and Mar join the holy man. The four begin to sing the rap song, "La Dee Dah Dee."

Suzanne and Max clap out the rhythm. Bindy looks around her at the Andean peaks. John photographs everyone.

JOHN: If these don't come out, nobody will ever believe us.

THE AMAZON, WHERE HOLLYWOOD FINDS MODELS FOR IMAGINARY BEASTS, AND AN ADVENTURE IN MUD. (SHARON WALKER)

Roy Blount Jr.

▼

AMAZON
ADVENTURE

Wild fish ripped my flesh. Let me qualify that.

A wild fish ripped my flesh. If there is one point that Ney Orlotegui, Amazon guide, would like to clear up ("When I had a
agent, I was going to swim in a twenty thousand–gallon tank with
thousands of piranha at Circus Circus in Las Vegas, but the guy
who had contact with my agent say, 'You commit suicide?' "), it
is that people go overboard when they talk about man-eating fish.

To tell the truth, when people ask me what the Amazon was like,
it is not man-eating fish that spring to mind. It is the mud. Strange
grey-green-blue-brown mud. But I tend to steer clear of the mud.

One small man-eating fish ripped my flesh. "You tell about that,
nobody gonna want to come," said Ney. It probably wouldn't have
ripped my flesh at all if.... It's a long story.

Traditionally, stories told by explorers back from the Amazon are hard to swallow. Those fierce women warriors for whom the Amazon is named? Fabricated by a sixteenth-century Spaniard. Those three-hundred-pound catfish that will drag children to the bottom of the river and gulp them whole? Well, those do exist. We ate part of one. And we found out that the Amazon is where Hollywood finds models for imaginary beasts: the wookies in *Star Wars* and the gremlins in *Gremlins*, for instance. We *owned* a gremlin, on our raft. It kept jumping into our meals and nestling in our armpits. And we could have picked up a wookie, but we didn't, we left it in the muddy village of Santa Maria, moaning.

The mud is what sticks with me. Two episodes in the mud. Ney, my son John and I in the mud twice—once wallowing like little kids, and once when I thought: "Someone could die like this."

The thing is, you probably want to hear about the man-eating fish. Okay. But I refuse to sensationalize it.

There I was, dog-paddling in the Huallaga, an Amazonian tributary in northern Peru. Our raft, the Yacu-Mama (named by Ney for a legendary Amazonian monster that is said to abduct people, down into the depths), was at anchor. Several of us explorers were in swimming. Ney had assured us that we needn't worry about what he referred to as "my piranha."

As long as we kept moving, he said, the kind of piranha that frequent this stretch of the river would rather eat something dead. "People come here, they make a documentary out of the piranha. They take a cow, they shoot pictures till they drown the cow. They use special pipes from the United States to blow bubbles. They buy one of the stuffed piranha, put it in the water and make its jaws move. Then they strip the cow, so it look beautiful, to the bone. That's false. That's why my piranha have gained so much fame."

Special pipes? This did not dispel footage of cow-devouring that held me rapt in my boyhood. But another explorer was asking about something even worse: the candiru, a toothpick-sized fish that introduces itself (strange phrase) into one or another of a swimmer's orifices, spreads open its set of spines, commences to grow in said orifice, and cannot be removed except by surgery. Was it true, in fact, that the candiru had such a soft spot in its heart for any old human entrance that it was capable of swimming up the stream of a person urinating into the river?

"Oh, yeaahhhh," said Ney. "They do that. Can . . . *dee* . . . ru. But thass just if you not wearing a bathing suit."

Room for clarification there, too. But deep down, in the Amazon, how much clarification could we stand?

So there we were, treading water, energetically, in the brown-green, pleasantly warm, unhurriedly inexorable current. And I felt a nibbling on my upper thigh.

I had been pecked at by fish before. I grew up being pecked at by fish, in waters of northern Georgia that were about this same color and temperature. I swam a few feet away.

I felt a sharper nibbling, in the same spot on my leg.

I thought to myself, this is just an hysterical piranha attack. I won't give in to it.

Then the nibbling got *fierce.*

And I hydroplaned back to the raft, yelling, "Fish! Fish!"

Nobody else had been attacked by fish. The others were still bobbing around, and now they were laughing.

I sat on the side of the raft. I pulled up the leg of my bathing suit.

And behold: ten or twelve spots of blood, growing.

People saw these! Heinz Kluetmeier, my fellow explorer, took pictures! Did anybody take pictures of the warrior maidens? No. But pictures exist of my bites.

"Sabalo," said Ney. A sabalo is not a man-eating fish. It is more or less what I would call a shiner. "This time of year, the dry season, those fish are starving," Ney said. "That is why. One hungry fish!"

I took his word for it. I had been attacked by a baitfish. At least I had demonstrably been attacked. When you wiped off the blood you could see the teethmarks. What kind of river was this, where you weren't safe from the *bait*?

At any rate, this boyhood rule applied: got to get back on that horse. I stood, semi-vindicated, and prepared to dive.

And something moved on my person. A cooler explorer would have said, "Heinz, get the camera." I said, "*Aauughhh!*"

And it jumped out of my pocket! People witnessed this! It glistened red, blue and voracious in the Amazonian sun! Eventually even Ney admitted it was a small piranha. (Later Julia Huaman Nolasco, his assistant, took me aside and confided, "Jou were very lucky. That was the fish that introduce himself into jour body." But I think she was just trying to make me feel better about having hollered "Fish! Fish!")

Flip, floop, it bounced off the side of the raft and disappeared into the murk of the Great Brown God.

I had a live Amazonian piranha in my bathing suit pocket for five solid minutes and lived to tell about it!

That is the kind of thing an explorer wants to dwell on. Not the mud.

We were the Emerald Forest expedition. Seven hundred miles in ten days along the Peruvian headwaters of the Amazon, through the heart of the rain forest, from Chasuta to Iquitos, on a raft handmade out of balsa logs, cane poles, wood poles, chainsawn planks and palm fronds.

Eight Peruvians. Ney, Julia, Ney's brother Aldo, crewwomen Lidia and Alicia, and boatmen Fermine, Antero (also known as Jack) and Nelson.

Nine gringos. Fred Bonati, former Marine pilot now a Northern California contractor and sailboatman. Hannah Carlin, British fashion consultant living in Houston. David Flint, graduation-picture photographer from Cincinnati. Fred's boyhood friend, the ominously named (for those who had read "Heart of Darkness") Jim Kurtz, now in investments in Arizona. Stephen and Carol Tatsumi, a cheerful young Southern California couple. Heinz, who taught innocent Amazonian children to point at me and say "Uooogly." My son John and I, at the time seventeen and forty-four respectively, awkward ages. I figured he and I needed an adventure together before he left the nest. He didn't seem to be so sure.

Most of us gringos had booked the trip through Sobek Expeditions, a California outfit that specializes in adventure vacations, but this particular tour was owned and operated by Ney, forty-seven, who grew up along the Amazon, lives in Florida now and is nimble to be so stocky. Dressed in a pith helmet and khaki shorts-and-shirt ensemble, and moving through the jungle in an odd preoccupied scuttle, with his head down into his shoulders and a look on his face of possible shrewdness, he invited comparison to Tattoo of "Fantasy Island," but he was a larger man than that and his face suggested a rounder, browner, vaguer Vince Edwards. Not an easy man to figure.

When our plane landed in Lima it was after the one A.M. curfew, the streets were empty except for soldiers with rifles and machine guns. Meeting us, Ney said we would be taken to a different hotel from the scheduled one, because of a revolutionary bomb threat. This

said, Ney and Julia left the airport-to-town bus and scooted off into the darkness—standing an excellent chance, Ney said, of being shot.

The next day we flew to Tarapoto, where we banqueted on excellent fish and hearts of palm and danced to pisco sours and the music of an eerie drum-and-whistle combo. "Now we a family," Ney said. On the third day we took minibuses to Chasuta, where the paved road ended, and the river was the highway.

N ey fielding the inevitable gringo question, whether we would acquire any authentic shrunken heads:

"Indians won't shrink your head anymore. Missionaries told them it was illegal. Now they wait till you die and then shrink your head.

"You go to the tourist hotel in Iquitos, white-man trader come to the hotel, says, 'I been in the jungle, got a shrunken head for five hundred dollars,'—it made in Japan! Says 'Taiwan' on the bottom!

"But if you tell the witch doctor *why* you need a head. . . . If you're patient with 'em, stick around. . . . Don't be mean with 'em. . . . And give 'em silver dollars 'cause they think paper money rot in the jungle. . . .

"But if you come into the jungle, *bambambam* shoot them, they prob'ly shrink your head."

I wrote that down, thinking it would be clearer later. We never met any witch doctors. Bad mechanics, yes; and John had the experience of bribing a policeman. But such head-hunters as may be left in the Amazon have retreated deep into the jungle, away from the sounds of motors and the promotions of such outfits as Green Hell Tours, which in the seventies (according to Alex Shoumatoff in *The Rivers Amazon*) brought tourists by the boatload to see a ceremony called "the plucking of the virgin's hair."

Native dress in Chasuta was pretty much the standard for villagers along the river: jogging shorts, patched T-shirts and either holey sneakers or flip-flops. I'm not saying we saw no primitivity: many of the villagers could not be dissuaded from shaking newly-snapped Polaroid pictures vigorously, which hasn't been necessary for years.

Then too, they lived in one-story huts whose walls were of flat, vertical three-inch-wide strips of cane (it grows broad in Amazonia), or occasionally of corrugated metal, and whose roofs were palm fronds or tin. Inside, the decor was pictures of Jesus and just about anything torn from newspapers or calendars: modest girlie photos, a two-page spread on Cheryl Ladd, a Mum deodorant ad, "The Anatomy of an Echinoderm." Along the main dirt street, Chasuta was in its second year of municipal electricity, which would come alive at dusk.

These villagers were predominantly old or middle-aged, or young mothers, or prime candidates for young motherhood, or little kids. Older children had to go to larger towns if they wanted to attend secondary school, and most of Peru's young men are drafted by the Army and taken into the big cities, where they discover boots, motorcycles and ice cream and lose their taste for the simple life. The villagers dwindle, the big cities swell, terrorists blow up a train or kill some policemen every so often (one of Ney's tour groups came trekking out of the jungle into an unprepared town and were taken for guerillas, had to lie on the ground with shotguns and machine guns held on them for a while), and the vast majority of people are poor.

But in the country fruits are handy (try and find an unpicked ripe banana near a trail). Jute, maize, rice, sugar cane and yucca grow quickly with little tending. People go out in canoes and return soon with ten-pound zebra-striped catfish. And piles of brilliant feathers next to charred spots mark snacks of opportunity. "Everything these people see, they kill and eat," Fred said.

"My first impression of the jungle was bananas and houseplants. Only way too big for a house or even a cathedral. A philodendron large enough to swallow a child."

Very appealing people, though. Clear handsome faces with smiles for us everywhere. At one time in history, the agency charged with protecting the Indians fed poisoned candy to inconveniently situated Indian children, and the kids in one village ran from us, saying (according to Ney) that we were Germans who would kidnap them for their fat. They were giggling, though. Uncorrupted-looking smiles abounded.

Chasutans led us up a mountain to swim in the pool below a fifty-foot waterfall (further along the river we would shower in falls warmed by a defunct volcano), and on the way down, as evening fell, one of them, named Marylou, got herself and Fred and Jim and me lost in the jungle.

Heinz and John and some local youths, full of beans, had *run* down the mountain toward the village, and Ney was shepherding other explorers. Fred, Jim and I assumed we were being led by Marylou. Every now and then she would stop and chuckle. Jim knew some Spanish (which nearly all the villagers spoke, proudly calling it *Castiliano*—it is not cool in the villages to be regarded as Indian). He asked Marylou where we were.

"*Yo no conosco,*" she said. That meant she didn't know. It didn't seem to bother her as much as it did us.

My first impression of the jungle was bananas and houseplants. Only way too big for a house or even a cathedral. A philodendron large enough to swallow a child, a forty-foot ficus tree, and something that seemed to touch Fred: pothos. Pothos on an enormous scale. Among us gringos Fred was the most into nature. He took offense when a Peruvian threw rocks at the only snake (an unimposing green one) we saw on the whole expedition.

Fred was the only one of us with jungle experience. He had bombed it during the Vietnam War. "The Southeast Asian jungle puts this to shame," he said. "Vegetation a hundred feet high. Beautiful country. We destroyed a lot of it. The jungle will come back, but I doubt the tigers and elephants will. I loved the flying. I didn't even mind bombing people. I just hated the dirty trick the system played on us. My father was in World War II. The President then, the system then, was pretty much ideal. That's not what I saw when I was in Vietnam. And then there was Watergate."

There we were, the houseplants closing in, darkness approaching, and personally I would have been glad to see Richard Nixon, if he knew the way to Chasuta. The path (or was it a path?) would peter out, Marylou would seem amused, and we would shout and not hear any animal sounds, even. (We were days further down the river before we heard jungle cries.) Two hours later we somehow made it to Chasuta's mini-outskirts. Marylou's mother was waiting with a machete, but I, at least, was so obviously grateful to see her—she was standing next to a man-made structure—that her suspicions were allayed. By this time John was dancing to a scratchy Stevie Wonder record with the daughter of the lieutenant governor. (There seemed to be a governor and a lieutenant governor for every forty or fifty people along the river.) I had the feeling this was not going to be one of those over-packaged tours.

"My father left me with the Campas Indians when I was thirteen," Ney said the next day as we jounced through rapids in a thirteen-meter-long dugout canoe (mahogany bottom built up with planks on the sides). There were twenty people on this boat, including a nursing mother and another hitchhiker, and three chickens and a dog. We were headed to where the raft awaited us.

"He got into hot water with the chief of the tribe. My father cheated him, didn't give him the merchandise he promised. My father traded with the Indians, and he would take me on trips. 'If you don't trust me,' my father said, 'I'll leave my son here, and I'll be back.'

"I waited six months. I was one of forty-eight kids my father had with different women.

He was sixty-four when he kidnap my mother, when she was sixteen. She was a Brazilian native, civilized. He came over from Spain in a small boat in 1922. He came to get the gold.

"Only good thing about him, he a gold prospector, a merchant, a lawyer, and he always got his way. We were wealthy people in the jungle. He put the gold in beer bottles under the house, and every two years he sell his gold and go to Spain and buy the most beautiful things for his wife and children. We lived at our gold mine in the headwaters of the Pachitea River, thirty days upriver from here. He never panned for gold, he held a shotgun on a hundred Indians while they panned for gold. There was an Indian who swallowed a nugget. My father stood there with a shotgun and said he was going to wait until that Indian passed that nugget. He did, twenty-four hours later. Then he took all the Indian's clothes and fired him.

"My father carry about five or six dynamites in his pocket, just for kicks. Sometimes he fish with it. Sometimes we fish with Indian poison. Take mashed potatoes, put a little poison in them, toss them on the water, the fish hit them, Pow, they jump around like crazy and you scoop 'em out before they die and cut their heads off so the poison don't get in the meat.

"I only had two years of school. My father teach me first grade. I wouldn't pronounce one word right, he come on top of me with a belt. He beat his kids—oh!

"When my father got to be eighty he wasn't right in the brain anymore. There's a legend about cutting the bull's ears and gold will come out. My father say, 'Ney, go get a saw, you take one end and I'll take another, bring a sack, we cut the bull, we have enough money to take the whole family to Spain.'

"My father travel the whole jungle here cheating people. He was so knowledgeable about the law. He name me for Marshall Ney, the French general at Waterloo. He was a fanatic about Waterloo. He could care less about another son. He left three of my brothers before me. I got scared with the Indians because this witch doctor, they would come to him, and a lady came with colic—she ate a lot of sugar cane and bar sugar. He tell that lady lay down, you got bad spirit in your stomach, and he cut a hole in her for that bad spirit to come out. With that the lady died.

"When I left there I was scared to death. I escape on a two-log raft. I went probably fifteen hundred miles, back home. My father wasn't there. My mother took all the gold and my brothers, and we abandon our ranch, we head to the big cities. We never saw lights, we never saw bicycles, never saw white people before. That was sad. I said, 'I want to go back.' I crossed the Andes by foot, came back, but it wasn't the same anymore. I missed my father, missed my mother, I missed my brothers, I was underage, I couldn't employ the Indians. I didn't have capital. So I started to a-benture."

He explored, he lived off the jungle, eventually he found his father in Iquitos. "He was amazing in his beliefs. He never believed in God. In his dying breath he said in Spanish, 'In God I . . .' and a dirty word. To me he was a great man. He was my father. Only difference between me and him, I am a very principled, religious, loveable man. I love people, I help them.

"He never tried to get back and see how his kids were doing. I found him when he was in the hospital dying. He was eighty-eight. He said, 'Which one are you?' I said, 'I'm Ney, the one you left with the tribe.' Out of the forty-eight kids he had, his sisters, brothers, not one would be at his bedside but me. I called them, they said no, because he was a mean man. They bring up the past.

"Then a missionary took me to Vicksburg, Mississippi, in his boat. Hired me to be the youngest sailor in the ship. On the way we stayed in Liberia for a year, thousands of Negro people pulled our ship to the shore.

(JACK HOLLINGSWORTH)

"I worked till my contract was over, then he sent me back to Peru. That wasn't fair, after I see the United States. I stow away in a merchant ship, three times. One time I didn't know which way was America, and I wind up in Italy. Every time in America I turn myself in to Immigration hoping they'd be nice people. Finally a man said do your service in your army, and if your intentions are honorable, you'll get into America. So I went to be a parachute, and I got seventeen jumps, and in 1967 the first letter came from Washington, that I had been forgiven for stowing away. In 1980 I became a citizen. I know it is not impossible to get anywhere a man want."

Before we reached the raft we met some men who were getting ahead in, alas, what is currently the most cost-effective way in Peru. Nominally they were salt miners, idling on the river bank. They shared with us their *aguardiente*, which means water with teeth and is home-made sugar cane rum, an intensely agreeable drink. They offered to sell us twenty-four kilos of cocaine, presumably unrefined coca paste, for nine million soles, about five hundred dollars. They said they had the stuff under chunks of salt there on the shore. Thanks to the coca trade, Ney finds it hard to hire boatman for a dollar a day.

"These men offer this drink to people on small raft going by," Ney said after we declined their offer. "The man on the raft got cocaine. They get him to talking, they take his cocaine and send him on or kill him."

By 1968, Ney says, he was a-benturing in the U.S. In an aluminum canoe, he started out on the Yellowstone river near Billings, Montana, and three months and five days later he was in New Orleans. Along the way he heard a speech by Ronald Reagan in Kansas City and painted "R. Reagan, 'El Hombre of To-Morrow' " on the side of the canoe. "I told the Republicans, 'If you want a sign on there it cost you three thousand dollars,' and they paid."

He was back and forth between his new home and his old. After Eric Fleming, the trail boss in TV's "Rawhide," drowned in a Peruvian rapid, Ney found the body. He says he took a raft from Belém, Brazil, across the ocean to Trinidad by himself. He did some guiding, kept going back to check on his ancestral gold mine, one thing and another.

Now, he says, "There are no more a-bentures. People gone everywhere. People gone to the moon! People go across the Atlantic in a bathtub! If I had twenty people to put up twenty thousand dollars each I'd do the original Kon-Tiki trip again."

There must be something nobody's done in the Amazon before.

"In the Amazon?" he says. "Commercialize."

The Amazon resists *constructive* commercialization. It can be ripped off for ores and coca, and in fact its flora and fauna are being cleared away by leaps and bounds, in the interest of profit. Enormous stretches of jungle are being burnt off to clear land for cattle to provide American fast-food hamburger meat. The smoke threatens to disrupt the ozone layer around the earth, which would change weather patterns disastrously. In the early eighties an ecologist predicted that the entire rain forest of Brazil, Peru, Ecuador and Colombia, the largest wilderness in the world, could be reduced to mud by the nineties.

That unarable mud, which lies a few inches below the enormously fertile but shallow layer of soil, swallows up planned long-term development. The American billionaire Daniel K. Ludwig realized a loss of $800 million when he pulled out of his Amazonian forestry-rice-and-mining project, which covered land the size of Connecticut.

So Ney has his work cut out for him, making a go of about eight tours a year along the Huallaga to the Mananon to the Ucalali to the Amazon proper, in Peru and sometimes on into Brazil. The economics of this operation are a mystery to me, especially after discussing them with Ney. All I know is that our expedition, whose price was $1,995 including airfare, was undercapitalized. Ney borrowed over four hundred dollars from us gringos in the course of the trip. He paid the builder of our raft a little over a thousand dollars. He sold it at the end of the trip for three hundred dollars. When his Coleman lantern broke down, Heinz and I bought a used one (which broke down) for about sixty dollars. Ney complained that Americans drank an awful lot of instant coffee at eight dollars a jar. And we kept running out of flashlight batteries, which meant that sometimes we travelled at night without navigation lights, because those lights were rigged up from flashlights appropriated from us explorers at unwary moments.

But none of us got sick—thanks to scrupulously prepared food and Ney's insistence that we take two Pepto-Bismol tablets a day. We hadn't even started feeling mutinous yet as we approached the place where the raft awaited.

"*Donde está la balsa grande?*" we cried to everyone we passed along the river as darkness fell, and then, at a place called Pellejo Island, we came upon her: the Yacu-Mama.

We clambered aboard. Eight meters wide by fifteen meters long, she floated on huge balsa logs, and she was made of *balina*-tree poles and planks, with rails of capirona wood, walls of *cana brava* cane, and a thatched roof of just-dry *yarina* palm fronds. There were fifteen-foot-long oars, the paddle-ends hand-carved from *renaco* wood, for steering. There was a kitchen area—a hand-made cookstove, mud laid down on poles so that wood could burn on top of the mud—and even a privy, with a real toilet seat and a tablecloth for a door. Most of this was lashed together with bark, though there were some nails.

Inside were two semi-private bedrooms, a big open area and a dining room with a tabletop that showed the marks of the chainsaw on its surface. Up top, reachable by ladder, was a bridge. Ney kept saying the Yacu-Mama was modeled after the Kon-Tiki raft, but what it looked like was an ark, a houseboat, a shaggy treehouse. What I would have called it when I was a boy was *neat*.

"This is the best raft I had!" said Ney.

It was neat.

We lived on it.

It floated on the four-miles-per-hour dry-season current, with intermittent push and positioning provided by a *peque-peque*, which is what Ney called the sixteen-horse, rope-cranked Briggs and Stratton motor with a ten-foot drive shaft attached. Ney kept saying, "I want to hear the *peque-peque*."

"That's right," Fred would say. "We were just beginning to hear birds. That noise really offends the sensibilities of a sailboatman."

So the *peque-peque* would fall silent. But not for long. But then too it wouldn't work for long either. Nor would the supplementary forty-horse Yamaha outboard that finally arrived from somewhere to replace the one that Ney said was stolen before it reached us.

"*Ha*-ha-ha!" Ney said when both motors were going at once, but that was seldom, because they kept breaking down and it is hard to get things fixed in Amazonia. There was an endless delay in the village of Lagunas as we waited for a mechanic to arrive and then as he cut a gasket from a cardboard box, a gasket that worked for a shorter time than it took to install.

It was never clear what our schedule was. "In Peru," Ney said, "you tell a guy you going to meet him at seven, he show up at nine, you have a fight. From that fight is born ten fights, everybody want to help. Now each of those guys is late to meet somebody else."

"I bought a monkey named Blanca for two hundred thousand soles, a turtle who never got named for fifty thousand, a little green parrot named Rosita for one hundred thousand, a puppy named Tipico for sixty thousand."

Here are some things I remember about our life on the water.

Our chickens clucking and scratching on the roof. We acquired these chickens for the equivalent of nine dollars each in the market at Yurimagua (where chicken feet and chicken *heads* were being cooked as snacks on braziers). One by one we ate them. We didn't eat the rooster—who crowed early in the morning, when Heinz didn't grab him and throw him in a sack first—until the last day. Ney identified with the rooster, and pouted when Heinz sacked him. When the rooster crowed Lidia would always echo him: "Chi-chimaraaada."

It wasn't just chicken we ate. Huge filets from horrible-looking catfish of various kinds, some fresh and some dried (the only portion I had trouble warming to was from a batch of insufficiently-dried that I'd seen Lidia scraping maggots off of). Potatoes and potatoish yucca, mangoes with lime juice, beans, rice, a vivid beets-and-peas-and-potato salad, various hearty soups (one of which was augmented by quantities of melting gnats one unusually buggy evening), and some red meat that Julia, when asked, said was "bief."

"It monkey meat," said Ney. "They change the name to protect the innocent."

From then on, David, who wouldn't eat the gnat soup on the grounds that he was unaccustomed to such things, wanted to know what everything was.

It wasn't just chickens we kept, either. I bought a monkey named Blanca for two hundred thousand soles, a turtle who never got named for fifty thousand, a little green parrot named Rosita for one hundred thousand, a puppy named Tipico for sixty thousand (to replace the puppy named Inca, who got so sick we left him with the coca-dealing salt miners), a marmoset for one hundred thousand.

The marmoset needed no name. He was a pistol. In the face he looked exactly like a movie gremlin. He was smaller than an explorer's hand but had more attitude than any four whole explorers put together. He would jump down onto the dinner table, wade right through somebody's beans and go headfirst into the lemonade. So during meals we kept him in a bag, where he expostulated like an arrested diplomat. One night he sat on the rafter above Jim's hammock and screamed, as if hailing a cab, until Jim stuck up his hand and the marmoset ran down his arm to his armpit, where he spent the rest of the night. The marmoset and the little green parrot were about the same size. Finding themselves on the same rafter, they fought toe to toe like King Kong and the dinosaur.

There were two macaws. They were purchased, on credit, by Ney, because macaws sell for over a thousand dollars in the States. The macaws kept to themselves on the roof. Their wings were clipped, but they kept escaping into the river, where they would be on the verge of drowning when John or Heinz or one of the boatmen would save them. One night there was a cold windstorm and the macaws were brought in and placed under my hammock. I didn't mind the marmoset in my underarm—if he tossed and turned I could always throw him over toward the next hammock, where Lidia and Alicia slept together head-to-toe—but macaws under my hammock gave me nightmares, and I woke up completely disoriented, thinking things had changed somehow, I'd been shanghaied; I woke up wild, prepared to fight, it was pitch dark, I stumbled to the side of the raft and there was Ney.

"Where are we?" I asked him.

"The Amazon," he said. The boatmen who were supposed to keep us going all night had gone to sleep (they huddled without sleeping bags along the raft's edge, drinking *coosi-wassi*, a formidable bark-and-sugarcane liquor, to ease their rheumatism). The wind had slowed us down, we had run aground, we only had four more hours of gas and Ney needed to borrow 380,000 soles from us to get two more barrels of gas.

I was glad I wasn't in his business.

"They all crooks on the river," he said. "The governor of a town in Brazil one time sold

NEY ORLOTEGUI—"NOT AN
EASY MAN TO FIGURE."
(COURTESY OF NEY ORLOTEGUI)

me two barrels half gas half water—the water goes to the bottom. I report him."

To whom?

"To the other governor."

There were long slow periods when we were drifting down along the wide brown-green, scum-flecked water, catching sight of gray or blue freshwater dolphins, looking at mud banks brightened by lime-green strips of young rice plants, waiting for Ney to give us a straight answer as to what we were going to do next.

During one of those periods Ney was lying on the bridge in the midday sun. Then he was up pacing, planning a crow's nest for the next raft, worrying about not going fast enough, making general business-administration statements: "I used to work for pleasure but I learned not to do that. Got to have capital." Then all of a sudden he was down the ladder and off the boat.

And wading to the riverbank. John and Heinz went off with him. Heinz ran ahead to get pictures of the raft from a distance. By the time I changed into my bathing suit the raft was a hundred yards from the shore. I swam in, and pretty soon Ney, John and I were in mud up to our ribcages.

This was great mud. Like modeling clay only thinner, like cake icing only thicker. There was firm footing underneath, and if we walked briskly the surface would just support our weight, so we could squooch in and out at will. We daubed each other, we turned ourselves into mudmen, we pretended to be descending into and then emerging from the primeval ooze.

"Now *this* is fun," John said. "What other guide . . . ?"

W e never knew what to expect. "What other guide . . . ?" remained the essential question, but it acquired less approving connotations.

To us gringos, with our support systems, the Amazon itself wasn't maddening. Repellent kept mosquitoes from being much of a problem to anyone except Stephen, who for some reason was a martyr to them. The heat wasn't punishing. There were card games and plenty of opportunities to stop and acquire beer and rum and Inca Cola. At night we could sing "Vaya Con Dios" and "Cielito Lindo" with Julia, Lidia and Alicia.

To us it was Ney who was maddening.

Ney, Jim, Fred and I are hiking through a stretch of jungle with a man from the nearest village (Ney knows a lot of people). The local guy hits a rubber tree with his machete and latex runs down. Ney hands Jim a guava fruit, he bites into it, passes it back to me without looking at it, I see it is crawling with worms. Local guy chops down a forty-foot palm tree at Ney's behest to get one heart of palm for salad. (I hit it a couple of licks and it's as hard as a railroad tie and clangs like metal.) We pass by a thorn tree with an orange impaled on it.

"What's that tree?" Fred says.

"Orange tree," says Ney, who seems to be in a hurry.

"With thorns? What's that, over there. *That* looks like an orange tree."

"Thass an orange tree," says Ney.

"But the fruit are yellow," says Jim.

"Yes. Grapefruit," says Ney.

"Oh," says Fred, picking one of the fruit. It is as big as a grapefruit. "But it smells like lemon."

"Yes, lemon," says Ney.

E veryone is grumbling. I talk to Ney on the bridge, ask him to brief us more often. Granted, it's difficult for him, because various of us explorers have various thresholds of adventure, but if he'd just. . . .

"I gonna really walk those waitresses," he says.

"Waitresses?"

"Yes. *Alpiniste.*"

"Alpinist waitresses?"

"Waitresses, bartenders, *all* walks of life. Gonna be my next group."

"Oh. What. . . ."

"I had all kinds of animals on the raft one time, capybara, ocelot, but the police say I got to register them. Where I gonna get birth certificates for all those animals?"

"What are we going to do next?"

"Three days off the raft, in the jungle."

"Three days?"

"Yeah. I never did it before."

"I'm not sure everybody—"

"We try it. If somebody don't like it, it's only an hour walk back to the raft."

"Well, you ought to tell them all that, then."

"Only thing, won't be any food on the raft."

"Well, then, how—"

"It's a spermint."

We got off the raft at a village called Esperanza and walked two hours into the jungle. Bromeliad growing on trees. Vegetation finally closing over our heads. A cypress big around as any California redwood, whose top we couldn't see and whose roots grew above the ground for great distances in all directions, because the soil was too shallow for them to grow downward.

Then we took dugout cedar canoes down the Rio Yanayaquillo. Along the way, some of us caught piranha—panfish-range in size—on cheap rods and reels (not nearly enough to go around), malfunctioning plastic bobbers and hooks so flimsy the piranha bit through them. (Cut-up savalo, or piranha, for bait.) I'll say this: Ney caught a strapping piranha on a hook that had no barb or point and hardly any crook left on it. I don't know how he did it. Ney could fish. Arranging for everybody else to catch fish, or to be happy while some caught fish, was another matter.

They were good fish to catch, the bigger ones fat and game as crappie, and sautéed with lemon they were good, if oily. (I'll also say this: thanks to Ney, I am the only person I know who has caught, and eaten, and been partially eaten by, piranha.) Ney would cut their lips away with a knife so we could see their teeth. If you held a leaf in front of its mouth, a caught piranha would take a semicircle out of it clean as a cookie cutter.

But we were out into some rough country now and we had no idea how long we were going to be there or under what circumstances. Suddenly Ney pulled us up onto a bar. We scrambled up it through sucking mud, and a whole new group of Peruvians materialized. In half an hour, with machetes, they had cleared a camping space and built a shelter for us. Impressive.

But what are our sleeping arrangements? We've brought sleeping bags, but now that we're not moving the mosquitoes are more intimidating, and Ney has been pooh-poohing talk of netting.

Time now to go off into the darkness hunting cayman. John, Fred, Jim, Stephen and I, in two dugouts with one paddle between us. I hold on to the second dugout so that it's pulled along by the strokes of a Peruvian in our prow, who holds a flashlight in his teeth, trying to catch the glint of cayman eyes along the banks, and a shotgun in his lap. And it's beginning to rain, so hard that before long the dugouts are within an inch of being filled with rainwater, inside, and the river water is within an inch of the gunwales, outside. I'm bailing with one hand, holding the other dugout with the other, my boots and the copious lap of my rainpants are full of water, and we don't see any cayman. Which are alligators. Nor do any of them see us, thank God.

We go back to camp. This is the dry season, but this is also a deluge. And the army-ant venom is beginning to kick in. Army ants are a good inch long. While the shelter was being built we saw a bunch of them running up a tree, and Ney said, "Less burn 'em up" and poured kerosene on them and tried to light it. I jumped in with David's cigarette lighter, and the ants got on me, biting me on each knee, through my rainpants, and on every knuckle of the left hand except one.

"Nothing in the jungle will bother you unless you bother it," Ney chose that moment to advise me. "I used to sell these ants. Suuuure. Six dollars for two of them. I advertise them in *Argosy* and *Field and Stream*. First you have to spray them once, with liquid starch, and they go into a comeback posture. Then you have to spray them again and they stay that way, only they fall all apart. Then you have to glue them together. I sell thousands of them. But they make me stop. I have to register, they say...."

Each of my army ant bites, when we come back from hunting cayman soaking wet, feels like I have been hit on that spot by a small ball-peen hammer.

There are nowhere near enough mosquito nets to go around, let alone hammocks. "If there's a hammock for everybody," says Ney, "where's de 'benture?"

He has a hammock. He ties it to our shelter, and gets in. The whole side of the shelter caves in.

I don't want to discuss that night's sleep any further. Sharing one single-size mosquito netting with John, wet, lying on palm-frond stems, mosquitoes getting in, ant bites throbbing.... I have slept in a foxhole with a moth in my middle ear, I have slept in an English Ford with angry dogs jumping up at the windows, I have slept under a desk on industrial carpet in a tweed suit and tie, but I think that night's sleep in the rain forest is the worst I ever had.

But when the night is over, it is no time to fade. This is our deepest penetration into the jungle, and Ney says if we keep going further up the Yanayaquillo we could see capybara (the world's largest rodent, big as a boxer dog only short-legged and portly), jaguar, who knows.

Half of the party returns to the raft, but John, Heinz, Fred, Jim, Ney, Julia, Fermin, the lieutenant governor of Esperanza (who serenades Julia with a song called "Culpado"), one of his constituents and I go on further. At last we get into country that approximates the Rousseau painting I'd imagined the Amazon to be: the waterway narrowing down to a lurky closeness; the vegetation arching over; the awful ratcheting noise of uncaptured macaws; a sound like wind or distant traffic that Ney says is monkeys; huge blue butterflies flashing artificially vivid, like the animated bluebirds painted onto the film in *Song of the South*. The unelected Esperanzan reaches abruptly under a stump and pulls out—what? What is that? A needle nose, an obscene (to my way of thinking) neck, a prehistoric aspect generally: the matamata turtle, which Hollywood hasn't caught up with yet.

In our dugouts, sitting on jammed-in sticks of cane, we limbo under limbs that lie a foot above the water, we keep floating forward as we step over logs, all the while catching the odd piranha and untangling the more frequent backlash.

And Ney keeps conferring with the lieutenant governor and then saying that further on, maybe an hour further, there could be anaconda, there could be pure Indian villages where they don't wear shorts....

And our fellow explorers, not to mention the whole kitchen operation, are back at the raft now, and we're not as far along toward Iquitos as we should be. If anything is clear, it is that we are not going to spend three days in the jungle; we are going back to the Yacu-Mama.

Fred said later, "I think we weinied out a little bit on the jungle." So did Daniel K. Ludwig.

"I have slept in a foxhole with a moth in my middle ear, I have slept in an English Ford with angry dogs jumping up at the windows, I have slept under a desk on industrial carpet in a tweed suit and tie, but I think that night's sleep in the rain forest is the worst I ever had."

Not that weinieing out, in itself, is a piece of cake. We canoe back to where we have to walk seven miles through mud, carrying packs, along a trail that we can't get lost on because Ney marked it on the way in. Right.

My feeling is, let's all stick together on the way back. John's feeling is, he wants to go full-tilt. Over a trail which, after that rain, is like the inside of an exotic alimentary canal—dank, dully glistening, sloshy, contracting, ingestive.

John and I have hung out with Steelers together, been to spring training together, swum in Georgia waters together, and one night when he was a little kid we walked on the tops of cars together, after *Singin' in the Rain*. Walking on cars together is when you are out with all your loved ones and feeling so good the sidewalk won't hold you. But forty-four and seventeen, father and son, are awkward ages. And I was damned if I was going to let him get lost in the jungle, on the one hand, or outwalk me, on the other.

He and I beat everybody else—except for the anonymous Esperanzan, who caught us just as John was hurtling into a wrong turn—out of the jungle by half an hour. "We're in Peru!" I was reminding John at the top of my voice, "Wait up!"—breaking my neck to keep him in sight or at least hearing, *sprinting* through foot-deep puddles and over thigh-level logs. At the point of the nearly-taken wrong turn, there was an altercation, loud on my part. Semi-vindicated, and pumped, I threw what might well be my last effective (*I* led the rest of the way out of the jungle, and just as—or just about as—fast) paternal tantrum. Sometimes you'd think I was as crazy as Ney's father.

Or at least that's one way of looking at it: I went wild because my son, whom I have proudly watched tackling people half again his size, was not afraid enough of the jungle to suit me. Not as afraid of it as I was, in other words. By the time he's my age the jungle may have been devoured, indirectly, by the customers of McDonald's, and I cost him a chance to be alone in it.

Or you could look at it this way: had I not been so obnoxiously paternal, my son would have been swallowed by that wrong turn. To my way of thinking, this view was supported, inadvertently, by Ney: *he* got lost on the way back. Granted, he made it back to the raft after a while. Fermin got so lost that darkness fell on him and we left him behind. The way Ney looked at it, Fermin had abandoned us. But some of us explorers imagined him thrashing around in circles in the dark. "He is not a jungle boy," said Julia. Granted, he caught up with us a couple of days later, down the river.

If a father could stay in touch *and* a son could be on his own. Life is muddy. I'll say this: I'll bet we picked up that Esperanzan's pace a little.

For the next two days John and I weren't on speaking terms, except when I congratulated him on saving one of the macaws from drowning. He and Heinz would swim alongside the moving raft, or man the steering oars, and do photography together, and in the villages John petted all the dogs (many of which looked almost as bad as the matamata turtle) and ran through the streets with flocks of little kids.

Ney had one more trek in mind. We were to walk a couple of hours across a neck of land and meet the raft, coming around the peninsula under brother Aldo's command, at the village of Nauta.

We disembarked. Moved easily over a long mud flat, through some farmer's rice field, to the high ground, where it struck Ney that we had disembarked in the wrong place. He ran off hollering, "ALDO!" Aldo (who incidentally believed he had malaria) eventually heard, and brought the raft back to the bank half a mile downriver.

So we cut across toward him, shaking our heads: Ney had done it again. John, Fred, Jim and I were ahead of the others.

The ground through here was softer. We began to have trouble walking. The mud pulled our shoes off, so we had to carry them. The raft was still a couple of hundred yards ahead and the going was slower and slower. We were up to our ankles. This stuff was less supportive than the fun mud, and it didn't seem to have the solid layer underneath—I tested, reaching down with one foot, something I soon regretted. Pretty soon we were up nearly to our knees, pulling ourselves along with our hands. "You know," I said to Fred, "I could see how an animal could get caught in this, and flounder and never get out."

Fred had been trained in the Marines that the way to negotiate quicksand was to get down flat on top of it and swim. But this wasn't quicksand, it was slow mud. The term "sinking sensation" took on a new meaning for me.

You had to push down hard to get any traction, but when you pushed down hard you got in deeper, and every time you pulled your hand or foot out it was heavier with mud.

Nobody made conversation. We labored. The more I strained, the more mired I got, and the more I tried to be casual and take it slow, the more time the mud had to draw me down.

Crawling now, I thought of the animals we were offered in the village of Santa Maria, a couple of days before. Everywhere we went, kids tried to sell us pets—a monkey with a cord around its stomach that looked like it had been there all its life (that was Blanca—we took the cord off after we bought her and in time she escaped), an unfledged baby bird whose rudimentary wings the kids made flapping motions with, and now here was some strange animal that ten or twelve kids were gathered around. They were smiling those fresh smiles, laughing innocently, and holding up this animal that I couldn't quite see. . . .

The group spread at my approach and held this animal up toward me—*and pulled something out of its stomach.*

It was nightmarish. Whatever the thing from the stomach was, the kids were playing roughly with it, tucking it back in and then pulling it back out—the thing was a fetus, still connected umbilically to its evidently marsupial mother's pouch.

"What is *that*?" I said.

"It's a monkey," said Ney.

"No, it's some kind of marsupial."

"Rat," said Ney.

"It's a Indian rabbit," said Julia.

"It's got *short ears*," I said.

"Squirrel. Indian squirrel."

I think it was a South American possum. Whatever it was, it was stuck where it didn't want to be. And so was the second animal we were offered there, the one that looked like a wookie in the face. It was a baby sloth. The kids who had it were tossing it around. Carol and John took it and cuddled it, but it seemed inconsolable. Set on the ground it would reach . . . out . . . its . . . arm . . . in . . . an . . . agonizingly . . . slow . . . and . . . hopeless . . . sort . . . of . . . move . . . toward . . . advancement, while emitting an unearthly noise, a long, slow, high-pitched *eeeeeeee.*

We thought of adopting this sloth but what it needed was its mother, and Ney said, "The two things in the jungle that got the most diseases: the sloth and the turtle." Of course we had just bought a turtle that morning at Ney's urging. But nobody wanted to hear that *eeeeeeee* on the raft at night.

I'm not saying we were in as bad shape as that sloth when we were in the bad mud, but we were proceeding with great difficulty. It came to me that I might actually not make it to the raft. I had reached the point where I was progressing about three inches every time I

reached forward, and I couldn't get one knee clear without getting the other one so deep that I couldn't get it anywhere near clear. I was still ten yards from the raft and the mud was getting softer.

Fred made it out under his own steam by carrying two flotsam logs with him, putting them down in front of him and pulling forward. John and the boatmen slithered right on out and came back with a rope to tow the rest of us out one by one.

My rainpants were full of mud and I saw that the flashlight in my waistband had been sticking straight down, adding a lot of drag. But I still felt dismayed. When I was eleven some of the other Boy Scouts had to hang back toward the end of our fifty-mile bike trip and walk with me up the steepest hills, and I'd been determined ever since not to let something like that happen again. Heinz would probably have made it in without a tow if he hadn't been carrying two cameras. I would have made it if I'd had two weeks. Maybe.

I sat on the side of the raft getting ten pounds of mud off myself and thinking that this was a hard old jungle. I had swum with piranha, played with fire and army ants, drunk beer fermented with spit (I didn't tell you about that—Ney didn't tell me about the spit until after I drank it). But this mud....

The others took their tows serenely. "Honey," said Carol, waiting for Stephen as he was brought in face-first through the glop.

"I'm home," Stephen said.

Hannah, who had said "Bloody hell" when she got her foot wet above Chasuta, came scudding in like a body surfer, as if the mud were a stylish element.

Ney was last. John hooked him up to the towrope and then pushed his face down into the mud. Ney laughed, everybody laughed. After all was said and done, "What other guide ... ?"

"When I saw you having trouble," Hannah told me, "I thought, 'This is serious.' " That helped my feelings some. It was also my sentiments exactly.

When we reached excursion's end in Iquitos—a city of 200,000, the largest city in the jungle—we ascended the mud slope into town by twenty trembling precipitous feet of metal stairway, which was only tenuously connected at a point halfway up and was secured only on one side at the top. Then, at last, pavement. Firm footing.

"They can't build a pier here," Ney said. "Rainy season, the river comes right into town. It going to carry the best hotel away. Thass right. The river turn the town to mud."

Man-eating fish are one thing. But if anybody tries to get you to go into a twenty thousand-gallon tank full of Peruvian *mud* at Circus Circus, say no. And don't go a-benturing in the Amazon without a stout rope and son.

HIKING TO BASECAMP (HARRY JOHNSON)

William Broyles

▼

CLIMBING ACONCAGUA

I am hanging, exhausted, by my fingertips from a rock ledge twenty-three thousand feet above sea level. First my right foot searches for a dimple in the rock to push from, fails, then my left foot does the same. Finally, my toe catches on a tiny protrusion. I take eight desperate breaths, then push. My left hand goes up to another rock, finds a hold. I breathe eight more times, trying to gather some last shred of strength, and pull.

Above me is more rock and, somewhere, the summit of Mount Aconcagua. Storm clouds are gathering. It is past five in the afternoon, and soon the temperature will fall to twenty below zero. I have climbed four thousand feet since six in the morning, the last thousand feet through a forty-five degree pitch of loose boulders.

For three days I have been unable to eat. I am dehydrated. My breathing comes in irregular gasps. My brain, starved for oxygen, has all but ceased to function. I have become senile, an old man. In the snow on the summit is the body of an Argentine who froze to death after reaching the top a few days before. Five other climbers have died on the mountain in the past month.

This is what mountain climbers call "a non-trivial situation." I have, however, never climbed a mountain in my life, and until a few weeks earlier I owned barely a pocket knife. I am also intensely afraid of heights, and break out in a sweat when I stand near a high window. I can't look down on a ski lift. I have nightmares about falling.

What am I doing here?

I had some reasons that made sense to me, at least at sea level, but the higher I climbed the less convincing they sounded. I had always thought of my life as going up, the direction of growth and progress. But as I approached my forties I began to realize that determination and ambition can sometimes lead up the wrong ladder. Because I had worked so long for success, because I had come to expect it and because I became all-too-accustomed to the trappings that go with it, I took longer than I should have to admit the truth: success was killing me.

Each morning I struggled into my suit and overcoat and picked up my briefcase, went to my glamorous job, and died a little. I was the editor-in-chief of *Newsweek*, a position that in the eyes of others had everything; only it had nothing to do with me. I took little pleasure in running a large institution. I wanted personal achievement, not power. For me, success was more dangerous than failure; failure would have forced me to decide what I really wanted.

The only way out was to quit, but I hadn't quit anything since I abandoned the track team in high school. I had also been a marine in Vietnam, and marines are trained to keep on charging up the hill, no matter what. But I *had* got up the hill; I just hated being there. I had climbed a wrong mountain, and the only thing to do was go down and climb another one. It was not easy: success in my new profession came more slowly than I had expected, and my marriage fell apart.

I needed something, but I wasn't sure what. I knew I wanted to be tested, mentally and physically. I wanted to succeed, but by standards that were clear and concrete, and not dependent on the opinion of others. I wanted the intensity and camaraderie of a dangerous enterprise. In an earlier time, I might have gone West or to sea, but I had two children and a web of responsibilities.

Climbing this mountain was the perfect thing. I could do it in a month, and it had the added advantage of forcing me to confront my deepest fear—of falling, being out of control, going down. I knew that just getting on the mountain would take all my courage, and I liked the idea of that.

A concagua (the name means rock sentinel) is in the southern Andes 670 miles west of Buenos Aires. Most atlases give its height as 22,835 feet, but the Argentines surveyed the peak recently and claim it is in fact 7021 meters, or 23,036 feet. Aconcagua is the tallest mountain in the Western Hemisphere and the tallest outside Asia. Climbers like those sorts of credentials; they were, in fact, exactly what attracted me.

For serious climbers Aconcagua is more a test of stamina, strength and endurance than skill. The final thousand feet of what is known as the Normal Route is an infamous steep gully of loose rock called the Canaleta; even veterans of Mount Everest consider the Canaleta one of the most demanding physical challenges in mountaineering.

The lack of dramatic technical problems tends to mask the danger of Aconcagua's extreme altitude and unpredictable weather. In a graveyard near the mountain are more than sixty markers in memory of climbers who have died there, and the actual number may exceed a hundred—more than have died on Mount Everest and K2 put together.

I signed up with Sobek Expeditions for a climb leaving at the end of January, then six weeks away. To get in shape, I began running in the mountains above Los Angeles. At first my legs and lungs rebelled against going uphill, but after a few weeks I was running eight miles a day, a pack loaded with rocks on my back. I was feeling strong and confident.

I read everything I could find about mountain climbing. One of my favorite books was *Seven Summits*, by Dick Bass, a Texas oilman and ski resort developer, and Frank Wells, a Hollywood executive. Bass and Wells were successful, self-assured men in their fifties, but like me they wanted more. Their dream was to climb the highest peak in each of the seven continents. Aconcagua was one of them.

I went to see Wells, now the president of the Walt Disney Company, in his office at the corner of Mickey Avenue and Dopey Drive in Burbank. Wells made it up six of those seven summits. I asked him why, given all his success, he would want to take such risks.

"In the beginning," he said, "I did it to set myself apart from everyone else. But by the end I was doing it for the mountains and for the people I climbed with. Unless you've been to the top, you can't explain it—but I can tell you there's nothing like it."

I spoke with Rick Ridgeway, a veteran climber and the co-author of *Seven Summits*. Ridgeway told me he was losing his interest in climbing big mountains.

"Too many objective conditions," he said.

"Objective conditions?" I asked.

"Yeah. Altitude, avalanches, storms, crevasses. You know, objective conditions."

Objective conditions. I liked the sound of that—a welcome relief from the subjective dangers of ordinary life: greed, envy, jealousy, ambition.

Wells had given me the name of Glenn Porzak, a lawyer in Boulder, Colorado, and the chairman of the expeditions committee of the American Alpine Club. Glenn was leaving in March for Makulu, the world's fifth highest mountain. Before dawn on Saturday morning we attacked a mountain northwest of Boulder. We ran the first few miles in our snowshoes, then, when snow gave way to steep rocks, we abandoned the snowshoes and kept climbing into the face of a blizzard. We couldn't see five feet and the wind was blowing so hard we could barely stand.

"What a great day!" Glenn said, rubbing his hands together. But finally the conditions managed to temper even Glenn's enthusiasm, and we went down without reaching the top.

The next day I journeyed to some rocks outside of town for my first lesson in rappelling. The other climbers scampered up a sheer cliff, as smooth as a marble table top. I somehow managed to reach the top, which was covered in ice and snow. I sat down, afraid to move. The edge of the rock formed a rough overhang, which then dropped more than forty feet to the ground.

Before I knew it I was standing at the overhang, the rope run through the carabiners on my waist harness. The rope was still slack; I couldn't believe it would hold me. I felt on the edge of space, not attached to anything. It was exactly the way all my nightmares of falling begin.

I took a breath and then I took a step backwards. The rope tightened and held. I let myself down, a few inches at a time. Suddenly, I was over the cliff and hanging in space. It worked! I let out the rope in bigger and bigger chunks, and too soon I was at the bottom, yelling for joy.

I scrambled back up the rock and stood again on the edge, confident this time. I stepped

"In an instant I was hanging upside down like a ham hung up to cure; blue sky was between my feet, my head aimed at the ground."

backward, leaned back—and my foot slipped. In an instant I was hanging upside down like a ham hung up to cure; blue sky was between my feet, my head aimed at the ground.

After a few anxious moments, I righted myself and carefully let myself down. Afterwards I was a little shaken, and my hands and knees were scraped and bleeding, but my heart was light and happy. I had felt fear on top of the rock, and for good reason: it was dangerous up there. But I realized I had not felt as close to death as I had felt each morning when I went to a job I hated.

One of the benefits of success is the chance to be protected, to have schedules and secretaries and comfortable places to live, shop, play and work—it is to presume to know the future. But that world can come unglued at any moment; its security is an illusion. On the mountain, I couldn't assume things today would be as they were yesterday. A mountain is intense, real; your life—and that of others—is in your hands.

Mountaineering is a sport of narrative, of beginning, middle, end; of form and structure. It is alien to the world of America's new literary elite, in whose work nothing ever happens—or matters. A mountain has no place for conceptual art, atonal music or deconstructionist literary theory. Climbing is the antithesis of post-modern. I began to think it was just what I needed.

After lunch I told Glenn about Aconcagua. Two groups would depart at the same time: one up the Normal Route, the other by way of the more difficult Polish Glacier route. I asked Glenn which one to take. Glenn had reached twenty-seven thousand feet on Everest, and has climbed more than seven hundred different peaks. He climbed Aconcagua by the Normal Route.

"If you want to get to the top, do the Normal Route. You pick the Polish Route, your chances go through the basement."

"But I'm not sure the Normal Route will be challenging enough," I said, in my ignorance.

He looked at me for a long time.

"Don't worry about that," he said.

We began our expedition in Mendoza, a town in the high Argentine desert at the foot of the Andes. In the hotel Harry Johnson, the expedition's leader, went through each of our packs to check our gear. Once I got on the mountain, anything not in my pack might as well not exist. There is a frontier self-sufficiency about it: you are responsible for your own survival, so I had to be prepared for any contingency. I also had to carry everything on my back—a powerful incentive to pare away everything that I didn't absolutely need.

On the bus to Puente del Inca at the foot of the mountain were twelve climbers and four guides. Harry would lead the Normal Route and Daniel Burrieza, one of Argentina's best climbers, would take the Polish Glacier route. I sat next to Ralph Gorton, thirty-one, a former college quarterback and basketball star. A knee injury had ended Ralph's athletic career; after it healed he took up mountaineering as an outlet for his competitive energies. Ralph's athletic abilities were obvious, but I felt reassured by the presence of his friend Mike Larrabee, fifty-three, who looked like a college professor who'd taken up tennis to keep in shape.

"Is Mike all that athletic?" I asked.

Ralph paused. "Well, Mike only won two gold medals at the Olympics in Tokyo. If he'd been athletic, he would have had three."

And so it went for the rest of the group: the bookish-looking doctor, Mitch Flores, who turned out to be one of the leading triathletes in Los Angeles; the quiet, laconic Gabe Papp, a mountaineering instructor; Harry Johnson himself, a wiry elf who came in twenty-ninth in

BROYLES (LEFT) WITH HIS PACK AND (RIGHT) WITH THE TEAM. (HARRY JOHNSON)

the Pikes Peak Marathon; his wife, Diane, just back from a winter ascent of Mount Rainier via the difficult Gibraltar Ledge route; Steve Selbrede, a 2:44 marathoner.

At least, I thought, I had a chance compared to Art Schultz and Kim Baldwin. At sixty, Art was the oldest member of the expedition; he turned out to be a highly competitive veteran of cross-country ski marathons around the world.

Kim, then? Small-boned, thin, and shy, she hardly looked the mountaineering type.

"Is Kim really up for this?" I asked Mitch.

"We'll see," Mike said. "She set the record in the Seal Beach Triathlon, and a few years ago she won the junior world windsurfing championship."

Was this the place for a forty-two-year-old jogger? I was beginning to wonder.

Halfway to Puente del Inca we stopped for Argentine barbecue. The local bus from the mountains arrived and some climbers staggered out, looking exhausted and dirty, with that same distant stare I remembered on the faces of the marines who were leaving Vietnam as I arrived. What had they seen, that I was about to see?

We talked to a young American who had just come off the summit. The news he had was about death.

"The weather's been bad," he said. "Two Japanese are still missing. A Frenchman and a Spaniard were swept away by an avalanche on the South Face. All they found was one glove. There's the body of an Argentine right on the summit."

We climbed back on the bus, sobered. Two Japanese. Missing. A Frenchman and a Spaniard, swept away by an avalanche—only one glove found. An Argentine. On the summit. Where we were going.

When we arrived at the hostel at Puente del Inca, I hiked up to the little church at the foot of the mountains. Nearby are the ruins of the old hotel, destroyed by an avalanche that leapt over the church and crushed the hotel. Inside I felt safe, protected, as if in the presence of some secret for appeasing the mountain.

Ralph, Mike Larrabee, Gabe Papp and Steve Selbrede were taking the Polish Route, and that night among their team there was mounting anxiety. Daniel had proposed a direct climb up a fifty-degree slope of ice. Ralph and Mike were skeptical; eighteen hundred vertical feet of ice that steep seemed too much to take on at twenty-two thousand feet. Ralph handed me a sweater he'd bought for his daughter.

"If anything happens to me," he said, "be sure my little girl gets this."

That night I weighed my pack on Mike's scale; forty-six pounds, not counting tents, food, stoves, and other community gear I'd carry.

Gabe and Ralph picked up my pack and put it on my back. The straps bit down into my shoulders; I could barely keep my balance. I walked down to the end of the hall and when I got back to the room I was out of breath. How was I possibly going to climb the fourteen thousand vertical feet between Puente del Inca and the summit?

That night I lay awake in my bunk, listening to the others breathe, worrying whether I was up to this. I thought of that body on the summit, lying there in the snow, a sentinel.

The next morning the Polish Route team, reassured of its option to take a safer route, jammed into the back of a truck and departed for their trailhead. As we waited for the truck to come back for us I talked to Harry.

Harry is thirty-one and since 1983 has owned Genet Expeditions of Talkeetna, Alaska. For all his familiarity with mountains and glaciers Harry grew up a few miles from me, in the bayous and inlets along Galveston Bay. And so we sat in the bar at Puente del Inca in the Andes and talked of gigging flounder and crabbing with mullet heads for bait, of water moccasin and alligator gar and killing fish with dynamite and treeing coons with Coleman lanterns.

We were interrupted by a mountain policeman, who summoned us to the stone police headquarters where the chief and some of his cohorts sat warming themselves in front of a fire. The Chief had a single request: take a silver cross to the summit and bury it with the Argentine climber whose body was lying there, frozen and abandoned.

"It is very hard for the widow," the chief said, "knowing he is there, unburied."

At that altitude, no one is strong enough to carry a body down the steep side of a mountain. We could only promise to bury it in a pile of rocks, off the summit.

As we squeezed into the truck, everyone was subdued. We were no longer simply an expedition. We were a burial party.

The truck let us out in a high mountain meadow dotted with grazing horses. Wildflowers were everywhere, each besieged by clusters of bees. We could hear the bells around the horses necks, and the sound of birds singing. To our right was the Horcones River, roaring in its gorge down from the peaks. Ahead were mountains capped with snow and clouds high above them.

As I stood there in the soft meadow, dressed only in shorts and a T-shirt, I realized that the high clouds were not that: they were the mountain, Aconcagua, looming above the smaller peaks, a huge mass of gray and white plumed by a streaming cloud that seemed torn out of the snowy summit. The mountain was still almost thirty miles away. I wanted to visualize myself on the summit, but it was too distant and too immense; my imagination failed.

As so I abandoned that distant goal for a more realistic one. I put on my pack and followed the others up the trail along the river—one step at a time.

The landscape was sheer and stark. High above us were striated ledges, massive rock cathedrals perched atop ridgelines fourteen thousand feet high. Buttes bathed in iron and copper ore rose out of great fields of scree scarred by the course of water and avalanche.

The wind began to howl down the valley. We could walk only by putting our heads down and leaning into it. Suddenly from nowhere came a hailstorm and we were pelted with stinging ice. In fifteen minutes the temperature dropped forty degrees and kept falling. Moments before we had been sweating. Now we were chilled to our bones. Finally we reached a little valley laced with waterfalls and carpeted with the last hardy remnants of grass. We had on all the clothes in our packs, but we were still shivering. We sat in the shelter of the rocks, former strangers, holding each other tight for warmth.

The next day we were up early. Twenty miles to go. We left the valley and emerged into the riverbed. The wind was worse, blowing down from the mountain like a message: stay away. With the wind came dust, clouds of it, choking and blinding us. I could walk only by pulling my bandana over my nose and mouth. Hours passed.

For the last six miles we began climbing in earnest, on narrow rock trails clinging to cliffs high above the river, twisting back and forth, sliding on loose rock, switchback after switchback. Aconcagua had disappeared. We were looking instead at Cerro del Cuerno, rising elegantly above a bed of snow at the end of the valley. But through gaps in the wall of peaks to the right, I could catch glimpses of something massive and mysterious. We were coming to it at last.

After another steep section across a barren moonscape of boulders we suddenly emerged at Plaza de Mulas, our base camp—two small ledges more than fourteen thousand feet above sea level, the same altitude as the summit of Mt. Whitney, the tallest mountain in the Continental United States. We had come five thousand vertical feet from Puente del Inca; we had nine thousand feet to go.

"**W**here's the mountain?" I asked Harry.

"You're under it," he said, gesturing behind him. I looked and there it was, rising above me in tier after tier of cliffs and rock, massive, endless, sublimely indifferent. I had to lean backward to see the top, and all at once it seemed vain and pointless to be pitching our tents on this tiny shelf. Who did we think we were?

Not five minutes after we arrived a figure came staggering off the mountain like a portent. Beneath his parka his face was frostbitten and white as ivory, cheekbones gleaming through the skin. His eyes were sunken, his lips cracked and grey. He walked awkwardly, as if his legs were stumps, and he held his hands out at an odd angle. He looked eighty years old.

He was in fact a Yugoslav in his twenties, and in a slow, halting voice he told his story to Mitch Flores, the doctor.

"We were caught in a storm just below the summit. We had to bivouac overnight at twenty-one thousand feet." He paused for breath. "You've got to come see my friend. He's much worse than I am."

Much worse? I could hardly believe it, but he was right. His friend was in a state of near shock. His hands were black and purple, the skin blistered and dead. There was nothing Mitch could do but send them down the mountain.

"He'll have to have the dead tissue cut away under sterile conditions," Mitch said. "He'll lose his fingers, but at least it looks like he'll keep his thumbs—that's what counts."

I had never given my fingers and toes a good deal of thought, but I was thinking how much I liked them. I had had romantic ideas about climbing a mountain. But the dead Argentine on the summit, the missing French and Spanish climbers, the frostbitten Yugoslavs—they no doubt had romantic ideas as well. To climb a mountain is to accept certain risks; I was being reminded that the risks were real.

We had spaghetti for dinner. It was delicious, but I had a hard time eating. I was in the throes of the first stages of altitude sickness. Above fourteen thousand feet, the air contains less than half the oxygen it does at sea level, and the body's ability to absorb the available oxygen is dramatically reduced.

If we had been transported directly from sea level to the summit of Aconcagua our bodies would have had only one response: unconsciousness followed by death. Given time, however, the body begins to adapt to high altitude, which is why high-altitude climbs are slow, careful projects. The process, acclimatization, is seldom a smooth one, and affects virtually all of the bodily functions. Severe headaches, shortness of breath, disorientation, loss of appetite, palpitations, nausea, insomnia, dehydration, clumsiness, and impairment of short term mem-

"That night the wind blew even harder. The ropes holding my tent creaked and moaned; the sides vibrated as if they were being hit by a giant fist."

ory are common symptoms. I would have them all.

The degree to which a climber suffers these symptoms is less a question of conditioning than genetics. For some climbers who adapt poorly, high altitude can quickly kill. With pulmonary edema, capillaries in the lungs burst, filling them with fluid; if the climber does not get down at once, he literally drowns. With cerebral edema, tiny blood vessels in the brain rupture and the climber becomes confused and disoriented and then loses consciousness. Cerebral edema can develop with frightening speed, even during sleep, when the symptoms can be masked until it is too late.

That night the wind blew even harder. The ropes holding my tent creaked and moaned; the sides vibrated as if they were being hit by a giant fist. At times the wind simply picked up the floor of the tent and shook it. The wind kept attacking me, searching me out, probing for weaknesses.

For a moment there was a lull, then I heard the wind coming down the mountain again like a jet engine taking off. I held my hands over my ears. Whenever I drifted off to sleep I was jolted awake by the image of my tent sailing over the nearby cliff. It was as if the mountain were trying to throw me off, as if I were a tiny irritant it wanted to be rid of.

I began to think perhaps this was all a big mistake. Faint, dizzy, nauseous and, I had to confess, scared, I resolved to go back down first thing in the morning. It was a wonderfully soothing idea. This wasn't like Vietnam; I could go home any time I wanted. Then I became angry with myself. I wasn't a quitter. At dawn I finally fell asleep, and when I woke up the sun had already begun to warm my tent. I was feeling better; the panic of the night before seemed a bad dream.

On the fourth day after leaving Puente del Inca we were to begin the move up to Nido de Condores ("Condor's Nest") at eighteen thousand feet, our next camp. We loaded our packs with extra tents, food, fuel, and high-altitude climbing gear. We would cache our supplies at Nido and return to base camp to rest and acclimatize before we climbed up for good. Every ounce of food or equipment we needed would go up the mountain on our backs. These "carries" are the essence of mountaineering. They allow the climber to survive at increasingly high altitudes. Before the summit come many days of painstakingly raising supplies higher and higher, step by burdensome step. You climb a mountain by building your own ladder.

We left for Nido before the sun hit our tents. The trail went all but straight up. I stopped constantly: to peel off my clothes in the sun, to put them back on when the wind picked up, to cover my feet with moleskin to ward off my developing blisters, to drink some water, to chew some raisins—anything to get relief from the weight of my pack.

I settled into a pace: step, breathe, step, breathe. My mind kept churning up strange fragments as I climbed: *The Book of Common Prayer*, poetry, obscure rock-and-roll lyrics, my children, women. When the fragments stopped coming I tried counting, then I began alphabetizing the months of the year, and the numbers from one to ten. Climbing a mountain is like being a prisoner of war. You have to fight to keep order in your mind, you even have to fight your mind itself—since the mind, being rational, wants to quit.

I began thinking about how different this mountain was from my career. I had worked hard, yes, but I had also vaulted over many others to reach the top—almost by magic. There was none of that here—no pushy kid getting a chance to direct, no favorite of the chairman on the inside track, none of the vagaries of ambition and success. There is, in fact, only one way to climb a mountain—one step at a time. There are no shortcuts. Good public relations doesn't help, nor does office politics or fast talking or good connections. No one can take the steps for you. You make it, or you don't.

NIDO DE CONDORES
(HARRY JOHNSON)

Because of my several stops, the strongest climbers had gotten considerably ahead of me. I knew that I should keep my own pace, but the competitor in me wanted to catch up. So I pushed myself—a mistake. In climbing mountains you don't compete with other climbers, only with yourself—and with the mountain. The climbers ahead of me were in their twenties and early thirties. They climbed mountains, ran marathons and competed in triathlons. I wanted to be young; they *were* young. Never had the difference between desire and reality been so powerfully etched in my mind.

I caught up with the others, and together we climbed another two thousand feet to the edge of a snowfield. Then the altitude hit me. My pack was a powerful hand pushing me down into the snow. Each step took tremendous effort. I had to breathe once, twice, three times, then concentrate as hard as I could, lift my foot up and set it down.

Halfway across the snowfield was a small rocky area. I decided I would try to make it there and then rest—a simple goal, but everything was conspiring against me: the glare from the snow, my fatigue, the altitude. I couldn't distract my mind any longer. Its message was clear. Stop. Go down. This is pointless. Make things easier. Set down your burdens. Ease your pain.

I wanted to listen, but the rhythm of breathing and then taking a step had taken on a force of its own, and I kept going. At last I reached the rocks, collapsed, and wriggled out of my pack. My breathing was arrhythmic and labored: instant emphysema.

I took a swallow of water and stood up. After considerable struggle, I got my pack back on. I kept thinking I was going to faint. I began my breathing pattern again—one, two—what comes next?—oh yes, three. The snowfield seemed never to end. After an hour I emerged at the foot of a rocky ridge, which I climbed with great difficulty—four breaths to the step now—but the ridge led only to another ridge. Despair. The summit of Aconcagua loomed directly above me. I couldn't bring myself to look at it.

I inched my way up the last ridge and emerged onto another snowfield. Nido de Condores. I had made it. I staggered over to where the rest of the group was unloading the supplies and simply collapsed. Harry took one look at me and told me to get back to base camp; he and the others would follow later.

I had to go lower, to find more oxygen to feed the starving cells of my mind and body. In fact, my mind had already shut down. I remember the snowfield going up, and I remember it going down, but I remember nothing about Nido de Condores. When I returned there three days later, it was as if I were seeing the place for the first time.

As I lay in my tent back at base camp, exhausted, trying to recover the luxury of automatic breathing, I realized how focused my life had suddenly become. Back in real life I had been waging a losing battle against distraction. The older I got, the harder it was for me to concentrate. Decisions were more difficult to make: the stakes were higher. Each choice meant others were foreclosed. But on the mountain there were no phone calls, no meetings, no other responsibilities—no choices. I was concentrating, thinking of nothing else. The only problem was, I could barely think at all.

That night I tried to tell a story at dinner, but I forgot the punch line. We talked about politics for a few minutes but I couldn't remember a single country in Central America. My mind had become a stranger.

I walked out under the stars, vomited up everything I had eaten that day, and then slept well, without dreams. The wind had died down. Perhaps the mountain was going to let us climb it after all.

The next day it became clear that I was not alone in feeling the altitude. Two Germans, experienced Alpine climbers, abandoned the mountain. Art, the oldest member of our group and a strong climber, had decided to go down, and several others were sick. For two days we stayed in camp.

I wandered from tent to tent, talking to my fellow climbers. For Kim Baldwin, twenty-six, this climb came at a crossroads in her life. She had just sold her interest in a windsurfing store, and she had yet to decide what to do next. The climb up to Nido was sobering for her. "I'm not sure what it's going to take to get me to the top. I'm used to going through the pain threshold, but being in shape is not what gets you up. The higher you get, the more mental it becomes."

Warren Cordner, fifty-nine, lives in Lake Tahoe. He sold his company, First Thrift of America, in 1979 and decided he wanted to "chase down some windmills—climb some mountains, run some marathons, the things I never got to do because I was working too hard. My friends think I'm nuts to do this. They say I don't want to get old—and they're right; I don't. Why should I? I'm going to get old kicking and screaming. I'd like to get to the top, but I've failed before. The trick to life is not to win—it's getting back up when you lose and trying again."

Warren's son Kelly, thirty-three, went to an exclusive Los Angeles prep school and has an M.B.A from UCLA. Kelly was the last climber to bed and the first one up, his infectiously enthusiastic voice the alarm clock for the camp. He has been hiking and climbing since he was eight, and is confident and unintimidated by the mountain or, one senses, by anything else; he seems immune to the altitude.

Ernie Fregoso, twenty-seven, grew up a runner and football player in the barrio of Anaheim, where all but one of his six brothers and sisters still live. He worked his way through high school in a tire shop, then took a semester of auto body in junior college. He was going nowhere when the father of one of his Anglo friends offered him a job selling real estate. A natural salesman, Ernie prospered, and soon he and his partner owned two real estate offices with more than thirty agents. Charismatic and funny, Ernie was the camp's entertainer.

"Before Christmas I had never been on a mountain," he told me. "But I was bored; everything had come too easily. I wanted something that looked like I couldn't reach. I'm determined to get to the top—I won't be pretty doing it, but I'll get there."

Michael "Mitch" Flores, thirty-five, is a pediatrician and a member of the teaching staff of Children's Hospital of Los Angeles. He was born in Mexico and came to Nevada when he was four. Mitch is intense and driven; since 1982 he has been competing in triathlons around the country.

"At first I would look up at the mountain and think, 'You're mine,' " he said. "I just knew I had it. But now I don't say that. Three people have died on the mountain since we got here. We're like ants compared to it. Nothing lives up there. Now I'm saying, 'Hey, mountain, I want to cooperate with you.' I've lost that arrogance."

Keith Rizer, forty-six, grew up, as Harry and I did, on the Texas Gulf Coast. Since 1963 he has lived in Alaska, where he is in the investments and insurance business. Keith was too sick to make it all the way to Nido the day before, and today he was barely able to get out of his tent.

"Right now my chances are about zero," he told me. "But if I just have enough time, I'm mentally tough enough to get there. The thing about climbing is that if you have any 'quit' in you, the mountain is going to find it."

Keith and I were talking in the kitchen tent while Harry and his wife Diane were making dinner. Diane is a marathoner and climber herself. She'd already climbed Aconcagua, and on this expedition was running base camp. Diane has watched hundreds of climbers on McKinley and Aconcagua. I asked her why she thinks men in their forties take up mountain climbing.

"There are two kinds of middle-aged climbers," she said. "One type does it to prove they're still young. That's the mid-life crisis category. The other type has been testing himself all his life—maybe not on mountains, but in his work or some other part of his life. They're the adventurers, the ones who've always been breaking away from routine to do what gives them joy."

"Which am I?" I asked her.

She paused in slicing potatoes and smiled. "You tell me," she said.

On the seventh day we were to move camp up to Nido. From there we would climb to Berlin Camp at 19,100 feet, and from Berlin, if the weather held, we would try to reach the summit. That night I made lists in my tent of what to take in my pack. I no longer trusted my mind to remember what I would need.

As I wrote, I noticed my fingernails were black. I was unspeakably filthy. My face was covered in whiskers and dirt. I stank. Every orifice was cracked and dry and raw. My teeth were moldy and my nose and ears filled with debris. Blisters oozed on my feet. Sex was a dim memory. Every meal began with a recitation of our ailments, about which our fellow climbers had a respectful and sympathetic curiosity. Medicines and advice were freely exchanged, belching and flatulence accepted without comment.

The morning was clear and cold, and the camp was a whirlwind of activity as we took down our tents and loaded our packs. Into mine went polypropylene and heavy wool socks, polypro and wool gloves and Gore-Tex mitten shells, polypro underwear tops and bottoms, Gore-Tex outer pants and coat, heavy down parka, down vest, medicine and first aid supplies, headlamp, knife, butane lighters, neoprene face mask, wool balaclava, gaiters, Patagonia pile pants and sweater, sleeping bag, notebook and Flair pens (ballpoints freeze), camera and extra film, snow goggles, sunblock, a small bag of valuables, and tapes for my Walkman: Bruce Springsteen and Buddy Holly for the tough going; Mozart and Handel for the more contemplative stages; Wagner for drama and Beethoven for the summit. I also had three bottles of water, a bag of food, some fuel, and the tent poles.

An hour into the climb I resented everything in my pack, every ounce of weight, just as I had come to resent the other distractions and burdens in my life. I had come to the mountain to be free, and I had ended up a pack animal. I was determined to climb at my own pace, stopping every hour or so to drink some water. I couldn't afford to pass out at Nido again. That would mean being sent back down; it would mean failure.

I joined two Frenchmen, parasailers from Chamonix. I found them oddly reassuring, as if the insanity of their mission gave a certain sanity to mine. After all, I was only climbing this mountain. They were going to fly off it.

I crossed the snowfield without incident, needing only one breath per step. I climbed the two ridges, and emerged on a barren, snow-filled basin in the shadow of the summit. The first climbers of our group were already unloading gear and putting up tents on some exposed rock next to a frozen lake.

I shared a tent with Mitch and Kim. The wind was blowing off the mountain again, and the temperature was well below zero. I had bizarre dreams: I was lost in a strange house, I was falling off the Empire State Building, I was wandering through New York City for hours with Bruce Springsteen on my back, trying to find the Meadowlands in a blizzard. I could feel the mountain right outside my tent, painfully close, like someone standing with his face right next to mine, staring.

The next morning we prepared to move up to Berlin. The climb was only twelve hundred vertical feet, so we could take our time and break camp slowly. Our packs were even heavier than the day before, since we had no cache at Berlin and had to carry all our food and fuel, in addition to the tents and personal gear we had carried before. I was feeling weaker; simply getting dressed and loading my pack left me dizzy.

The climb was steep but uneventful. I had to stop twice to get my breath and choke down some water. Each time, I was unable to put my pack back on without several minutes of intense, exhausting effort, fighting to keep my balance on the steep slope.

By 2:30 we reached Berlin camp, a squalid collection of old huts perched amid garbage and excrement. I choked down some instant split pea soup and lay down in the tent next to Kim, who was trying to nurse her headache. Suddenly, nausea came over me. I climbed over Kim and staggered toward some rocks, inadvertently interrupting the videotaping of Ernie's account of the climb ("I'm standing in front of the El Torito here at nineteen thousand feet . . .") and allowing Mitch to capture my tortured heaves on video.

Harry came over and gave me a suppository, since the pills I had been taking for nausea were simply being regurgitated with everything else. I crouched behind the rock and tried to insert it, but the suppository was frozen.

"Are you going to make it?" Harry asked me, meaning, Should I send you down?

"I don't know," I said. "But if I can eat some oatmeal in the morning I'm going."

I was discouraged, but also relieved because I was protected from failure. If I didn't make it, I had my excuse: no food for days, sick, exhausted—why it's a wonder he got as high as he did. I could hear myself explaining how hard I'd tried, but there was nothing I could do.

Kim and I weren't the only ones feeling sick. Keith had struggled into Berlin long after dinner and had gone straight to his tent, unable to eat or even to move. Bruce Barron, our second guide, had serious congestion in his lungs. At nineteen thousand feet, such symptoms can quickly develop into pulmonary edema. Even though it was almost dusk, Bruce shouldered his pack and went back to base camp. As I watched him go I wondered if I should be with him.

I lay in the tent with Kim and Mitch, the windsurfer from Palos Verdes, the doctor from Zacatecas, our bodies sandwiched together.

"This is it," Mitch said, "this is what we came for."

"Be quiet, Mitch," Kim said, "I want to sleep."

"I'm going to make it. I'm going to make it." I realized that was me talking, and they were the last words I heard until Kelly's voice woke me at four.

I got up slowly, my mouth dry, my head heavy and thick. Where was I, exactly, and what was I doing? Oh yes, it came to me through the mist: I'm climbing a mountain. I didn't feel fear or even much anticipation. I only knew I had to begin getting ready. I had gone to sleep in the underwear and pile pants and jacket I would wear on the climb, so I taped my feet with moleskin, pulled on my heaviest socks and my boot liners, threw my parka over my shoulders, and limped over to the hut, where I sat, exhausted from the effort of getting dressed. I was too tired to force my liners into the stiff plastic boots.

The night was clear and cold, and the stars shone with a furious intensity. I wanted to brush my teeth, but it was pointless: there was no water yet and besides, my toothpaste would still be frozen. After Harry melted some snow I began to eat hot water mixed with instant oatmeal. I had to chew each bite eight or nine times in order to swallow. The taste was metallic; I could feel my stomach gathering its protest.

I wanted to travel as lightly as possible, since we would be returning to Berlin at the end of the day. I wore everything I had except my parka, which I put in my pack, along with my Walkman, some emergency medical supplies, and my knife. At the last minute, as everyone else was headed out of camp, I stuck in my head lamp, just in case it was dark when we came down. I didn't bother with food—I knew I wouldn't be able to eat anything, but I did bring two bottles of melted snow.

All my life I had been accumulating things, people, ideas, achievements. As I set off up the mountain, I realized I was at last embarking on a venture where nothing I had accumulated would do me the slightest good. I couldn't show the mountain my resume or my BMW or tell it I was a good father. The mountain didn't care; it was simply there. I wanted to be on its top, gravity wanted me at its base. I was either going to make it or I wasn't, sick or not sick, food or no food. Yes or no.

Blessed, terrible clarity.

We fell into line and moved out, casting strange moonshadows on the snow and rock. I kept thinking of dawn patrols in Vietnam, but there I always felt my senses heightened, my body one vibrating nerve ending. Here I felt almost nothing—I was numb and withdrawn, driven deep into myself.

As the light dawned we were climbing the switchbacks to the Independencia hut at twenty-one thousand feet, and I was falling behind. At nine I reached Independencia, a tiny A-frame with no roof, supposedly the highest permanent structure in the world. I fell onto the rocks and begin to retch—so much for keeping the oatmeal down. My pack was intolerably heavy, so I stashed the parka and the Walkman under some rocks, to pick up when I returned.

"As I set off up the mountain, I realized I was at last embarking on a venture where nothing I had accumulated would do me the slightest good."

I couldn't listen to music anyway. My mind wouldn't have tolerated the noise.

I felt as if I were in a dream, each footstep pulling me up to some goal I no longer knew or understood or even particularly agreed with. I wanted just to lie there on the rocks, but somehow I began to climb again, one foot, then the other. Three breaths to the step already, and not even to the Canaleta.

Above Independencia I crested a ridge and then began a long traverse across a steep moraine that fell off thousands of feet to the right. I crossed a snow field, and the one look down I took made me sick again. No triumphant chords of Beethoven's Ninth. No romantic communion with God and nature. I didn't even see the mountains around me, only the toes of my boots moving over rock and snow, a constant, hypnotic rhythm.

The trail stopped. I looked up and saw an endless expanse of loose rock and snow, going what seemed straight up, finally disappearing into the clouds. I was at the foot of the Canaleta.

The rocks were jumbled and balanced like some huge house of cards, massive yet fragile—an avalanche waiting to happen. It looked like something fluid and powerful, even alive. Altitude, fear, fatigue, storm and accident: we had overcome them all. Here was the last barrier: a river of loose scree and boulders stretching up more than a thousand feet, with no way around—only through.

I remember reading Glenn Porzak's account of climbing Aconcagua back in 1974. He thought the Canaleta would never end; before he reached the summit he was taking eight breaths to a step. Eight! Breath, breath, breath, breath, breath, breath, breath, breath. Step. Then again. Breath, breath. . . .

When I read those words in the quiet security of my house in Los Angeles I could hardly believe them. Eight breaths to a step? But as I looked up at the Canaleta, mustering all my strength simply to stand, eight breaths to the step seemed like an achievement. Only eight?

Up the middle went the faint hint of a trail in the loose scree. I kicked my toe into it, hoping for a foothold. Three feet above me, the rock started to slide. As I watched, the toe I had kicked in slid past my other foot and I began to slip backwards. It was like climbing up a down escalator. There was a touch of hell about it: instead of having to roll a rock uphill, we had to keep climbing a falling mountain.

Around me I could see the other climbers, in various stages of their struggle. I tried going to the right, then to the left, then up the middle. I felt I was going nowhere. I was already taking six breaths a step. The summit was far above me, lost in clouds amid two large outcroppings to my left. I felt panic coming over me.

"Help!" I yelled, "Help! I'm lost! Which way do I go?"

But my voice was weak from fatigue and dehydration, and the wind snatched it away. I felt totally alone. I realized that no one was going to help me, that I was responsible for myself, and that if I made it or didn't make it the credit or blame would go only to me.

My will, however, was eroding. I wanted only to go down. Down was hot food and water and showers and sit-down toilets and my sleeping bag. Down was this ordeal being over. But I couldn't turn back. The idea of "up" was so powerful that it kept my feet moving, kept my hands reaching for the rocks above me, pulling me up even after I slid backwards.

It was not particularly heroic. I wanted to turn around with all my heart, and I kept trying to. But I simply couldn't. I just kept going, picking out a rock, struggling to get over it, hoping it didn't begin to slide, getting my arms around it, my feet on it, pushing up—then picking out another rock and breathing six, seven, eight, nine times until I had the strength to stretch out again.

I tried to urinate; it was a pitiful flow, the color of strong iced tea. I was sick again—my vomit the color of prune juice, or was it blood? I was beyond caring. The only way out was up. I kept going, ten breaths now to a step, desperate when I slipped backwards, so many breaths just to get back to where I was.

I had been in the Canaleta for almost three hours, when I looked to the left and saw Ernie trying to make his way up some cliffs. Climbers from the Argentine army's elite mountain unit were there too, but they seemed stuck. After another hour I finally reached the base of the cliffs, and just then one of the Argentines dislodged a rock.

Hypnotized, I watched it hurtle toward me in slow motion. It bounced into some ice, rocketed up and over a cliff, then hit some boulders. It began the size of pea, then became an orange, a grapefruit, a small melon. My brain was sending impulses to my arms and legs, but I couldn't move. Suddenly, in a whoosh the rock was by me, missing by inches.

I kept climbing, pulling myself up the cliffs, lying gasping on the ledges. Mitch and Kim materialized out of the clouds, headed down. At 22,500 feet, Warren turned back. That left Kelly, Ernie and me. I finally reached the Argentines, who seem glued to the boulders.

"To the summit, which way?" I gasped.

One of the Argentines pointed to the left, the other to the right. I couldn't see the summit, only clouds and rocks.

I kept moving, although I had no concept of where I was going or how much farther it was. I was, totally and completely, a prisoner of the principle of "up." Every time I pulled up to a new ledge, my arms felt as if they would never be able to move again. Then I breathed, ten, twelve times, lifted my arms, and pulled myself up again. A handhold, pull, step, handhold, pull, don't forget to breathe. Do it again, forever.

Suddenly two boots appeared in front of my face. I looked up. It was Harry.

"I thought you'd gone down," he said, his voice quiet and hoarse.

I shook my head. Harry took a minute to survey the situation. It was getting late, the clouds were building, we should go down. But I was so close, very close.

"Let's go," he said, and headed back up. I tried to follow him. He was just at the end of my vision, perched on a rock like a leprechaun. I breathed carefully, eight times, looked around the rock, located a handhold, pulled. Then I did it again with a foot and pushed. An eternity passed. Harry was on another rock above me.

"Find it," he said. "Find the strength. You can do it."

I kept going, trying to get to him. But every time I should have reached him he was always higher, beyond me. An hour passed. Finally I stood beside him. Above my head was a ledge.

"Up there," Harry said.

I pulled myself up, using my knees on the rock, and scrambled on to yet another ledge, this one covered in snow. I lay gasping for breath.

I looked around for the next place to go up, for the next handhold, the next step, the next series of breaths, the cycle that never ended.

But it had. There was no more up.

I was on the summit.

The clouds had blown away and the sky for a moment was blue. I was on top of the Western Hemisphere, quite probably higher at that moment than any other human being on solid ground in the world. The Andes stretched out in all directions. To my right was the breathtaking cliff of the South Face, falling off ten thousand feet into the mists below. I knew the view was spectacular, that I should concentrate on it, absorb it, enjoy it.

All I could do, however, was *feel*: I felt the wind, the cold, the blueness of the sky, the whiteness of the snow and the clouds. Those feelings were the only connections I had to my body. The summit was thirty feet away in a bed of snow, marked by a crude tubular cross three feet high. I walked slowly and carefully over to it and sat down. Harry appeared and put his arms around me.

"You did it," he kept saying, "You did it."

I had expected some epiphany, some magic moment filled with insight into man and nature, into ambition, success, and the fruits of human endeavor. I thought none of those things. In fact, I thought nothing. My mind was as blank as the great fields of snow on the South Face. On a ledge about six feet down was a pile of rocks.

"That's where we buried the body," Harry said. "Can't you imagine how it happened? He was exhausted, even more tired than you are, so he just probably decided to lie down for a minute and take a rest. The odd thing is he was trying to take off his clothes, as if at the moment he froze to death he felt warm. And there was a smile on his face. He probably never even knew he was dying. It just felt so good to lie down."

I could imagine it. I felt out of place on the summit. I knew I didn't belong there. I wasn't sure if any of us did.

I had begun my climb in green pastures, surrounded by life. My step was springy, my mind clear. I was ending it weak and bent, lungs gasping for breath, my mind senile. I had thought to recover my youth; instead I saw myself as an old man.

I had climbed toward not life but death, a death I hadn't met before. This death wasn't an invigorating presence to be fought and cheated, as I had fought it in Vietnam or in rock climbing. This was death by old age and exhaustion, numbing and final—death as a soothing blessed relief, the smile on the face of the frozen Argentine.

I didn't want to linger. I only wanted down.

"Let's go," I said. I had been on the summit less than ten minutes.

We felt our way down the Canaleta slowly and carefully. The rocks kept quivering under my feet. I expected the whole thousand feet to give way at any moment.

"Are you okay?" Harry asked me at the bottom of the Canaleta.

"Sure," I said.

"I'm going on ahead to check on the others. Just keep moving. It's about seven o'clock now. You should be down to Berlin in an hour or so. If you're not there by nine, I'll come look for you."

I nodded. No problem. Down was easy. I made my way carefully along the ridge to Independencia, where I picked up my parka and Walkman and sat down. All of a sudden my eyes were heavy, my bones and muscles seemed just so grateful to be resting. It felt good, so good, to stop. Then I remembered the Argentine on the summit. I got to my feet and kept going. Five minutes later, there was Ernie, standing in the middle of a series of switchbacks.

"Hey, I think I'm lost!" he yelled.

We stood in the middle of the slope and looked around. The trail kept going down to a ledge, then went both ways. The rocks at the bottom didn't look familiar, but another rock higher up did.

"It's down and to the left," I said.

"You sure it's not up there?" Ernie asked me.

I looked back at the familiar rock. I didn't want it to be there; I didn't want to climb back up—wasn't, in fact, sure I could.

"Maybe," I said. "We better check them both out."

Ernie went down to the intersection and then turned left, disappearing over the ledge. I

took off my pack and inched my way back up, sideways, one step at a time. I couldn't see another trail, so I walked back down to where I had left my pack. It was getting dark and clouds were gathering. I started to shiver. After about twenty minutes, Ernie reappeared.

"I went way down the trail and didn't recognize a thing," he said. "Maybe it's to the right."

"No, it's to the left—I think."

It was beginning to sink in. We were lost at twenty-one thousand feet. Night had fallen and a storm was coming in. We had no tent, no sleeping bags. We couldn't go wandering around in the dark. The trails were too steep, and somewhere below us could be glaciers and crevasses.

Snow began to fall. My feet were feeling numb. I gave Ernie my extra pair of gloves. We sat down very close to each other and draped the parka over our shoulders and set the pack across our legs. I had the headlamp, which I began shining up. Every now and then Ernie would stand up and yell, "Harry!"

The wind began to blow harder and the snow came thicker, wet and cold. The temperature was already ten below zero and dropping fast. Ernie and I took inventory of our supplies. We had a knife and the light, which was good, but we didn't have the Bic lighter; it lay in my tent at Berlin, jumbled into a sack with my toothbrush and my Lomotil. If we had the lighter, we could have built a fire with some boards from the Independencia hut.

We decided to stay put until eleven and then try to make it up to Independencia and bivouac, just as the frostbitten Yugoslavs we had met our first day had done. Our yells went unanswered. My little light seemed pitifully weak as it shone up into the snow.

Ernie and I put our arms around each other, I the overeducated Oxford graduate with the fancy résumé, he the possessor of one semester of auto body in junior college. On the surface we had little in common, but that night we were each prepared to do anything for the other. We didn't talk much. We were caught in the open in a storm at twenty-one thousand feet—it was hard to make conversation around that fact.

So this is the way it ends, I was thinking. After all the struggle and all the ordeal, after *succeeding*, to get lost on a simple, routine trail going down, the easiest part of the trip. We didn't know how far we were, in fact, off the real trail, which meant we weren't sure if Harry could find us, particularly if the snow kept coming down.

The dangers were only vaguely real to us; we made no connection between fatigue and altitude and cold and death. It was nothing like war, where no one ever doubts bullets and bombs can kill. But that body was on the summit; six climbers were dead in the past month. Mountain climbing is a high stakes game. By stupidly getting lost, Ernie and I had put our bets on the table.

"HARRRRRRRRY!" Ernie yelled again.

It was after ten. My pack was covered with snow.

I thought about my children, about my work, about people I loved, about my life and what I had made of it: not clear, orderly thoughts, just crude pictures, feelings really. My mind was too burdened for anything profound. It had enough to do simply keeping me awake. To stay awake was to stay alive.

10:30.

I kept shining my light up. It seemed pointless. If they were going to find us, they would have by now. On the other hand, I had total faith in Harry. I knew, somehow, he'd come.

"What's that?" Ernie said.

"What?"

"That noise."

"It's the wind."

"No, I heard something. Listen."

I listened. I did hear something. Someone was yelling. And there, down below, was a light!

Ernie leapt to his feet, stumbling over the rocks, and I was right behind him.

A figure emerged from the snow.

"Harry?" Ernie yelled.

"Is Bill with you?" A voice answered.

"Yeah," Ernie said, "but what about me?"

"You'll never guess who this is," the voice said, in a Spanish accent. "It's Daniel."

Daniel? Daniel. The guide from the Polish Glacier team. Had we wandered all the way around the mountain to the Polish Glacier? How did he find us? Our questions poured out.

"Later. We talk later. Let's get to camp."

Ernie and I followed him down, our headlamps shining in the falling snow. My legs moved automatically. I was beyond fatigue. By midnight we were back at Berlin. Mitch checked us over quickly while Daniel went to find Harry, who had gone down to Nido de Condores looking for us. The Polish Glacier team, it turned out, had abandoned their attempt and traversed the mountain while we were trying for the summit, and they were in camp as well.

"You've got to get right into your sleeping bag," Mitch said, as he checked my pulse and examined my fingers and toes. Mitch put me between Kim and him for warmth. I was hardly prone before my eyes closed, and a deep sleep came over me, the sleep I had been yearning for all day.

During the night I kept dreaming someone was choking me; finally I woke up with Mitch's hands at my throat.

"You've got severe Cheyne Stokes breathing," he told me, describing a breathing arrhythmia at high altitudes that involves taking three or four breaths and simply stopping breathing. Usually the breathing reflex recovers and the breathing begins again, but not always.

"I'm just lying here listening to you," he said, "and each time you stop I sit up and take your pulse. Once or twice I thought you'd died on me, but your pulse is still strong."

I had a hard time going back to sleep after that, but I woke up feeling clearheaded, stronger and hungry. My body had finally adapted to the altitude—a day too late.

I was tired but exhilarated. I had made it to the summit, and, more important, I had made it down. It was a good, clean feeling, unspoiled by my stupidity in getting lost. Mitch and Kim were lying in their sleeping bags, also awake.

"We made it," Mitch said.

We just smiled at each other. There were no other words to say.

As we were inching our way back to base camp, the Frenchman finally took off from Nido de Condores in his parasail. He soared down almost five thousand feet before crashing unhurt into the mountain just outside base camp—narrowly missing, in the process, Ernie Fregoso.

"This mountain is out to get me," he said. "It hates me because I'm Mexican."

The next day we waited at base camp for the climbers still on the mountain. Daniel woke up with severe pain in his liver; Ralph gave up his own shot at the summit and escorted him down. A few hours later Gabe and Keith arrived, after being turned back by a storm just short of the Canaleta.

Of the sixteen of us who had begun the climb, six made it to the summit: Harry Johnson, Kim Baldwin (the first, after Harry, to the top), Ernie Fregoso, Kelly Cordner, Mitch Flores, and me. The result wasn't particularly just or logical. Novices made it, while some of the expedition's most experienced climbers didn't. Everyone had worked hard and given the climb all they had. If a few things had happened differently, the list would have had other names, and we all knew it.

The next day we returned to Puente del Inca, laughing and joking as we walked. Behind us the mountain steadily receded into the clouds. Late in the afternoon, we came to the first meadow. After so many days of seeing only rock, ice, and snow, the green of the grass was almost blinding. We were back in the land of the living.

Why had I done it? Not, I think, because it was there, the enigmatic reason given by George Mallory when asked why he climbed Everest. I did it because I was there. The mountain cared nothing for me—it was, after all, made of rock. When I began, I felt some deep tie to it, as if it were alive. But back at Base Camp I realized that it had given me nothing, that all I learned I had brought with me.

And then I read what else Mallory had said: "Something in man responds to the challenge of this mountain and goes to meet it: the struggle is the struggle of life itself upward and forever upward.... What we get from this adventure is sheer joy. And joy is, after all, the end of life. We do not live to eat and to make money. We eat and make money to enjoy life."

Mallory was last seen, shrouded in clouds, as he headed for the summit of Everest in 1924, in the midst of what gave him the most joy in life. For the ordeal I had just undergone joy might seem an odd description. But as I prepared to go down off the mountain that is what I felt: the joy of accomplishment, of having been tested—the joy of a survivor.

The cares and complications of my life had receded into the valleys. I had been to the mountaintop.